Grammar Links 2

A Theme-Based Course for Reference and Practice

SECOND EDITION

M. Kathleen Mahnke
Saint Michael's College

Elizabeth O'Dowd
Saint Michael's College

M. Kathleen Mahnke
Series Editor

Houghton Mifflin Company   Boston   New York

Publisher: Patricia A. Coryell
Director of ESL: Susan Maguire
Senior Development Editor: Kathleen Sands Boehmer
Editorial Assistant: Evangeline Bermas
Senior Project Editor: Margaret Park Bridges
Senior Manufacturing Coordinator: Marie Barnes
Marketing Manager: Annamarie Rice
Marketing Associate: Laura Hemrika

Cover image: Stock Illustration Source © 2003 David Ridley, *Multicultural Figures*

Photo Credits: p. 1, left: © JFPI Studios, Inc./Corbis; p. 1, right: © Allana Wesley White/
Corbis; p. 43: Printed by permission of the Norman Rockwell Family Agency Copyright
© 1958 the Norman Rockwell Family Entities; p. 45: Maynard Owen Williams/Getty Images;
p. 56: Philip Baird/AnthroArcheArt.org; p. 85: Chad Baker/Getty Images; pp. 101, 143: AP/
Wide World Photos; p. 125: Karl and Jill Wallin/Getty Images; pp. 133, 235, 249, 269:
© Bettmann/Corbis; p. 176: © Richard T. Nowitz/Corbis; p. 180: Pat Eriksson/Getty Images;
pp. 189, 315, 367: Corbis; p. 224: © Michael Cole/Corbis; p. 233: © Beth Wald/AURORA;
p. 243: © Peter Harholdt/Corbis; p. 248: © Lake County Museum/Corbis; p. 273: Philip
Habib/Getty Images; p. 284: © Douglas Kirkland/Corbis; p. 287: Aitch/Getty Images;
p. 296, top: Rohan/Getty Images; p. 296, middle: David Job/Getty Images; p. 296, bottom:
Timothy Laman/Getty Images; p. 299: Paul and Lindamarie Ambrose/Getty Images;
p. 314: John Elk III; p. 361: Andersen Ross/Getty Images; p. 366: © Ed Kashi/IPN/AURORA

Printed in the U.S.A.

Library of Congress Control Number: 2003115072

ISBN: 0-618-27413-8

123456789-HES-08 07 06 05 04

Introduction

WELCOME TO *GRAMMAR LINKS*!

Grammar Links is a comprehensive five-level grammar reference and practice series for students of English as a second or foreign language. The series meets the needs of students from the beginning through advanced levels:

- *Grammar Links Basic*: beginning
- *Grammar Links, Book 1*: high beginning
- *Grammar Links, Book 2*: intermediate
- *Grammar Links, Book 3*: high intermediate
- *Grammar Links, Book 4*: advanced

Available with each *Grammar Links* student text are an audio program and printable Web-based teacher's notes; the teacher's notes are accompanied by the answer key and tapescripts for each book. Tests and other materials are also available on the Houghton Mifflin Website and are described below. In addition, *Grammar Links 1–4* feature workbooks for further practice of all grammar points introduced in the student books.

NEW IN THIS EDITION

- A fresh, new design with eye-catching art, realia, and a focus on ease of use
- Streamlined, easy-to-read grammar charts showing structures at a glance
- Succinct explanations of grammar points for easy understanding
- Simplified content coverage accompanied by vocabulary glosses to let students focus on grammar while learning about topics of interest
- An even greater number and variety of activities than before, now signaled with icons for easy reference:

    Listening activities for receptive practice of grammar structures in oral English

    Communicative activities that lead to fluent use of grammar in everyday speaking

    Writing activities for productive practice of targeted structures in extended written discourse

    Links to the World Wide Web for:
    - Model paragraphs for writing assignments
    - Practice tests, both self-check tests for student use and achievement tests for teacher use
    - Links to interesting sites related to unit themes for further reading and discussion
    - Vocabulary flashcards for review of the content-related vocabulary that is used in text readings and exercises
    - Much more! See for yourself at www.hmco.com/college/esl.

TO THE TEACHER

Series Approach

Recent research in applied linguistics tells us that when a well-designed communicative approach is coupled with a systematic treatment of grammatical form, the combination is a powerful pedagogical tool.

Grammar Links is such a tool. The grammar explanations in *Grammar Links* are clear, accurate, and carefully sequenced. All points that are introduced are practiced in exercises, and coverage is comprehensive and systematic. In addition, each grammar point is carefully recycled in a variety of contexts.

The communicative framework of *Grammar Links* is that of the theme-based approach to language learning. Unlike other approaches, theme-based models promote the development of both communicative and linguistic abilities through in-depth contextualization of language in extended discourse. The importance of this type of contextualization to grammar acquisition is now well documented. In *Grammar Links*, content serves as a backdrop for communication; high-interest topics are presented and developed along with the grammar of each chapter. As a result, *Grammar Links* exercises and activities are content-driven as well as grammar-driven. While learning about adjective clauses in Book 3, for example, students explore various aspects of the discipline of psychology. While they are practicing gerunds and infinitives in Book 2, they read about successful American entrepreneurs. And while practicing the simple present tense in Book 1, students learn about and discuss North American festivals and other celebrations. Throughout the series, students communicate about meaningful content, transferring their grammatical training to the English they need in their daily lives.

Complementing the communicative theme-based approach of the *Grammar Links* series is the inclusion of a range of successful methodological options for exercises and activities. In addition to more traditional, explicit rule presentation and practice, we have incorporated a number of less explicit, more inductive techniques. Foremost among these are our discovery exercises and activities, in which students are asked to notice general and specific grammatical features and think about them on their own, sometimes formulating their own hypotheses about how these features work and why they work the way they do. Discovery exercises are included in each unit opener. They are frequently used in chapter openers as well and are interspersed throughout the *Grammar Practice* sections, particularly at the higher levels.

In short, the *Grammar Links* approach provides students with the best of all possible language learning environments—a comprehensive, systematic treatment of grammar that employs a variety of methods for grammar learning within a communicative theme-based framework.

About the Books

Each book in the *Grammar Links* series is divided into approximately 10 units. Each unit looks at a well-defined area of grammar, and each unit has an overall theme. The chapters within a unit each focus on some part of the targeted unit grammar, and each chapter develops some specific aspect of the unit theme. In this way, chapters in a unit are linked in terms of both grammar coverage and theme, providing a highly contextualized base on which students can build and refine their grammatical skills.

Grammar coverage has been carefully designed to spiral across levels. Structures that are introduced in one book are recycled and built upon in the next. Students not only learn increasingly sophisticated information about the structures but also practice these structures in increasingly challenging contexts. Themes show a similar progression across levels, from less academic in Books 1 and 2 to more academic in Books 3 and 4.

Grammar Links is flexible in many ways and can be easily adapted to the particular needs of users. Although its careful spiraling makes it ideal as a series, the comprehensive grammar coverage at each level means that the individual books can also stand alone. The comprehensiveness and careful organization also make it possible for students to use their text as a reference after they have completed a course. The units in a book can be used in the order given or can be rearranged to fit the teacher's curriculum. Books can be used in their entirety or in part. In addition, the inclusion of ample practice allows teachers to be selective when choosing exercises and activities. All exercises are labeled for grammatical content, so structures can be practiced more or less extensively, depending on class and individual needs.

Unit and Chapter Components

- **Unit Objectives.** Each unit begins with a list of unit objectives so that teachers and students can preview the major grammar points covered in the unit. Objectives are accompanied by example sentences, which highlight the relevant structures.

- **Unit Introduction.** To illustrate grammar use in extended discourse, a reading and listening selection introduces both the unit grammar and the unit theme in a unit opener section entitled *Grammar in Action*. This material is followed by a grammar consciousness-raising or "noticing" task, *Think About Grammar*. In *Think About Grammar* tasks, students figure out some aspect of grammar by looking at words and sentences from the *Grammar in Action* selection, often working together to answer questions about them. Students induce grammatical rules themselves before having those rules given to them. *Think About Grammar* thus helps students to become independent grammar learners by promoting critical thinking and discussion about grammar.

- **Chapter Introduction.** Each chapter opens with a task. This task involves students in working receptively with the structures that are treated in the chapter and gives them the opportunity to begin thinking about the chapter theme.

- *Grammar Briefings.* The grammar is presented in *Grammar Briefings*. Chapters generally have three or four *Grammar Briefings* so that information is given in manageable chunks. The core of each *Grammar Briefing* is its **form** and **function** charts. In these charts, the form (the *what* of grammar) and the function (the *how, when,* and *why*) are presented in logical segments. These segments are manageable but large enough that students can see connections between related grammar points. Form and function are presented in separate charts when appropriate but together when the two are essentially inseparable. All grammatical descriptions in the form and function charts are comprehensive, concise, and clear. Sample sentences illustrate each point.

- *Grammar Hotspots. Grammar Hotspots* are a special feature of *Grammar Links*. They occur at one or more strategic points in each chapter. *Grammar Hotspots* focus on aspects of grammar that students are likely to find particularly troublesome. Some hotspots contain reminders about material that has already been presented in the form and function charts; others go beyond the charts.

- *Talking the Talk. Talking the Talk* is another special feature of the *Grammar Links* series. Our choice of grammar is often determined by our audience, whether we are writing or speaking, the situations in which we find ourselves, and other sociocultural factors. *Talking the Talk* treats these factors. Students become aware of differences between formal and informal English, between written and spoken English.

- *Grammar Practice.* Each *Grammar Briefing* is followed by comprehensive and systematic practice of all grammar points introduced. The general progression within each *Grammar Practice* is from more controlled to less controlled, from easier to more difficult, and often from more receptive to more productive and/or more structured to more communicative. A wide variety of innovative exercise types is included in each of the four skill areas: listening, speaking, reading, and writing. The exercise types that are used are appropriate to the particular grammar points being practiced. For example, more drill-like exercises are often used for practice with form. More open-ended exercises often focus on function.

  In many cases, drill-like practice of a particular grammar point is followed by open-ended communicative practice of the same point, often as pair or group work. Thus, a number of exercises have two parts.

  The majority of exercises within each *Grammar Practice* section are related to the theme of the unit. However, some exercises depart from the theme to ensure that each grammar point is practiced in the most effective way.

- **Unit Wrap-Ups.** Each unit ends with a series of activities that pull the unit grammar together and enable students to test, further practice, and apply what they have learned. These activities include an error correction task, which covers the errors students most commonly make in using the structures presented in the unit, as well as a series of innovative open-ended communicative tasks, which build on and go beyond the individual chapters.

- **Appendixes.** Extensive appendixes supplement the grammar presented in the *Grammar Briefings*. They provide students with word lists, spelling and pronunciation rules, and other supplemental rules related to the structures that have been taught. The appendixes are a rich resource for students as they work through exercises and activities.

- **Grammar Glossary.** A grammar glossary provides students and teachers with definitions of the grammar terms used in *Grammar Links* as well as example sentences to aid in understanding the meaning of each term.

Other Components

- **Audio Program.** All *Grammar Links* listening exercises and all unit introductions are recorded on audio CDs and cassettes. The symbol 🎧 appears next to the title of each recorded segment.

- **Workbook.** *Grammar Links 1–4* student texts are each accompanied by a workbook. The four workbooks contain a wide variety of exercise types, including paragraph and essay writing, and they provide extensive supplemental self-study practice of each grammar point presented in the student texts. Student self-tests with TOEFL® practice questions are also included in the workbooks.

- **Teacher's Notes.** The *Grammar Links* teacher's notes for each student text can be downloaded from <http://www.hmco.com/college/esl/>. Each contains an introduction to the series and some general and specific teaching guidelines.

- **Tapescript and Answer Keys.** The tapescript and the answer key for the student text and the answer key for the workbook are also available at the *Grammar Links* Website.

- **Links to the World Wide Web.** As was discussed above, the *Grammar Links* Website www.hmco.com/college/esl/ has been expanded for the second edition to include student and teacher tests, teacher notes, model writing assignments, content Web links and activities, and other material. Links are updated frequently to ensure that students and teachers can access the best information available on the Web.

TO THE STUDENT

Grammar Links is a five-level series that gives you all the rules and practice you need to learn and use English grammar. Each unit in this book focuses on an area of grammar. Each unit also develops a theme—for example, business or travel. Units are divided into two or three chapters.

Grammar Links has many special features that will help you to learn the grammar and to use it in speaking, listening, reading, and writing.

FEATURE	BENEFIT
Interesting Themes	Help you link grammar to the real world—the world of everyday English
Introductory Reading and Listening Selections	Introduce you to the theme and the grammar of the unit
Think About Grammar Activities	Help you to become an independent grammar learner
Chapter Opener Tasks	Get you started using the grammar
Grammar Briefings	Give you clear grammar rules in easy-to-read charts, with helpful example sentences
Grammar Hotspots	Focus on especially difficult grammar points for learners of English—points on which you might want to spend extra time
Talking the Talk	Helps you to understand the differences between formal and informal English and between written and spoken English
Grammar Practice	Gives you lots of practice, through listening, speaking, reading, and writing exercises and activities
Unit Wrap-Up Tasks	Provide you with interesting communicative activities that cover everything you have learned in the unit
Vocabulary Glosses	Define key words in readings and exercises so that you can concentrate on your grammar practice while still learning about interesting content
Grammar Glossary	Gives you definitions and example sentences for the most common words used to talk about English grammar—a handy reference for now and for later
Websites	Guide you to more information about topics of interest
	Provide you with self-tests with immediate correction and feedback, vocabulary flashcards for extra practice with words that might be new to you, models for writing assignments, and extra practice exercises

All of these features combine to make *Grammar Links* interesting and rewarding—and, I hope, FUN!

M. Kathleen Mahnke, Series Editor
Saint Michael's College
Colchester, VT USA

ACKNOWLEDGMENTS

Series Editor Acknowledgments

This edition of *Grammar Links* would not have been possible without the thoughtful and enthusiastic feedback of teachers and students. Many thanks to you all!

I would also like to thank all of the *Grammar Links* authors, from whom I continue to learn so much every day. Many thanks as well to the dedicated staff at Houghton Mifflin: Joann Kozyrev, Evangeline Bermas, and Annamarie Rice.

A very special thanks to Kathy Sands Boehmer and to Susan Maguire for their vision, their sense of humor, their faith in all of us, their flexibility, their undying tenacity, and their willingness to take risks in order to move from the mundane to the truly inspirational.

Author Acknowledgments

We would like to express our appreciation to the following individuals who helped to make this book possible:

Our valiant editor, Karen Davy, who worried, teased, and stretched our efforts toward a product we could be proud of.

The staff at Houghton Mifflin for their constant patience and encouragement.

The other *Grammar Links* series authors for their commitment and their camaraderie.

Our friends and colleagues at Saint Michael's College, who provided support in their invaluable ways.

In addition, we are grateful to the following members of the revision advisory board:

Marianne Grayston, Prince George's Community College
Cristi Mitchell, Miami-Dade Community College
Terry Robinson, University of Texas, Brownsville
Oscar Vera, University of Texas, Brownsville

Finally, our warmest gratitude goes to our close families and friends for feeding, sustaining, and worrying about us through the writing and production process: Wayne Parker, Greg Mahnke, Paddy and Mary O'Dowd, the Olivers of La Luz, New Mexico, and, last but not least, Tina, Amelia, and Cosmo.

Thanks, one and all!
M. Kathleen Mahnke and Elizabeth O'Dowd

Present Time

TOPIC FOCUS
People and Personalities

UNIT OBJECTIVES

- **the simple present tense**
  (George *lives* alone. He *doesn't make* friends easily.)

- **adverbs of frequency with the simple present tense**
  (You *often* talk about your personality. You're *always* happy.)

- **the present progressive tense**
  (I *am* not *enjoying* my job. I'*m looking for* a new job.)

- **choosing between the simple present and the present progressive**
  (They usually *worry* a lot. They *aren't worrying* today.)

- **verbs with stative meaning**
  (Kim *likes* parties. She *has* an outgoing personality.)

Grammar in Action

Reading and Listening: Good Stress, Bad Stress

Professor Larson is giving a class lecture about people and personalities.
Read and listen.

Good morning, class. Today we are starting a new topic. The topic is stress. Stress is our response to a threat or a new situation. The world is changing very fast, and there are always new threats and new situations. So stress is becoming a problem for all of us.

What do you know about stress? What does it do to you? Most people think all stress is bad. That's not true. There is good stress, and there is bad stress. Here's an example of each:

Meet John and Jane. John has a new job. He likes it very much. He's learning new things every day. Does this cause stress? Yes. But it's good stress.

Jane is working, too. She's working very hard, but she's having problems. Her boss doesn't like her. Does she like her job? No. She hates it. This is causing stress, and it is bad stress.

Bad stress usually affects our personality in negative ways. It often changes us. Optimists become pessimists. Organized people become disorganized. Patient people become impatient. People with bad stress are often angry and tired. They look and feel unhappy. Sometimes they don't think clearly; they forget important things and remember unimportant details. Bad stress is a bad thing.

There are many ways to relieve bad stress. For example, do you get enough sleep and exercise every day? I hope so. We need sleep and exercise. Do you have free time every day? This is also important. You need free time for relaxation. Sleep, exercise, and free time make our lives less stressful.

Do you have questions? No? Okay, then. That's it for today. Remember—I am preparing a short test for you. That's for . . . yes . . . for tomorrow. And your paper is due next Tuesday. And your class project is due next Wednesday. Enjoy your stress-free day!

---

threat = danger. *optimist* = a hopeful person; a person who expects the best.
pessimist = a person who expects the worst. *relieve* = reduce or lessen.

Think About Grammar

A. Complete these sentences from Professor Larson's lecture.

1. Today we **are** _____ a new topic.

2. The world **is** _____ very fast.

3. I **am** _____ a short test for you.

Look at the words you wrote. These are the main verbs. The main verbs in these

sentences end with the same three letters. What are they? _____

Look at the **boldfaced** words. These are the auxiliary verbs. What are the auxiliary

verbs in these sentences? _____ _____

_____

B. Complete these sentences from the lecture.

1. He _____ it very much.

2. She _____ it.

3. It often _____ us.

4. They _____ important things.

5. I _____ so.

6. We _____ sleep and exercise.

7. You _____ free time for relaxation.

Some of the verbs end in -*s*. Write those verbs here. _____

_____ _____

Circle the subjects that go with this -*s* ending.

    I   You   He   She   It   We   They

Simple Present Tense; Adverbs of Frequency

Introductory Task: What Kind of Personality Do You Have?

A. Try this test.

Write this sentence: **I am a student.**

_____

Compare your handwriting to the samples below. Does it look more like the sample

in a, b, or c? _____

Handwriting sample		Slope	
a. *I am a student.*	Backward slope	\	
b. *I am a student.*	Forward slope	/	
c. *I am a student.*	Upward slope	|	

B. Graphologists study handwriting. Sometimes they study the "slope" of the handwriting. They believe handwriting shows a person's personality. Look at this chart.

Handwriting Personality Chart	
Slope	**Personality**
Backward slope: \	You are shy and quiet. You usually think first and speak later. You don't often show your feelings.
Forward slope: /	You are confident and outgoing. You speak openly. You rarely hide your feelings.
Upward slope: |	You are in between. You sometimes feel shy, and you are sometimes very outgoing.

1. Look at your handwriting. Think about the chart. Do the graphologists describe your personality correctly? Circle your answer.

   Yes, they do.   No, they don't.

2. Discuss as a class: Do you believe the graphologists?

See the *Grammar Links* Website for more about handwriting and personality.

Simple Present Tense I

FORM

A. Affirmative Statements

SUBJECT	VERB
I	
You	**work.**
We	**match.**
They	
He	
She	**works.**
It	**matches.**

B. Negative Statements

SUBJECT	*DO NOT/DOES NOT*	BASE VERB
I		
You	**do not**	
We	**don't**	**work.**
They		**match.**
He		
She	**does not**	
It	**doesn't**	

(See Appendix 1 for the simple present tense of *be*.)

FUNCTION

A. Habits and Routines

The simple present describes **habits** and **routines**.

PAST   NOW   FUTURE

often watch

We often **watch** the news on TV.

She **takes** swimming lessons.

B. General Truths

The simple present describes **things that are generally or always true**.

PAST   NOW   FUTURE

water helps plants

Water **helps** plants grow.

Scientists **study** the natural world.

1. Spelling rules for third person singular (*he, she, it*) simple present verbs:

   - Most verbs: verb + -*s*.

     work → work**s**, play → play**s**

   - Verbs ending in -*ch, -s, -sh, -x,* or -*z*: verb + -*es*.

     catch → catch**es**, wash → wash**es**

   - Verbs ending in consonant + -*y*: Change -*y* to -*ies*.

     study → stud**ies**, carry → carr**ies**

   - Some irregular verbs.

     go → **goes**, do → **does**, have → **has**

2. Remember! Use -*s*/-*es* only for third person singular.

   Jane like**s** her new dress.
      NOT: Jane ~~like~~ her new dress.

   I like my new dress.
      NOT: I ~~likes~~ my new dress.

(See Appendix 2 for pronunciation rules for the simple present tense.)

GRAMMAR PRACTICE 1

Simple Present Tense I

1 **Affirmative Statements:** The Right Job

A. Certain personalities seem right for certain jobs.

> Line A: Complete the first statement with *be*. Complete the second statement with the simple present of the verb in parentheses.

> Line B: Match the jobs in the box with each personality type. Write a sentence with *be*.

an artist	a mechanic	a race car driver	✓ teachers
a comedian	a nurse	✓ a scientist	

1. A. He __is__ very curious. He __researches__ new facts and information.
      (research)

   B. __He is a scientist.__

2. A. We __are__ patient. We __explain__ things gently again and again.
      (explain)

   B. __We are teachers.__

3. A. You _____ funny. You _____ people laugh.
      (make)

   B. _____

4. A. He _____ adventurous. He _____ danger.
   (enjoy)

   B. _____

5. A. You _____ creative. You _____ beautiful pictures.
   (paint)

   B. _____

6. A. I _____ good with my hands. I _____ cars and trucks.
   (fix)

   B. _____

7. A. My sister _____ very kind. She _____ all night with
   (stay)

   sick people.

   B. _____

B. What is a good job for you? Why? What type of personality do you have?
Write the name of the job. Use the jobs in Part A or your own ideas. Then write
about your personality. Follow the example.

Example: **JOB:** _manager_____

_I'm outgoing. I like people._____

JOB: _____

1. I _____. I _____.

2. I _____. I _____.

3. I _____. I _____.

See the *Grammar Links* Website for a test to help you find the right job for
your personality.

2 Verb Endings: More About Personalities

Write sentences about people with different types of personality.

1. outgoing
   a. This person/have many friends
      _This person has many friends.__
   b. He/speak openly to people
      _He speaks openly to people.__

2. organized
   a. This person/have good
      organizational skills
      _This person_____
      _____
   b. She/use time wisely
      _She_____
      _____

3. impatient
   a. This man/hurry all the time
      _____
      _____
   b. He/rush around
      _____
      _____

4. self-centered a. This boy/try to get attention   b. He/think about himself

_____   _____

_____   _____

5. pessimistic a. This girl/worry a lot   b. She/expect problems

_____   _____

_____   _____

6. obedient a. This person/follow rules   b. He/obey the law

_____   _____

_____   _____

3 Negative Statements: Graphology

Try some graphology. Study the handwriting and statements in Column A. Then write statements about the personality types and handwriting in Column B.

A   **B**

Grammar is interesting!   *Grammar is interesting!*

1.   **outgoing**   **shy**

  a. These letters slope forward.   _These letters don't slope forward._

  b. This person is outgoing.   _This person isn't outgoing. She's shy._

Grammar is interesting!   *Grammar is interesting!*

2.   **organized**   **disorganized**

  a. I leave big spaces between words.   _____

  b. I'm organized.   _I'm not_   _. I'm_   .

Grammar is interesting!   *Grammar is interesting!*

3.   **impatient**   **patient**

  a. These words jump up and down.   _____

  b. This person is impatient.   _This person_   .

                                   _He's_   .

Grammar is interesting!   *Grammar is interesting!*

4.   **pessimistic**   **optimistic**

  a. Their lines slope downward.   _____

  b. They are pessimistic.   _____

_____

4 **Affirmative and Negative Statements:** Graphology—Fact or Fiction?

Complete the passage. Use the simple present tense.

Graphologists _study_ handwriting. They _____ a
          1 (study)   2 (match)

person's personality with his or her writing. But this _____
                                              3 (not / work)

for everybody.

For one thing, people's personalities _____ always the same.
                                          4 (not / be)

My friend Kim always _____ with a backward slope, and graphologists
                               5 (write)

_____ her she is shy. But Kim _____ always shy. In class,
       6 (tell)   7 (not / be)

she _____ quietly and she _____ questions.
     8 (sit)   9 (not / ask)

She _____ her classmates and _____ to understand
     10 (watch)   11 (try)

the teacher. But Kim also _____ to a lot of parties, and at parties, she
                        12 (go)

_____ the same personality. She _____ a
  13 (not / have)   14 (dance)

lot, and she _____ funny jokes! Kim _____ actually very
        15 (tell)   16 (be)

outgoing and not shy at all!

GRAMMAR BRIEFING 2

Simple Present Tense II

FORM

A. *Yes/No* Questions and Short Answers

QUESTIONS			SHORT ANSWERS				
DO/DOES	SUBJECT	BASE VERB	YES			NO	
Do	I			I			I	
	you			you	**do.**		you	**do not.**
	we			we			we	**don't.**
	they	**work?**	Yes,	they		No,	they	
Does	he			he			he	**does not.**
	she			she	**does.**		she	**doesn't.**
	it			it			it	

(continued on next page)

B. *Wh-* Questions and Answers

Wh- Questions About the Subject

QUESTIONS			ANSWERS
WH- WORD	VERB + *-S/-ES*		
Who	**eats**	fish?	I do.
What	**matches**	these shoes?	Your new dress matches them.

Other Wh- Questions

QUESTIONS					ANSWERS
WH- WORD	*DO/DOES*	SUBJECT	BASE VERB		
Who/Whom*	**do**	you	**see?**		Professor Larson.
What	**do**	they	**want?**		Some soup.
Where	**does**	he	**live?**		He lives on Main Street.
When	**does**	it	**snow**	here?	It usually snows in November.
How often	**do**	you	**eat**	fish?	Two or three times a week.

Whom is more formal than *who*.

GRAMMAR PRACTICE 2

Simple Present Tense II

5 **Short Answers:** You're the Expert!

What are the habits of people with these personalities? Write short answers.

1. shy   Do we speak openly? _No, we don't._

2. disorganized Do these people have poor organizational skills? _____

3. patient   Does she hurry and rush a lot? _____

4. quiet   Does he try to get attention? _____

5. friendly   Do they like other people? _____

6. generous   Do you share your things with other people? _____

7. honest   Do I tell the truth? _____

Contents

6 *Yes/No* Questions and Answers: The Right Job for Jack

A. Jack Carter is very unhappy at his job. He needs help. Complete the conversation.
Change each statement in parentheses to a *yes/no* question, and write short answers.

Jane: Hello, Mr. Carter. My name is Jane Mooney. I'm your career counselor.

    Do you have a problem _____?
                                      1 (You have a problem.)

Jack: Yes, __I do_____. I don't like my job! I really need a new job.
                  2

Jane: Okay, but I need some information about you.

_____?
             3 (You like meeting new people.)

Jack: No, _____. I prefer time alone or with my family.
          4

Jane: _____?
       5 (You enjoy working with numbers.)

Jack: No, _____! I'm not good with numbers! I always make mistakes.
        6

Jane: Okay. Well, that's important, then! _____?
                                 7 (You like the outdoors.)

Jack: Yes, _____. I love the peace and quiet of the countryside.
         8

Jane: I see. That's also very important information. Just a few more questions.

_____?
         9 (Your wife works.)

Jack: Yes, _____.
        10

Jane: _____?
       11 (She likes her job.)

Jack: No, _____. She is too busy.
        12

Jane: _____?
       13 (You have children.)

Jack: Yes, _____. We have two children.
        14

Jane: _____?
        15 (They go to school.)

Jack: No, _____. They finished school, and now they work.
             16

Jane: By the way, Jack. What is your job now?

Jack: I work for a large company in New York City. I meet a lot of people, and I work with

numbers all the time. You see, I really need a new job!

B. Discuss as a class: Does Jack's job fit his personality? Why or why not? What is a
good job for Jack?

7 *Wh-* Questions: An Interesting Job

Learn more about career counselors. Read the answers. Write the questions.
Use the words given.

1. Q: *Where do you find career counselors* _____?
                     (Where / you / find / career counselors)

   A: In many places.

2. Q: _____?
                     (Who / hire / them)

   A: Employment offices often hire them. Sometimes colleges and universities hire them, too.

3. Q: _____?
                     (What / be / their job)

   A: They help people match their personality with good jobs.

4. Q: _____?
                     (Who / ask / them for help)

   A: All kinds of people. Young people and old people. People without jobs and people

   with good jobs.

5. Q: _____?
                     (When / people / go to career counselors)

   A: They go to career counselors when they need a job or when they don't like their job.

6. Q: _____?
                     (How often / career counselors / really help people)

   A: They help people quite often.

7. Q: Career counseling sounds interesting. I want to be a career counselor.

   _____?
                     (What / I / do)

   A: You need to go to school.

8. Q: _____ ?
       (What / I study)

   A: Many things, including psychology.

9. Q: _____ ?
       (What / be / psychology)

   A: Psychology is the study of personalities.

Adverbs of Frequency with the Simple Present Tense

FORM

A. Adverbs of Frequency with *Be*

Adverbs of frequency usually come **after** *be*.	She **is usually** outgoing.
	They **aren't often** here.
	Jane and Dick **are always** happy.

B. Adverbs of Frequency with Other Verbs

Adverbs of frequency usually come **before** other verbs.	Kim **frequently goes** to parties.
	We **sometimes go** together.

FUNCTION

Telling How Often

Adverbs of frequency tell **how often** something happens:

100% of the time

always
almost always
usually
often, frequently
sometimes, occasionally
rarely, seldom
hardly ever
never

0% of the time

1. *Rarely, seldom, hardly ever,* and *never* are already negative. Don't use *not* with these words.

   We **rarely** go shopping alone.
     NOT: We ~~don't~~ rarely go shopping alone.

   We **never** eat alone.
     NOT: We ~~don't~~ never eat alone.

2. *Ever* means "at any time." Use it in questions and in the phrase *hardly ever.*

   Do you **ever** eat meat?

   We **hardly ever** eat meat.

GRAMMAR PRACTICE 3

Adverbs of Frequency with the Simple Present Tense

8   **The Meaning of Adverbs of Frequency:** Surprise Personality!

  A. Some people's personalities don't match their jobs. Kim is at a party. She is talking to a famous Hollywood actor, George Giantmuscle. She gets quite a surprise. Read the conversation.

George at Work

George at Parties

Kim: Excuse me, but aren't you . . . ?

George: Uh . . . yeah. George Giantmuscle. Hi.

Kim: Oh, I don't believe it! I'm so happy to meet you. I watch your movies all the time!

George: Really?

Kim: Yes. I love the movie with the wild horse on Fifth Avenue. How did you ride that horse?

George: Oh, that's my stuntman. I don't ride horses. I don't like big animals.

Kim: Oh, I see. Hmm . . . Well, do you go to a lot of parties?

George: Some, but only with my mother. She goes to a lot of parties, and she occasionally

takes me with her.

Kim: You're so famous. I bet you meet new people all the time.

George: Yes, I often meet people, but I don't often have time to make friends. I work all the time.

Kim: Ah. Um . . . Well, do you ever dance?

George: Not very often. I'm not very athletic. Maybe I'm just shy. Oh, here comes my mother.

Time to go. Goodbye.

B. Look again at the conversation in Part A. How often do these things happen? Circle the correct adverb of frequency.

1. Kim watches George's movies.	(Always)	Often	Sometimes	Seldom	Never
2. George rides horses.	Always	Often	Sometimes	Seldom	Never
3. George goes to parties with his mother.	Always	Often	Sometimes	Seldom	Never
4. His mother goes to parties.	Always	Often	Sometimes	Seldom	Never
5. George meets new people.	Always	Often	Sometimes	Seldom	Never
6. He makes friends.	Always	Often	Sometimes	Seldom	Never
7. He works.	Always	Often	Sometimes	Seldom	Never
8. He dances.	Always	Often	Sometimes	Seldom	Never

C. What surprises you about George, the actor? Write two sentences. Use an adverb of frequency in each sentence.

1. _He seldom makes friends._

2. _____

3. _____

9 Adverbs of Frequency: My Friend George

Now Kim is telling her friend about George Giantmuscle. Listen to the conversation and write the verbs and adverbs you hear.

Kim: Rosa, _do___1___ you _ever___2___ watch George Giantmuscle videos?

Rosa: _____3____. I _____4____ usually _____5_____

out to movies. He's that big tough guy, right?

Kim: Right. You _____6_____ him on television.

Rosa: Uh-huh. He _____7_____ onto the stage, and everyone screams.

Kim: Well, I know him. We're friends.

Rosa: No! Why _____8_____ you _____9_____ all the luck?

I _____10_____ famous people.

Kim: Well, of course not. Famous people _____11_____ all their

time in the library, and you _____12_____ there!

10 Adverbs of Frequency: More About George

Complete the conversation with the words in parentheses. Put the adverbs in the correct place.

Rosa: Well, what's George Giantmuscle like?

Kim: Guess what! He's really shy. He _is usually___1 (be / usually)___ at work, so he _____2 (have / hardly ever)_____

time for friends. His mother _____3 (take / sometimes)_____ him to parties.

Rosa: That's amazing. He _____4 (be / always)_____ so adventurous and

confident in his movies.

Kim: Well, people _____5 (surprise / sometimes)_____ you.

Rosa: Hmmm. I wonder. Does he have a girlfriend?

Kim: Forget it, Rosa. He _____6 (have / never)_____ time for friends!

11 Adverbs of Frequency: More About You

Work as a class or in small groups. Do this exercise quickly! Take turns asking one another questions with *Do you ever . . . ?* Answer with adverbs of frequency.

Example: Student 1: *Jan, do you ever go to the library?*
Student 2: *No, I hardly ever go to the library. Pedro, do you ever fall asleep in class?*
Student 3: *I occasionally fall asleep in class. Mimi, . . .*

Never	Hardly ever	Rarely Seldom	Sometimes Occasionally	Often Frequently	Usually	Almost always	Always

0%   100%

go to the library	go horseback riding	study all night
fall asleep in class	tell jokes	rush all day
go to the movies	forget people's names	watch the sunset
go to parties alone	forget your telephone number	cry at movies
worry a lot	send letters from a computer	jog before class

12 Simple Present and Adverbs of Frequency: Your Dream Job

Write a paragraph about your dream job. Talk about what you usually, always, sometimes, etc., do at this job. Use the simple present tense and adverbs of frequency.

See the *Grammar Links* Website for a complete model paragraph for this assignment.

Example: *I work in a plant nursery. This is my dream job. I usually work five days a week. . . .*

Check your progress! Go to the Self-Test for Chapter 1 on the *Grammar Links* Website.

Present Progressive Tense

Introductory Task: Pessimists and Optimists

A. Chip and Chuck are taking a vacation. Read their postcards.

Dear Dan and Eve,

How's it going back in sunny California? We're doing okay. Our ski instructor is trying hard with me, but I'm not learning very fast! At the moment, we're sitting in a cafe. It**'s snowing** hard outside, and the wind is blowing. The radio **is playing** some terrible country and western music. Some of the people in our group **are telling** bad jokes. Others **are singing** loudly! We'll be home next Friday. I'm counting the days!

Love,

Chuck

Dan and Eve Stoddard
560 Elm Street
Los Angeles, CA 90065

Dear Dan and Eve,

We're having a great time in Colorado! We**'re learning** a lot about skiing, and we're making some good friends. Right now, we're sitting in a cozy cafe near the ski slopes. The snow **is falling** in big, beautiful flakes outside, and lively music **is playing** in the background. We**'re telling** funny jokes and singing. I'm not thinking about work or school or anything! It's a good life.

Love,

Chip

Dan and Eve Stoddard
560 Elm Street
Los Angeles, CA 90065

country and western music = music from the southern and western parts of the United States. *cozy* = comfortable and warm. *lively* = full of energy.

B. Chip and Chuck have different personalities. One is an optimist: He always sees the good side of life. The other is a pessimist: He always sees the bad side. Who is the pessimist? Who is the optimist? How do you know? Copy the sentences from the postcards. Use the **boldfaced** verbs.

I know that _____ is the pessimist because he says:

1. About skiing: _I'm not learning very fast._

2. About the snow: _____

   _____

3. About the music: _____

   _____

4. About the jokes: _____

   _____

I know that _____ is the optimist because he says:

1. About skiing: _____

   _____

2. About the snow: _____

   _____

3. About the music: _____

   _____

4. About the jokes: _____

   _____

Present Progressive Tense I

FUNCTION

A. Actions Happening at the Moment

The present progressive (also called present continuous) describes **actions happening at the moment of speaking**. These actions are often **temporary**. Common time words and expressions used with this meaning of the present progressive include *now*, *right now*, and *at the moment*.

I **am writing** postcards right now.

Snow **is falling**.

PAST   NOW   FUTURE

am writing right now

B. Actions Happening over a Longer Time

The present progressive describes **actions happening over a longer period of time**. These actions are also often **temporary**. Common time words and expressions used with this meaning of the present progressive include *these days*, *this year*, *this semester*, *this week*, *today*, and *this afternoon*.

We **are staying** in a hotel this week.

They **aren't skiing** this afternoon.

PAST   NOW   FUTURE

this week

are staying

Present Progressive Tense I

1 Present Progressive Meanings: Learning to Be an Optimist

Read the letter. Underline the present progressive verbs. Write *N* (for "now") above present progressive verbs that describe what is happening right now. Write *L* above verbs that describe what is happening over a longer period of time.

Dear Mom and Dad,

Guess what! This semester, I'm learning to be a better athlete. I'm taking classes with Dr. Sydney Bennett. He's a very famous psychologist. Dr. Bennett is writing a book called "Optimism for Athletes." He's working with other psychologists here. They are teaching special mental and physical exercises to athletes. They believe these exercises make people optimistic. It's incredible! All their athletes are becoming champions!

Right now, I'm sitting outside the classroom. I'm waiting for Dr. Bennett. And I'm writing this letter. I'm also practicing some of Dr. Bennett's techniques. I'm relaxing my shoulders, but I'm sitting up straight. I'm breathing deeply. I'm thinking happy thoughts. In fact, I'm thinking about you guys! Are you having a good week? Are you relaxing and enjoying yourselves? Or are you working too much, as usual?

Well, Dr. Bennett is coming now. I miss you. Write soon.

Love,

Kurt —the optimist and future Olympic champion!

Present Progressive Tense II

FORM

A. Affirmative Statements		
SUBJECT	*BE*	BASE VERB + *-ING*
I	am 'm	
You We They	are 're	working.
He She It	is 's	

B. Negative Statements		
SUBJECT	*BE* + *NOT*	BASE VERB + *-ING*
I	am not 'm not	
You We They	are not 're not aren't	working.
He She It	is not 's not isn't	

(See Appendix 3 for the spelling rules for *-ing* verb forms.)

GRAMMAR PRACTICE 2

Present Progressive Tense II

2 **Affirmative Statements:** Optimists Win!

Complete the sentences with the present progressive of the verbs in parentheses.
Use full forms, not contractions.

Chip and Chuck __are taking__ skiing lessons right now. Poor Chuck __is doing__ badly.
             1 (take)   2 (do)

But maybe that's because he _____ like a pessimist! He _____ to fall, so
                                  3 (ski)   4 (expect)

his legs _____ and he _____ his balance. But Chip _____
               5 (shake)   6 (lose)   7 (use)

his body like an optimist. He _____ himself, and he _____ confidently.
                                  8 (enjoy)   9 (ski)

His arms and legs _____ together. He _____ his mind and body.
                      10 (work)   11 (use)

His mind _____ to his body: "Relax! Enjoy! Be positive!"
           12 (say)

3 Affirmative Statements with Contractions: Learning to Win

Kirk is helping a friend play tennis. Complete their conversation with the present progressive of the verbs in parentheses. Use contractions ('m, 's, or 're).

Kirk: Look at me. What am I doing?

Friend: You __'re staring__ at the ball.
                  1 (stare)

Kirk: Good. Now, breathe deeply.

Friend: I am. I __'m breathing__ deeply and slowly.
                  2 (breathe)

Kirk: Good. Now think about the present.

Friend: Okay. I _____ about the present moment.
                  3 (think)

Kirk: Are you relaxing your muscles?

Friend: Yes. I _____ my muscles.
                  4 (relax)

Kirk: Okay. Now look at the other player over there. She _____
                                                                      5 (rest)

         between shots. Why? Because she . . .

Friend: I know. She _____ energy.
                       6 (save)

Kirk: Energy. That's important. And those players always miss the ball, but what are

         they doing?

Friend: They _____ at their mistakes.
                  7 (smile)

Kirk: Right. Are you smiling? Good. And what are you expecting?

Friend: I _____ a perfect shot.
              8 (expect)

Kirk: That's it. Now you _____ like an optimist . . . and
                                  9 (act)

         a winner.

4 **Negative Statements with Contractions:** Optimistic Tennis

Use the words in parentheses to make negative sentences. Use contractions (*'m not, 're not/aren't, 's not/isn't*).

1. They're thinking about the present moment.

   They're not thinking about the future. OR They aren't thinking about the future.
   (not / think about the future)

2. They're staring at the ball.

   _____
   (not / look at each other)

3. She's expecting a perfect shot.

   _____
   (not / worry about her shot)

4. I'm breathing deeply and slowly.

   _____
   (not / breathe fast)

5. You're smiling at your mistakes.

   _____
   (not / get angry)

6. I'm resting between shots.

   _____
   (not / waste energy)

7. We're acting like optimists.

   _____
   (not / act like pessimists)

See the *Grammar Links* Website for more information about psychology and sports.

5 **Writing Sentences:** The Good Side

A. These situations are stressful, but maybe they have a good side. Write a sentence about the good side of each situation. Use the present progressive.

1. Your car isn't working, so you walk to school.

   I'm getting good exercise.

2. Ali's teacher is giving him a lot of homework.

   _____

3. Bob is jogging, and it's snowing now.

   _____

4. Our neighbors are playing loud music next door.

   _____

5. You're spending this weekend alone.

   _____

6. Carolyn is dieting, and it's very difficult!

   _____

7. I'm not going out much these days.

   _____

8. We're waiting for a plane, and it's three hours late.

   _____

9. Dr. Bauer's students are finding a lot of stress in their lives.

   _____

B. Share your sentences with the rest of the class. Discuss: Who is the most optimistic? Why?

Present Progressive Tense III

FORM

A. Yes/No Questions and Short Answers

QUESTIONS			SHORT ANSWERS*					
BE	SUBJECT	BASE VERB + -ING	YES			NO		
Am	I			I	am.		I	am not.
								'm not.
	you			you			you	are not.
Are	we		Yes,	we	are.	No,	we	're not.
	they	working?		they			they	aren't.
	he			he			he	is not.
Is	she			she	is.		she	's not.
	it			it			it	isn't.

*Use contractions only in negative short answers, not in affirmative short answers.

(continued on next page)

B. *Wh-* Questions and Answers

Wh- Questions About the Subject

QUESTIONS			ANSWERS
WH- WORD	BE	BASE VERB + *-ING*	
Who	**is** / **'s**	**working?**	Chuck is.
What	**is** / **'s**	**happening?**	Not much!

Other *Wh-* Questions

QUESTIONS					ANSWERS
WH- WORD	*BE*	SUBJECT	BASE VERB + *-ING*		
Who/Whom	**is** / **'s**	Chuck	**calling?**		He's calling his friend.
What	**am**	I	**eating?**		Fish.
Where	**are**	you	**going?**		I'm going to the bank.
How	**are**	they	**doing**	today?	Great!

Present Progressive Tense III

6 ***Yes/No* Questions and Answers: I'm Changing My Life!**

Read the conversation. Complete the *yes/no* questions and write short answers.
Use contractions in negative short answers.

Lizzy: So tell me about this new book. <u>Are you reading</u> it now?
    1 (you / read)

Kathy: Yes, <u>I am</u> . It's called *Teach Yourself Optimism*. It's great.
    2

Lizzy: Oh, I have a book like that. It's called *Optimism for Athletes*.

    _____ about the same book?
        3 (we / talk)

Kathy: No, _____ . At least, I don't think so.
        4

Lizzy: Well, _____ you?
        5 (it / help)

Kathy: Yes, _____! It's giving me confidence.
        6

Lizzy: _____ this book?
        7 (a lot of people / buy)

Kathy: Yes, _____ . It's a bestseller.
        8

Lizzy: Kathy, look out the window! Is that Bob? _____ in the snow?
$\underset{\text{9 (he / jog)}}{}$

Kathy: Yes, that's Bob. He's reading the book, too. It's really helping him. He's exercising and

dieting and . . .

Lizzy: Kathy, look over there, at that table. That's Carolyn! _____
$\underset{\text{10 (she / eat)}}{}$

pizza for lunch?

Kathy: No, _____ . She's eating salad. She's reading the book, too.
$\underset{\text{11}}{}$

She's dieting and feeling very positive about it.

Lizzy: I'm exercising and dieting, too. But it's not doing any good.

Look! _____ thinner?
$\underset{\text{12 (I / get)}}{}$

Kathy: Oh, Lizzy. You're not overweight.

Lizzy: Yes, I am. I'm fat, and I'm getting fatter.

Kathy: Lizzy, you're talking like a pessimist! You really need this book!

7 *Wh-* Questions: Report the Conversation

Complete the questions with the present progressive.

1. Q: Who _is talking to Lizzy?_____ A: Kathy is talking to Lizzy.

2. Q: Where _____ A: They are sitting in a restaurant.

3. Q: What _____ A: They're talking about a new book

4. Q: What _____ A: The book is helping Kathy.

5. Q: Who(m) _____ A: The book is helping Kathy, Bob, and Carolyn.

6. Q: Where _____ A: Bob is jogging in the snow.

7. Q: What _____ A: Carolyn is eating salad.

8. Q: How _____ A: She's feeling very positive about her diet.

_____

9. Q: How _____ A: Lizzy is feeling pessimistic.

10. Q: What _____ A: She is complaining about her diet.

11. Q: What _____ A: Kathy is saying, "You need the book!"

	WRITING	SPEAKING
1. Use contractions of *wh-* words + *is* in speaking and informal writing.	Who**'s** eating with us tonight?	Who**'s** eating with us tonight?
2. Use contractions of *wh-* words + *are* or *am* only in speaking.	Who **are** you inviting?	Who**'re** you inviting?
	What **am** I doing here?	What**'m** I doing here?

8 **Contractions and Full Forms:** The Help Yourself Show

🎧 A psychologist is speaking on a TV talk show. Listen to the interview, and write the full forms of the words you hear.

Interviewer: Dr. Bauer, thank you for coming on the Help Yourself Show. <u>How are</u>
    ₁

you doing? _____ happening at your clinic these days?
                2

Dr. Bauer: Well, you know, I'm teaching people about stress.

Interviewer: And _____ you doing that?
              3

Dr. Bauer: Positive visualization.

Interviewer: Positive what?

Dr. Bauer: Visualization. Making pictures with our minds. For example, think about this. You and I

    are waiting for an important job interview. _____ you doing?
                            4

    _____ you feeling?
       5

Interviewer: My hands are shaking. I'm worrying about the interview.

Dr. Bauer: Right, and that's not helping you. Now. _____ I doing?
6

I'm visualizing. I'm making a picture in my mind. _____ this
7

picture taking me? Into the interview room. _____ I seeing?
8

The interview is going well. The interviewer is smiling and saying, "You're perfect for

this job." That's positive visualization.

Interviewer: Wow! So _____ coming to your clinic?
9

Dr. Bauer: People. Lots of people. I'm helping people every day.

9 | Present Progressive: Positive Visualization

 Imagine a stressful situation. Use a situation from the box or think of your own
situation. Visualize a positive picture about this situation. What is happening? Write a
paragraph about this picture. Use the present progressive.

Possible Situations	
the dentist office	learning to ski
the TOEFL exam	your first week in a new country
a long international plane flight	your first date with a new person
an operation in a hospital	a job or college interview
your first day of class	

Example: The Dentist's Office
I'm sitting in a comfortable chair. I'm listening to soft music on the radio.
Am I worrying? No, I'm not. . . .

See the *Grammar Links* Website for a complete model paragraph for this assignment.

Check your progress! Go to the Self-Test for Chapter 2 on the *Grammar Links* Website.

Chapter 3

Simple Present and Present Progressive

Introductory Task: Changes

A. Many things change our personality and habits—sometimes only for a few hours; sometimes forever.

Read about the changes in these people. Underline the **boldfaced** verbs that describe their usual habits and routines. Circle the **boldfaced** verbs that describe what is happening to them now.

1. Yoko **is** usually very sociable. She **goes** to a lot of parties and makes friends quickly. But this month she is acting very quiet. She**'s losing** her confidence. (Why? This is her first month in a new country. It's stressful.)

2. Carolyn and I almost always **work** very fast and **have** lots of energy. These days, we**'re working** slowly, and we**'re making** mistakes. (Why? Our diet **is making** us tired. We **aren't eating** right.)

3. You often **act** nervous and tired. But right now you **are acting** quiet and calm. (Why? You**'re listening** to relaxing music right now.)

4. Greg **is** usually very organized. He **concentrates** well and **does** a lot in a short time. Right now, he**'s trying** to work, but he **is not concentrating**. (Why? It's late at night, and Greg is a "morning person." He works better in the morning.)

B. Look at the verbs you circled and underlined in Part A. Then read the statements below and check the correct box.

1. The **boldfaced** verbs that describe usual habits or routines are in the
   ❑ simple present tense.   ❑ present progressive tense.

2. The **boldfaced** verbs that talk about what is happening now, this month, or these days are in the
   ❑ simple present tense.   ❑ present progressive tense.

Simple Present Versus Present Progressive

FUNCTION

A. Simple Present

1. The simple present describes **habits**, **routines**, and things that are generally true.

PAST	NOW	FUTURE

get up

They **get up** at 7:30. (routine)

PAST	NOW	FUTURE

stress makes us tired

Stress **makes** us tired. (generally true)

2. Adverbs of frequency (see Chapter 1) often occur with the simple present.

They **usually** get up at 7:30.

3. Other time expressions also occur with the simple present. They include *every day, in the afternoon, at night, most of the time,* and *on Saturdays* (or other days).

They get up at 9:00 **on Saturdays.**

B. Present Progressive

1. The present progressive describes **temporary actions** happening at the moment of speaking or over a longer period of time in the present.

PAST	NOW	FUTURE

he's concentrating

Shh! He**'s concentrating**. (moment of speaking)

PAST	NOW these days	FUTURE

we're working

We**'re working** slowly these days. (longer time)

2. Time expressions often occur with the present progressive. They include *these days, (right) now, today, tonight, this week, this semester, this month* and *this year.*

Right now, she's working.

We're living at home **this year.**

Simple Present Versus Present Progressive

1 **Simple Present Versus Present Progressive: What Changes Personality?**

Circle the correct verb form in the sentences.

1. a. Food (**gives** / is giving) people energy.

   b. But Tom and I (diet / are dieting) this week.

   c. Today we (try / are trying) to eat very little food, but it is difficult.

2. a. Color sometimes (changes / is changing) our personality.

   b. Psychologists say that bright colors often (make / are making) people active and nervous.

   c. For that reason, libraries and hospitals (don't usually paint / aren't usually painting) their walls red.

3. a. Alice (wears / is wearing) a blue dress right now.

   b. She likes blue. It always (makes / is making) her feel calm and relaxed.

4. a. People often (act / are acting) differently in new situations.

   b. For example, Yoko (lives / is living) in a new country this month.

   c. She (acts / is acting) quiet and shy these days.

5. a. I sometimes (get / am getting) tired when the weather is hot.

   b. I (get / am getting) very tired today. It is very hot and hazy.

6. a. Psychologists generally (try / are trying) to help people with personality problems.

   b. They sometimes (help / are helping) people change their personalities and behavior.

7. a. Relaxation (saves / is saving) energy.

   b. It (helps / is helping) people feel positive.

   c. Listen to your breathing. Look at your hands. (Do you relax / Are you relaxing) right now?

2 **Simple Present and Present Progressive: A New Situation**

A. Yoko usually has a routine. But today she is doing something different. Complete the sentences about Yoko. Use the simple present and the present progressive.

USUALLY		TODAY
Eat breakfast with her family	8:00 a.m.	Skip breakfast
Walk to the office	8:45	Catch the fast train downtown
Meet with clients all morning	9:00–12:00	Sit quietly at a desk
Go home for lunch	12:15 p.m.	Buy lunch in the school cafeteria
Answer letters and phone calls	1:00	Go to a laboratory and listen to tapes
See her friends after work	5:00	Go home
Go out in the evening	7:30	Work at her computer

1. Yoko usually _eats breakfast with her family_____.

   Today _she is skipping breakfast_____.

2. It's 8:45. She usually _____.

   At the moment, _____.

3. She usually _____ all morning.

   This morning _____.

4. _____ for lunch.

   Today _____.

5. In the afternoon, _____.

   This afternoon _____.

6. It's 5:10 now. She usually _____ at this time of day.

   Today _____.

7. Most of the time, she _____.

   This evening _____.

B. What is Yoko doing now? Why is her routine changing? What do you think?
Discuss as a class. Do you all agree?

---

3 Simple Present and Present Progressive: There and Here

A. What do you usually do on vacation, at home, with friends, or at work? What are you
doing here today? Write a paragraph about the differences. Use the simple present
and the present progressive. Use the verbs in the box or use verbs of your own.

drink	go	read	visit
eat	live	speak	watch
enjoy	play	study	wear

Example: I usually take a vacation every summer. I visit my parents in China.
          This summer, however, I'm not taking a vacation. . . .

See the *Grammar Links* Website for a complete model paragraph for this assignment.

B. Exchange papers with a partner. Read your partner's paragraph. Share three ideas
about your partner with the class.

Example: On vacation, my partner often wears shorts. She's not wearing shorts now.
          She's wearing a skirt.

Verbs with Stative Meaning

FORM and FUNCTION

A. Overview

Some verbs have stative (not active) meanings. Verbs with stative meaning describe states, not actions. Some common verbs with stative meaning are:

IDEAS	ATTITUDES	EMOTIONS	POSSESSIONS	SENSES	DESCRIPTIONS
forget	need	hate	have	hear	be
know	want	like	owe	see	cost
remember		love	own	smell	look
think				sound	seem
understand				taste	weigh

B. Simple Present Tense for Verbs with Stative Meaning

We usually use the **simple present** with verbs with stative meaning. We rarely use the progressive.

You **seem** nervous at the moment.
   NOT: You ~~are seeming~~ nervous at the moment.

C. Verbs with Both Stative and Active Meanings

Some verbs have both a stative and an active meaning. When they have an active meaning, they can be in the progressive.

Stative meaning: Arnold **looks** happy.
   (He seems happy.)

Active meaning: He **is looking** at his mother.
   (He is watching his mother.)

Stative meaning: I **think** he's wonderful.
   (In my opinion, he's wonderful.)

Active meaning: I **am thinking** about Arnold.
   (My mind is focusing on him.)

1. Use the simple present with *have* when it means "own" or "possess."

> I **have** a car.
>   NOT: I ~~am having~~ a car.
>
> She **has** a lot of free time.
>   NOT: She ~~is having~~ a lot of free time.

2. In certain special expressions, you can use the progressive with *have*: *have a good time, have trouble, have a problem, have dinner.*

> Frank **is having a good time** tonight. He is enjoying himself.
>
> Gloria **is having trouble** with her car.

GRAMMAR PRACTICE 2

Verbs with Stative Meaning

4 **Stative and Active Meaning:** Life with Gloria

A. Read the passage. Circle the verbs with stative meaning.

Gloria Jones (is) very tired tonight. Her eyes are heavy, and she is yawning.
Gloria needs sleep. Gloria's pillow feels soft and comfortable. The music on
her radio sounds soothing. The cool air from the open window smells fresh.
Gloria has a perfect place to sleep! But she isn't sleeping tonight. She is thinking
about her problems.

B. Circle the correct form of the verbs in parentheses.

Gloria (wants / is wanting) help with her problems. She is writing a letter to
1
Miss Know-It All. Miss Know-It-All (has / is having) an advice column in the local
2
newspaper. This (is / is being) Gloria's letter.
3

Dear Miss Know-It-All:

Help! I (have / am having) some problems, and I
4
(don't know / am not knowing) what to do. I
5
(need / am needing) some advice. I (think / am thinking)
6   7
you can help me.

First of all, my job (is / is being) a problem. These days,
8
I am working all the time. I usually (love / am loving) my job,
9
but, this is too much!

I also (have / am having) no appetite these days. Food
10
(doesn't look / isn't looking) good to me, and most food
11
(doesn't smell / isn't smelling) and (doesn't taste / isn't tasting)
12   13
so great, either. So I (don't eat / am not eating) these days, and
14
I (lose / am losing) weight.
15
I (think / am thinking) about going to a doctor, but that
16
(costs / is costing) a lot and I (am / am being) too busy. So
17   18
I hope you can help me instead. Please answer this letter.

What is my problem? What is your advice?

Wasting away in Washington,

Gloria Jones

Gloria Jones

C. Complete the letter. Use the simple present or present progressive of the verbs in parentheses.

Dear Miss Know-It-All:

We _**want**_____ your advice. We _____ a dear
     1 (want)   2 (have)

friend named Gloria. She _____ usually a happy and outgoing
                           3 (be)

person, and we _____ her very much! But Gloria's personality
              4 (like)

_____. She _____ angry and
    5 (change)   6 (seem)

nervous these days. She often _____ important meetings, and
                 7 (forget)

she always _____ too many things to do. Gloria never
         8 (have)

_____ time for her friends. She never _____ to
    9 (have)   10 (remember)

call us! These days, Gloria _____, and she
                11 (not / eat)

_____ well, either. We are worried about her.
    12 (not / sleep)

We _____ Gloria. Can you help us?
      13 (not / understand)

We _____ you give good advice.
    14 (know)

Worried in Washington,

Gloria's friends

---

 5 **Simple Present or Present Progressive:** Excuse Me?

Work with a partner. Complete the telephone conversation. Use the simple present or the present progressive of the verbs in parentheses.

1. Teenager: Mom, the phone's for you. It's Billy.

   Mom: Hello, Billy! _Are you having_____ a good time in Florida?
                     a (you / have)

   Billy: Great! But _I don't have_____ any money. I need $300.
                  b (I / not have)

2. Student 1: This homework is so difficult!

   Student 2: _____ about it too much! Just relax. It's easy!
               a (you / think)

   Student 1: Really? _____ it's easy?
               b (you / think)

3. Mr. Jones: Jack? This is Mr. Jones from the manager's office. _____ at

                               a (I / look)

              your sales report right now.

    Jack: Oh, hi, Mr. Jones. _____ okay?

                             b (it / look)

    Mr. Jones: Yes, pretty good!

4. Man: We have a nice new sports car on sale.

    Woman: _____ about the cost. What about a used car?

                  a (I / think)

    Man: Sorry. _____ the used cars are all sold.

                      b (I / think)

5. Woman: My cat is sick. _____ terrible. She needs an

                     a (She / look)

    appointment with the doctor today.

    Receptionist: _____ at the appointment book right now. Is two o'clock okay?

                  b (I / look)

6   **Editing: A's and B's**

Read about personality types. Draw a line through the incorrect **boldfaced** verbs. Write the correct verb form above the line. There are six incorrect verbs. The first correction is done for you.

                                                      divide

Different people **have** different reactions to stress. Medical scientists usually ~~**are dividing**~~
                  1   2

these reactions into two groups: Type A and Type B. Type A people always **feel** a lot of
                                                                                  3

pressure from stress. Type B people **are** more patient and relaxed.
                      4

Frank is a Type A person. He **is having** a new job. There **is being** a lot of stress at his
5   6

job. What is he doing about it? He **is seeming** angry all the time. He **is fighting** with his
7   8

new boss. Joyce is a Type B person. Sometimes she **is hearing** her neighbors' loud music at
9

night. In fact, this **is happening** tonight. What is she doing about it? She **is listening** to
10   11

relaxing music through her earphones. Type B personalities almost always **are reacting** to
12

stress in a calm way. Type A personalities usually **have** trouble with stress.
13

 See the *Grammar Links* Website for more information about Type A and Type B
personalities.

---

7 **Simple Present and Present Progressive:** Your Personality Type

Which personality type do you think you are, A or B? Why? Write a paragraph. Use the
simple present and present progressive.

Example: I think I have a Type A personality. I worry a lot. I'm worrying right now
about my grammar test tomorrow. . . .

 See the *Grammar Links* Website for a complete model paragraph for this exercise.

---

8 **Stative and Active Meanings:** Personal Profiles

A.

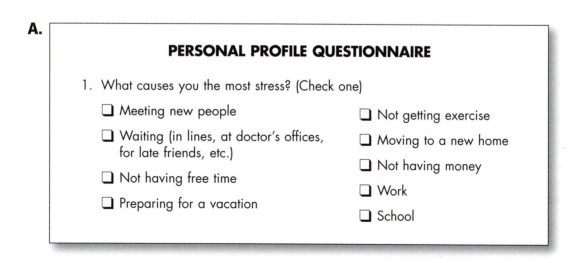

PERSONAL PROFILE QUESTIONNAIRE

1. What causes you the most stress? (Check one)

❏ Meeting new people   ❏ Not getting exercise

❏ Waiting (in lines, at doctor's offices,   ❏ Moving to a new home
for late friends, etc.)
❏ Not having money
❏ Not having free time
❏ Work
❏ Preparing for a vacation
❏ School

 See the *Grammar Links* Website for more information about stress.

2. What happens to you when you have stress? What happens to your health? How do you look? How do you feel? Write three sentences. Use verbs with stative meaning. Use the words in the box or use your own ideas.

angry	grouchy	out of sorts	sad	sore
anxious	nervous	pale	sick	tired
exhausted	out of control	restless	sleepless	unhappy

Note: Are any of the words and expressions above new to you? Find them in your dictionary.

When I have too much stress:

My neck is tight and sore.

I look pale and tired.

a. _____

b. _____

c. _____

3. What do you do to relieve stress? Write three sentences about your habits and routines. Use the simple present tense.

I take a warm bath.

I go for a long walk.

a. _____

b. _____

c. _____

 B. Share your answers with a partner. Do you have any of the same answers? Share these answers with the class. Which answer is the most common for each question?

Check your progress! Go to the Self-Test for Chapter 3 on the *Grammar Links* Website.

Wrap-up Activities

1 Letter Home: EDITING

Correct the errors in this e-mail message. There are 12 errors with simple present, present progressive, and adverbs of frequency. The first error is corrected for you.

To: lrbrocopp@aol.com
From: Amy_Brocopp@smcvt.edu
Subj: Hello from school

Dear Mom and Dad,

How are you? Thank you for the photos. They are beautiful, and you
                          seem
all ~~are seeming~~ fine. Little Maria is looking so tall now!

I miss you, but I am having a great time at school. We are having a good

grammar teacher. She is nice, but she give us a lot of homework. And she

doesn't never finish class on time. I sitting in grammar class at the

moment. The teacher is talking, and I fall asleep. You ask often me: "You

are okay?" The answer is: Yes, I'm. I'm eating in the school cafeteria

these days. I like the pizza! I am thinking it tastes good, and it don't cost

too much.

Goodbye for now. I love you all.

Amy

2 Me or Not Me? WRITING/SPEAKING

Match the paper with the person.

Step 1 On a piece of paper, write three statements about yourself and your personality. Use at least one present progressive verb and one simple present verb. Try to use a verb with stative meaning.

Step 2 Work in a team of four or five. Put your papers together in a bag.

Step 3 Student A: Take a paper from the bag and read the statements aloud. Ask questions to match the paper with the person. That person then becomes Student A.

Step 4 Continue until all students have a turn and all people and papers have a match.

Example statements on paper: I never go to parties.
I'm living in a dormitory right now.
I love dogs.

Possible questions: Who never goes to parties?
Jorge, are you living in a dormitory right now?
Do you love dogs?

3 Advertisements: WRITING/SPEAKING

Work in teams of three or four. Write an advertisement for a product that helps with stress or personality problems.

Step 1 Use one idea from Box 1, one idea from Box 2, and one idea from Box 3.

Step 2 Write the advertisement. Add your own description. (For example, how does it look? What is the price? How does it taste, feel, or smell? What does it do?) Use the simple present and the present progressive.

Step 3 Share your advertisement with the rest of the class.

Example:

> DO YOU FEEL NERVOUS AND ANGRY THESE DAYS? The Mind Massager is helping millions of people. People are relaxing and enjoying life.
>
> This wonderful little radio weighs only 50 grams. It goes inside your hat and plays soft music. It sounds wonderful!

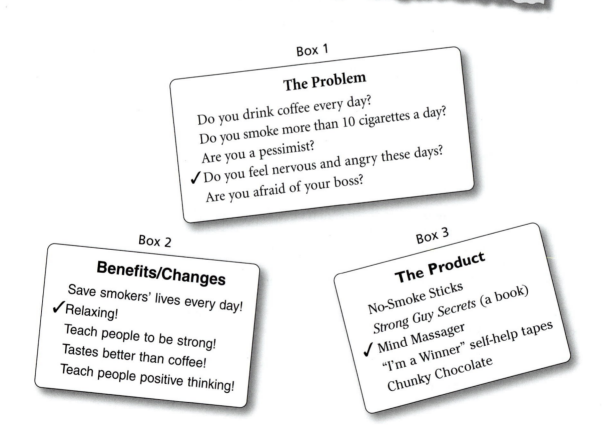

Box 1

The Problem

Do you drink coffee every day?
Do you smoke more than 10 cigarettes a day?
Are you a pessimist?
✓ Do you feel nervous and angry these days?
Are you afraid of your boss?

Box 2

Benefits/Changes

Save smokers' lives every day!
✓ Relaxing!
Teach people to be strong!
Tastes better than coffee!
Teach people positive thinking!

Box 3

The Product

No-Smoke Sticks
Strong Guy Secrets (a book)
✓ Mind Massager
"I'm a Winner" self-help tapes
Chunky Chocolate

4 **Where Are You Going?** WRITING/SPEAKING

Step 1 Look at this picture by the famous American artist Norman Rockwell. Write a paragraph about the picture. Describe the people in the picture. Why are they together? What are they doing? What are they thinking about? Use the simple present and the present progressive.

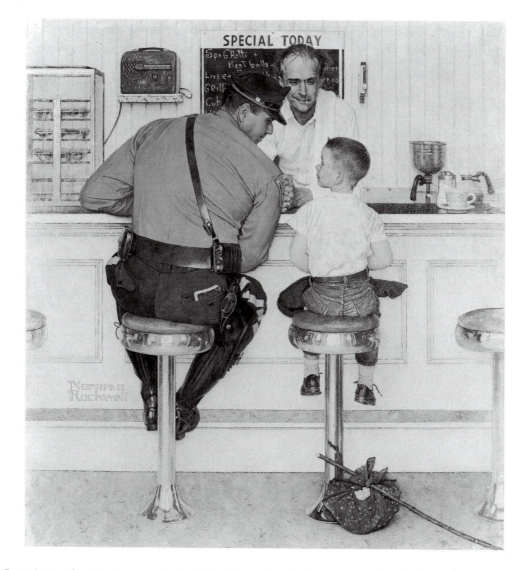

Step 2 Read your paragraph to your classmates. Compare your descriptions.

Example: This is a picture of a policeman and a little boy. They are in a restaurant. The policeman is talking to the little boy. . . .

 See the *Grammar Links* Website for a complete model paragraph for this activity. Go to the *Grammar Links* Website to see more Norman Rockwell paintings.

5   **More About You:** SPEAKING/LISTENING

Step 1 Prepare a short talk about your best friend. Why is this person your best friend? What do you usually do together? What is your friend (probably) doing today?

Step 2 Give your talk in class. Bring along a photo if you can. If possible, tape-record your talk.

Step 3 Listen to your recording. Did you use the simple present tense? The present progressive? Adverbs of frequency?

Past Time

TOPIC FOCUS
Unsolved Mysteries

UNIT OBJECTIVES

■ **the simple past tense**
(He *lived* a long time ago. He *wrote* about mysteries.)

■ ***used to***
(He *used to* travel a lot, but he doesn't travel now.)

■ **the past progressive tense**
(The sun *was shining* that morning.)

■ **choosing between the simple past and the past progressive**
(They *were standing* on the beach. Suddenly, they *saw* a ship.)

■ **the simple past and the past progressive with *while* and *when***
(She *was talking while* I *was cooking*. *When* the phone *rang*, I *answered* it.)

Grammar in Action

 ## Reading and Listening: Unsolved Mysteries

Read and listen.

1   People love stories about ancient history—stories from thousands of years ago. Many of these stories are mysteries. We have a lot of questions about them. Are they all true? What really **happened** to the people and places in these stories?

2   For example, Plato **was** a Greek philosopher. He **lived** and **died** more than 2,000 years ago. He **described** a beautiful continent in the Atlantic Ocean. Plato **called** this continent Atlantis. The Atlantean people were fighting a war with Greece when a terrible earthquake **destroyed** the continent. Atlantis **went** down to the bottom of the sea forever.

3   Was Plato telling the truth when he **wrote** about Atlantis? In ancient times, historians **were** not very scientific. They sometimes used to write from opinion and imagination; but the mystery of Atlantis did not end with Plato.

4   In the middle of the twentieth century, two modern Atlantis stories **became** famous. In one story, the Atlanteans **worked** with the ancient Egyptians. They **helped** the Egyptians build their pyramids. In another story, Atlantis **had** a big magnetic solar crystal. The Atlanteans used this crystal for energy. When the earthquake happened, the crystal **fell** into the ocean, into an area called "The Bermuda Triangle." Thousands of years later, in modern times, many ships and airplanes **disappeared** in this area. Did the magnetic crystal destroy them?

Big Magnetic
Solar Crystal

5   Did Atlantis really exist? Who **built** the pyramids? What happened in the Bermuda Triangle? We don't know the answers to these questions. All these stories are unsolved mysteries.

See the *Grammar Links* Website for more information about Atlantis, the pyramids, and the Bermuda Triangle.

Think About Grammar

A. The simple past tense forms of these verbs are **boldfaced** in the passage. Find them and write them below.

Regular Forms		Irregular Forms	
happen	_happened_	be (is)	_was_
live	_____	go	_____
die	_____	write	_____
describe	_____	be (are)	_____
call	_____	become	_____
destroy	_____	have	_____
work	_____	fall	_____
help	_____	build	_____
disappear	_____		

All **regular** simple past verbs end with the same two letters. What are they? _____

B. Complete this sentence from the passage (paragraph 2).

The Atlantean people _____ _____ a war with Greece
_{action 1}

when a terrible earthquake _____ the continent.
_{action 2}

Circle the correct answer.

Action 1 started _____ action 2.

a. before

b. after

c. at the same time as

Chapter 4

Simple Past Tense; *Used To*

Introductory Task: The Curse of King Tutankhamen

A. Read and listen. Underline all the **regular** simple past tense verb forms.

King Tutankhamen was a boy king in ancient Egypt.

He died in 1323 BC. His people buried him in a
large stone tomb. Some people say the Egyptians
wrote a terrible warning—a curse—on his tomb.
The warning said, "Open this tomb and die!"

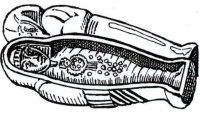

No one opened the tomb for more than 3,000 years.

Then, in 1923, Lord Carnarvon, a British archeologist, opened the tomb. A team of
40 people helped him. On February 22, Carnarvon walked into King Tutankhamen's
tomb. He looked at all the treasures inside. A beautiful mask of gold covered the boy
king's body. Jewels were all around him.

A few weeks later, a mosquito bite killed Lord Carnarvon in Egypt. In England,
his dog fell down dead on the same day. In the next seven years, 22 other men from
Carnarvon's team died mysteriously!

More recently, in 1972, a plane carried King Tutankhamen's treasures out of
Egypt. Soon after that, the pilot and engineer had heart attacks and died.

The ancient Egyptians wanted to protect King Tutankhamen's tomb. Did their
terrible curse end the lives of all these people?

---

tomb = a place to bury people who have died. *archeologist* = a person who finds and
studies things from the ancient world. *treasures* = very valuable things. *mask* = a cover
that shows the shape of the body.

B. According to some people, the curse on King Tutankhamen's tomb said, "Open this
tomb and die!" Discuss as a class: Do you believe the curse? Did it come true?

Simple Past Tense I

FORM

A. Regular and Irregular Verbs

1. All **regular** past tense verbs end in *-ed*.
   (See Appendix 4 for spelling rules for the simple past tense.)

   work → work**ed**, live → liv**ed**, study → studi**ed**, wait → wait**ed**

2. The *-ed* ending is pronounced /t/, /d/, or /ɪd/.
   (See Appendix 5 for pronunciation rules for the simple past tense.)

   work/**t**/, live/**d**/, wait/**ɪd**/

3. Many common verbs have **irregular** simple past forms.
   (See Appendix 6 for a list of irregular verb forms. See Appendix 7 for the simple past tense of *be*.)

   have → **had**, go → **went**, do, → **did**

B. Affirmative Statements

SUBJECT	VERB	
I		
You		
He		
She	**lived**	there.
It	**went**	away.
We		
They		

C. Negative Statements

SUBJECT	*DID NOT*	BASE VERB	
I			
You			
He			
She	**did not**	**live**	there.
It	**didn't**	**go**	away.
We			
They			

FUNCTION

Past Actions and States

1. The simple past describes actions and states that began and ended at some time or during some period in the past:

I **saw** her last night.

He **lived** a long time ago.

2. Common time expressions used with the simple past include *yesterday*, (*two days*) *ago*, *this* (*morning*), *last* (*night*), *for* (*three years*), *at* (*two o'clock*), and *on* (*Thursday*).

   We worked **for three hours**.

   He died **on Saturday**.

Simple Past Tense I

1 **Pronunciation:** Tutankhamen's Tomb

 A. Listen again to "The Curse of King Tutankhamen" from page 48. Above each verb you underlined, write the sound you hear: **/t/** (as in *helped*), **/d/** (as in *died*), or **/ɪd/** (as in *visited*).

Example:

$\quad$ *d*
He di̱e̱d in 1323 BC. . . .

 B. Read "The Curse of King Tutankhamen" aloud to a partner. Help each other pronounce the past tense verbs correctly.

2 **Affirmative Statements (Regular Verbs):** The Rest of the Story

Learn more about King Tutankhamen's curse. Complete the stories. Use the simple past tense of the verbs in parentheses.

1. The Soldier's Story (AD 56)

   One morning, my friend and I _visited_ King Tutankhamen's tomb. We
   $\qquad$ a (visit)

   _____ the door and _____ inside. A snake
   $\quad$ b (open) $\qquad$ c (walk)

   _____ up at us from King Tutankhamen's body. My friend
   $\quad$ d (look)

   _____ the snake. But two weeks later, a terrible sandstorm
   $\quad$ e (kill)

   _____ my friend in the desert. He _____ forever.
   $\quad$ f (bury) $\qquad$ g (disappear)

2. The Farmer's Story (AD 1560)

   I found the tomb many years ago. I was excited, and I _____ my wife.
   $\qquad$ a (call)

   We _____ to go into the tomb. But we _____ at the
   $\quad$ b (want) $\qquad$ c (look)

   warning on the tomb, and we _____ outside. After that, nothing
   $\qquad$ d (stay)

   _____ to us. My wife _____ and _____
   $\quad$ e (happen) $\qquad$ f (live) $\qquad$ g (work)

   with me for many happy years. She _____ six months ago.
   $\qquad$ h (die)

3 Affirmative Statements (Irregular Verbs): Ancient Mysteries

Complete the sentences with the simple past tense of the verbs in parentheses. Use Appendix 6 and Appendix 7 to help you.

1. The ancient Egyptians _built_____ (build) the pyramids.

2. These pyramids _____ (be) stone buildings.

3. They _____ (have) a square base and four triangle-shaped sides.

Square = □   Triangle = △

4. The Egyptians _____ (put) their kings and queens in the tombs in the pyramids.

5. They _____ (leave) jewels and useful objects next to the kings and queens.

6. Other ancient people _____ (do) different things to protect their dead.

7. For example, they _____ (take) the bodies to caves.

8. They _____ (write) stories on the walls of the caves.

9. Many centuries later, Hollywood _____ (make) many movies about ancient mysteries.

10. For example, many people _____ (see) the "Indiana Jones" and "The Mummy" movies.

11. Indiana Jones _____ (be) a famous scientist. He _____ (go) to dangerous places with ancient curses.

12. The Mummy was a dead body from ancient Egypt. It _____ (come) back to life in the twentieth century and _____ (become) very dangerous.

4 Regular and Irregular Simple Past: Time for a Race

A. How many verbs can you think of? Divide into two teams and stand in two lines. The first person in each team writes a **regular** simple past tense verb on the board and runs to the back of the line. The next person writes a different verb. Continue the game until one team can't think of more verbs or for 10 minutes.

B. Now play the game with **irregular** simple past tense verbs.

5 Negative Statements: Curse or Common Sense?

Read these warnings. Then look at each picture and write what the people **didn't** do.

WARNINGS:

✔ Give the waiter a good tip!

Eat right and exercise!

Stay out of the sun!

Take a road map!

Pay the rent on time!

Look right and left before crossing the street!

Lock the door!

Confirm the reservation!

1. _She didn't give the waiter a good tip._____

2. _____

_____

3. _____

_____

4. _____

_____

5. _____

6. _____

7. _____

8. _____

6   Time Expressions with Simple Past: Personal History

Write a paragraph about your past life. Write at least five sentences. Use time expressions (see the examples in the box).

Example: I came to the United States five years ago.

| last Tuesday | a long time ago | in 1999 |
| yesterday | this morning | for many years |

See the *Grammar Links* Website for a complete model paragraph for this assignment.

Simple Past Tense II

FORM

A. *Yes/No* Questions and Short Answers

QUESTIONS			SHORT ANSWERS					
DID	SUBJECT	BASE VERB	*YES*			*NO*		
	I			I			I	
	you			you			you	
	he			he			he	
Did	she	go?	Yes,	she	did.	No,	she	didn't.
	it			it			it	
	we			we			we	
	they			they			they	

B. *Wh-* Questions and Answers

Wh- *Questions About the Subject*

QUESTIONS		ANSWERS
WH- WORD	PAST FORM OF VERB	
Who	**went?**	She did.
What	**disappeared?**	The ship disappeared.

Other Wh- Questions

QUESTIONS				ANSWERS
WH- WORD	*DID*	SUBJECT	BASE VERB	
Who(m)	**did**	they	**help?**	They helped their friends.
What	**did**	he	**do?**	He worked.
Where	**did**	you	**go?**	Home.
How	**did**	it	**disappear?**	Very fast.

GRAMMAR PRACTICE 2

Simple Past Tense II

7 *Yes/No* **Questions and Answers:** My Secret Past

On a piece of paper, write a statement about your past life (you can use one from your paragraph in Exercise 6). Put your papers together in a bag. Take a paper from the bag. Ask *yes/no* questions to match the paper with the person.

Example: Q: Did you come to the United States many years ago?
A: Yes, I did./No, I didn't.

8 ***Wh-* Questions: Doctor Fossil, It's a Curse!**

Complete the *wh-* questions in the conversation. Use the simple past tense of the verbs in parentheses.

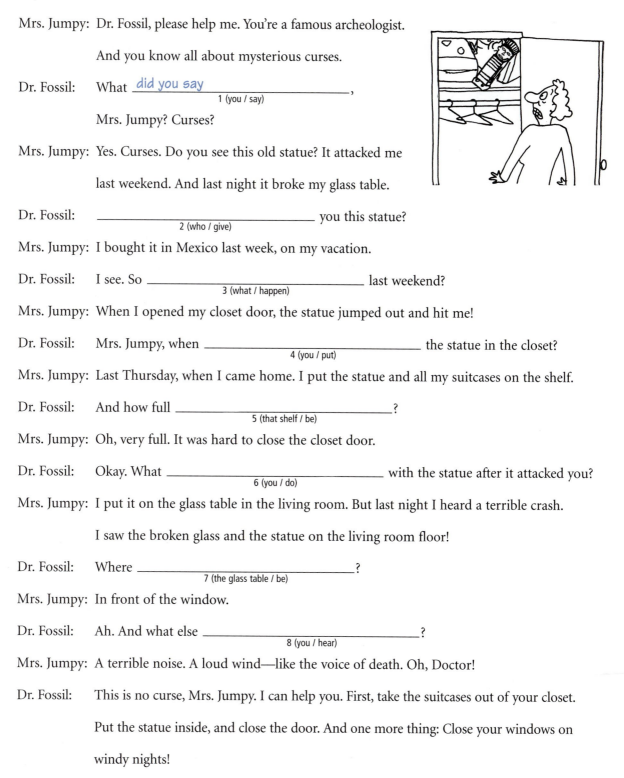

Mrs. Jumpy: Dr. Fossil, please help me. You're a famous archeologist.

And you know all about mysterious curses.

Dr. Fossil: What _did you say_____ ,
 1 (you / say)

Mrs. Jumpy? Curses?

Mrs. Jumpy: Yes. Curses. Do you see this old statue? It attacked me

last weekend. And last night it broke my glass table.

Dr. Fossil: _____ you this statue?
 2 (who / give)

Mrs. Jumpy: I bought it in Mexico last week, on my vacation.

Dr. Fossil: I see. So _____ last weekend?
 3 (what / happen)

Mrs. Jumpy: When I opened my closet door, the statue jumped out and hit me!

Dr. Fossil: Mrs. Jumpy, when _____ the statue in the closet?
 4 (you / put)

Mrs. Jumpy: Last Thursday, when I came home. I put the statue and all my suitcases on the shelf.

Dr. Fossil: And how full _____ ?
 5 (that shelf / be)

Mrs. Jumpy: Oh, very full. It was hard to close the closet door.

Dr. Fossil: Okay. What _____ with the statue after it attacked you?
 6 (you / do)

Mrs. Jumpy: I put it on the glass table in the living room. But last night I heard a terrible crash.

I saw the broken glass and the statue on the living room floor!

Dr. Fossil: Where _____ ?
 7 (the glass table / be)

Mrs. Jumpy: In front of the window.

Dr. Fossil: Ah. And what else _____ ?
 8 (you / hear)

Mrs. Jumpy: A terrible noise. A loud wind—like the voice of death. Oh, Doctor!

Dr. Fossil: This is no curse, Mrs. Jumpy. I can help you. First, take the suitcases out of your closet.

Put the statue inside, and close the door. And one more thing: Close your windows on

windy nights!

9 *Yes/No* and *Wh-* Questions: The Mystery of the Mayans

A. The Mayans, like the Egyptians, were ancient pyramid builders. Write *yes/no* or *wh-* questions about the Mayans. Use the information given.

1. The ancient Mayans lived in southern Mexico and Guatemala.

   Q: *Where did the ancient Mayans live?*_____

   A: In southern Mexico and Guatemala.

2. They lived there from 2000 BC to AD 1542.

   Q: _____

   A: From 2000 BC to AD 1542.

3. They built beautiful pyramids.

   Q: _____

   A: Beautiful pyramids.

4. Workers, noblemen, and priests lived in Mayan society.

   Q: _____

   A: Workers, noblemen, and priests.

5. The workers built the pyramids.

   Q: _____

   A: Yes, they did.

6. The noblemen wrote laws for the people.

   Q: _____

   A: The noblemen.

7. The priests didn't work in the fields.

    Q: _____

    A: No, they didn't. They organized religious services.

8. In 1542, the Mayans disappeared.

    Q: _____

    A: In 1542.

9. They didn't leave any information about their disappearance.

    Q: _____

    A: No, they didn't.

10. The forest buried their beautiful cities and pyramids.

    Q: _____

    A: The forest.

> *noblemen* = people from families with a high social position. *priests* = men who perform religious duties for a society.

B. What is the mystery of the Mayans? Write a question about the mystery. Then share your question with a partner. Do you have the same question?

See the *Grammar Links* Website for more information about the Mayans and their civilization.

GRAMMAR BRIEFING 3

Used To

FORM

A. Affirmative Statements

SUBJECT	*USED TO*	BASE VERB	
He	used to	live	here.
We			

B. Negative Statements

SUBJECT	*DID NOT*	*USE TO*	BASE VERB	
He	did not	use to	live	here.
We	didn't			

C. *Yes/No* Questions and Short Answers

QUESTIONS				SHORT ANSWERS	
DID	SUBJECT	*USE TO*	BASE VERB	*YES*	*NO*
Did	we	use to	live	here?	Yes, we **did**. No, we **didn't**.

(continued on next page)

D. *Wh-* Questions and Answers

Wh- Questions About the Subject

QUESTIONS				ANSWERS
WH- WORD	*USED TO*	BASE VERB		
Who	**used to**	**be**	famous?	Colorado Jones did.
What		**happen**	a lot?	He used to travel.

Other Wh- Questions

QUESTIONS					ANSWERS
WH- WORD	*DID*	SUBJECT	*USE TO*	BASE VERB	
What	**did**	he	**use to**	**do?**	Travel.
When		they		**go?**	A long time ago.

FUNCTION

Past Habits and Routines

Used to describes past habits and routines that are no longer true in the present. *Used to* makes it easy to compare the past with the present.

past	present
I **used to** travel a lot, but I **don't travel** anymore.	

GRAMMAR **HOT**SPOT!

1. Use the base form of *used to* in negative sentences and in questions with *did*.

   I **didn't use to** watch TV.
     NOT: I didn't ~~used~~ to watch TV.

   What **did** you **use** to do?
     NOT: What did you ~~used~~ to do?

2. *Use* is a regular main verb. It has a different meaning from *used to*.

   I **used** your pen.

Used To

10 *Used To*: Changing Lifestyles

Two conversation partners are talking about Jorge's new class. Complete the conversation with the correct forms of *used to* and the verbs in parentheses.

Elizabeth: The students in your class are very interesting. I'm sure they have many stories to tell.

Jorge: That's right. We all __used to live__ in different countries, and we
1 (live)

__didn't use to be__ students. But life is changing for us now. For example, Brigitte
2 (not / be)

_____ in a bookstore in France. Now she wants to be a banker.
3 (work)

Elizabeth: And what _____? Where
4 (Antonio / do)

_____?
5 (he / live)

Jorge: Well, Antonio _____ a banker in Guatemala. Now he wants to
6 (be)

buy a bookstore in New York City!

Elizabeth: Really? And your teacher said something about actors in your class. Who

_____ actors?
7 (be)

Jorge: Mariko and Kenji, from Japan.

Elizabeth: _____ in Tokyo?
8 (they / work)

Jorge: No. They _____ much time in Tokyo.
9 (not / spend)

They _____ around Japan. But now they want to open a
10 (travel)

flower shop in Kyoto.

Elizabeth: And what about you?

Jorge: Well, I _____ Spanish in Puerto Rico. But now I want to go
11 (teach)

home and teach English.

11 *Used To*: Changes in My Life

A. Write six sentences about changes in your own life. Use *used to*. Write at least three negative sentences. Use verbs from the box or use your own ideas.

be	go	live	talk to
feel	have	see	work

Examples: I used to have a dog, but now I have no pets.
I used to live in a small town, but now I live in a city.

B. Share your sentences with a partner. Ask and answer questions about your past lives.

Examples: A: What kind of dog did you use to have? B: A small brown one.
A: Did you use to like the small town? B: Yes, I did.

C. Work in small groups. Find one change that is the same for everyone in your group. Share it with the whole class.

Example: Our parents used to bring us to school, but now we come alone.

TALKING THE TALK

	WRITING	SPEAKING
1. In speaking, contractions of *wh-* words + *did* are common. *Did you* is often pronounced *didja* or *ja.*	Did you see it?	Did**ja** see it?
	When did you go?	When **ja** go?
	What did he do?	What**'d** he do?
	Who did she see?	Who**'d** she see?
2. In speaking, *used to* is often pronounced *useta.*	He used to travel a lot.	He **useta** travel a lot.

12 Contracted Forms: A Changed Man

An archeologist is speaking on a radio talk show. Listen to the interview and write the full forms of the words you hear.

Interviewer: Dr. Colorado Jones! We're happy to have you on our show tonight. Tell us about your exciting life. You love to explore the secrets of the ancient world, right?

Dr. Jones: Well, I ___used to___ ₁ love traveling. But I stopped all that a long time ago. It was a great life. I saw the world. I traveled to pyramids, temples, ancient cities . . .

Interviewer: So _____ ₂ travel with?

Dr. Jones: By myself. Alone. I _____ ₃ need company in those days.

Interviewer: _____ ₄ feel lonely sometimes?

Dr. Jones: No, I never _____ ₅ think about it.

Interviewer: So what happened? _____ ₆ get tired of it?

Dr. Jones: No, my wife didn't like it.

Interviewer: Your wife? _____ ₇ get married?

Dr. Jones: About 10 years ago.

Interviewer: And _____8_____ meet her?

Dr. Jones: In a travel agency! I only _____9_____ two agencies in all my

              traveling years, and she _____10_____ work in one of them.

Interviewer: So _____11_____ give up all those adventures for love?

Dr. Jones: No, I didn't give them up. Now I can see the world and have a family life too!

              My father-in-law found the way.

Interviewer: _____12_____ he do?

Dr. Jones: He bought us a television and a VCR as a wedding gift!

13 **Simple Past Tense and *Used To*: Explain This!**

  Work in small groups. Write a story to explain the picture. Write at least six sentences. Use the simple past tense and *used to*. Explain these mysteries: Where were these people? Who was the woman? Why was the man in the box? Did she use to know him? What happened next?

Example: Maria and Bill used to work together in the city museum. . . .

See the *Grammar Links* Website for a complete model paragraph for this assignment.

Check your progress! Go to the Self-Test for Chapter 4 on the *Grammar Links* Website.

Past Progressive Tense; Simple Past and Past Progressive; Past Time Clauses

Introductory Task: The Flying Dutchman

Read the true story below. Each underlined sentence tells about two actions. Which action started first? Write *1* above the first action and *2* above the second action.

1. In 1580, a Dutch ship was traveling from Holland to Indonesia.
   $\overset{2}{\text{It disappeared}}$ in a storm while it was $\overset{1}{\text{passing}}$ South Africa.

2. A few years later, some sailors met the ship again.

   They were sailing in the Atlantic Ocean when they saw the ship.

3. It was moving fast toward them.

   When the sailors saw this, they tried to send a signal to the ship.

4. While they were shouting and waving, it disappeared.

5. The ghost ship appeared again in the eighteenth and nineteenth centuries.

   When people heard about the ship, they called it "the Flying Dutchman."

---

sailors = people who work on ships. *signal* = message. *ghost* = a dead person who appears again in the world.

🌐 See the *Grammar Links* Website for more information about the Flying Dutchman.

Past Progressive Tense I

FORM

A. Affirmative Statements

SUBJECT	PAST OF *BE*	BASE VERB + *-ING*
I		
He	was	
She		
It		moving.
You		
We	were	
They		

B. Negative Statements

SUBJECT	PAST OF *BE* + *NOT*	BASE VERB + *-ING*
I		
He	was not	
She	wasn't	
It		moving.
You		
We	were not	
They	weren't	

(See Appendix 3 for the spelling rules for *-ing* verb forms.)

FUNCTION

A. Actions in Progress in the Past

The past progressive describes actions **in progress** (not completed) at a specific time in the past. The action started **before** the specific time and might continue **after** the specific time.

PAST 6:00   NOW   FUTURE

was shining

The sun **was shining** at six o'clock.

B. Actions Happening over a Longer Time in the Past

The past progressive also describes actions happening over a longer **period** of time in the past.

PAST 6:00   12:00   NOW   FUTURE

was studying

I **was studying** last night from six o'clock till midnight.

Past Progressive Tense I

1 Affirmative Statements: A Strange Scene

In March 1939, some people saw the Flying Dutchman again, near a beach in South Africa. Joanna, a South African woman, described the scene. Complete her story with the past progressive of the verbs in parentheses.

At six o'clock, the sun __was shining_____. Some children
_____ 1 (shine)

_____ in the sand. I _____
2 (play)   3 (lie)

in the sun. Then I noticed the people around me. They _____
4 (look)

at the sea. A woman _____ at a ship. The ship
5 (point)

_____ toward the beach. It _____
6 (come)   7 (rain)

hard around the ship. The ship's sails _____ in the wind. It looked
8 (blow)

like the ship _____.
9 (fly)

2 Affirmative and Negative Statements: What Really Happened?

Tom and Joanna are trying to remember what they saw on the beach. They don't agree. Complete their conversation with the past progressive of the verbs in parentheses.

Tom: I remember it exactly! I __was swimming_____ in the ocean with Kate.
1 (swim)

The ship __wasn't moving_____. It was cloudy around the ship, but it
2 (not / move)

_____. One man _____
3 (not / rain)   4 (wave)

at the ship.

Joanna: No, you're wrong! I saw the ship first. You and Kate _____.
5 (not / swim)

Both of you _____ into the sea. The ship
6 (walk)

_____ still. The storm _____
7 (not / stand)   8 (push)

it very fast. That man _____ at the ship. He
9 (not / wave)

_____ you and Kate! But you
10 (call)

_____ attention to him.
11 (not / pay)

Past Progressive Tense II

FORM

A. *Yes/No* Questions and Short Answers

QUESTIONS			SHORT ANSWERS					
PAST OF *BE*	SUBJECT	BASE VERB + *-ING*	YES			NO		
Was	I		Yes,	I		No,	I	
	he			he	**was.**		he	**was not.**
	she			she			she	**wasn't.**
	it	**moving?**		it			it	
Were	you			you			you	**were not.**
	we			we	**were.**		we	**weren't.**
	they			they			they	

B. *Wh-* Questions and Answers

Wh- *Questions About the Subject*

QUESTIONS			ANSWERS
WH- WORD	PAST OF *BE*	BASE VERB + *-ING*	
Who	**was**	**moving.**	I was.
What			The ship was.

Other Wh- *Questions*

QUESTIONS				ANSWERS
WH- WORD	PAST OF *BE*	SUBJECT	BASE VERB + *-ING*	
What	**was**	it	**doing?**	It was moving.
When	**were**	you	**watching?**	Yesterday.
Where	**were**	they	**going?**	Home.
How	**was**	it	**moving?**	It was moving fast.

Past Progressive Tense II

3 *Yes/No* **Questions and Short Answers:**
The Disappearance of Flight 19

A. At 2:00 p.m. on December 5, 1945,
five U.S. Navy planes (Flight 19) left the
Fort Lauderdale Navy base in Florida.
They never came back. Read this report
from the Navy base captain.

Flight 19 was doing a short training exercise over the Atlantic Ocean.
At first, we were receiving good radio contact with Flight 19. The planes
were flying fast, at 200 miles per hour. Then, at 2:30, the commander of
Flight 19 reported problems. His compass was not working. His radio
was giving him trouble, too. From 3:45 until 4:15, we had no contact.
During that time, our radio officer was trying to make contact, but he
was not getting an answer. He was starting to worry. Finally, at 4:15,
he received this message from the flight commander: "I don't know
our location." The last message, at 4:25, said, "We're in trouble. I think
we are . . ." The commander never finished the message.

> *compass* = an instrument that shows direction.

B. Ask the captain about his report in Part A. Write *yes/no* questions with the words
given. Then read the story again and write short answers.

1. Flight 19/do/a short exercise?

   Q: Was Flight 19 doing a short exercise?

   A: Yes, it was.

2. you/receive/good radio contact at first?

   Q: Were you receiving good radio contact at first?

   A: Yes, we were.

3. the planes/fly/slowly?

   Q: _____

   A: _____

4. the commander's compass/work/at 2:30?

   Q: _____

   A: _____

5. his radio/work/well?

   Q: _____

   A: _____

6. your radio officer/try/to make contact from 3:45 till 4:15?

Q: _____

A: _____

7. he/get/an answer?

Q: _____

A: _____

8. he/start/to worry?

Q: _____

A: _____

4 *Wh-* **Questions:** The Bermuda Triangle

Flight 19 was flying in the Bermuda Triangle, a dangerous area of the Atlantic Ocean. Christopher Columbus wrote about the Bermuda Triangle in 1492. Read the notes from his journal. Write *wh-* questions about the **boldfaced** words. Use *where, who, what,* or *when.*

1. At that time, I was sailing **west from Europe.**

   Where were you sailing? _____

2. **My men and I** were looking for a new way to the Indies.

   _____

3. **On October 11,** we were traveling in good weather.

   _____

4. Then we came into a terrible place. **Strange things** were happening.

   _____

5. Bright lights were flashing **in the sky.**

   _____

6. **White water** was bubbling in the sea.

   _____

7. I noticed my compass. The needle **was jumping around.**

   _____

8. I looked at my companion. He was covering **his face** with his hands.

_____

9. The other men were watching **me**. They were waiting for instructions. But I was frightened too.

_____

5 *Wh-* **Questions:** What Were You Doing?

A. Work with a partner. Take turns asking and answering questions about times in your lives. Use ideas from Columns A and B or use your own ideas.

Example: A: *What were you thinking about five minutes ago?*
B: *My lunch.*

A	B
Where / live?	five minutes ago
What / think about?	last night at midnight
What / do?	last year
Who / teach you?	three years ago
Who / live with?	at 3 o'clock this morning

B. Write the most interesting answer here. Then share it with the class.

Example:

Last year, Ernesto was living on a boat in Florida.

_____

_____

GRAMMAR BRIEFING 3

Simple Past Tense Versus Past Progressive Tense

FUNCTION

A. Simple Past

Use the simple past for actions or states that began and ended in the past. The action or state is **completed**.	I **explained** it to my friend last night. (I finished explaining.)

(continued on next page)

B. Past Progressive

1. Use the past progressive for actions **in progress** (not necessarily completed) in the past.

   I **was explaining** it to my friend last night. (Perhaps I didn't finish.)

2. The past progressive often **describes a scene**. It gives **background information** for stories. The simple past gives the **action** of the story.

   The sun **was shining**. We **were swimming**. (background description)

   Suddenly, a strange ship **appeared**. We **swam** back to the beach. (action)

GRAMMAR HOTSPOT!

Use the simple past (not past progressive) for verbs with stative meanings.

(See Chapter 3 for more on verbs with stative meaning.)

They **had** a good map.
   NOT: They ~~were having~~ a good map.

GRAMMAR PRACTICE 3

Simple Past Versus Past Progressive Tense

6 **Simple Past Versus Past Progressive:** Mystery in My Living Room

Read the sentences below. Check (✓) the sentences that describe completed actions.

1. Last night, I stayed up late. ___✓___

2. I was watching a murder mystery on TV. _____

3. I watched the movie for about an hour. _____

4. Halfway through the movie, I was falling asleep. _____

5. So I went to bed. _____

6. I closed my eyes and fell asleep. _____

7. Suddenly, big, scary monsters were running after me. _____

8. They were laughing and showing their long teeth. _____

9. I woke up and ran into my parents' bedroom. _____

10. They said, "No more mystery movies for you!" _____

Simple Past Versus Past Progressive: A Careful Man

A. Complete the conversation with the simple past or past progressive of the verbs in parentheses.

Jorge: Do you want to hear a joke?

Liz: Okay.

Jorge: Well, one day Christopher Columbus and his men _were sailing_ _____ in the
1 (sail)

Atlantic Ocean. Suddenly, they _noticed_ _____ a small boat in the
2 (notice)

distance. The man in the boat _____ a big basket of fish on top
3 (hold)

of his head! Columbus and his men _____ the man onto their
4 (take)

ship. Then Columbus asked him, "What _____ you

_____ out there?" The man _____:
5 (do)   6 (answer)

"Yesterday morning, I _____ near my island. A big storm
7 (fish)

_____ my boat all the way out here."
8 (push)

"But what about that basket on your head?"

"Oh, I _____ my boat. You see, my boat is very light, and the
9 (help)

basket is very heavy. I _____ the boat to sink. So I
10 (not / want)

_____ to carry the basket myself!"
11 (decide)

B. Work in small groups. Can you explain the joke? What was the man's mistake?
Share your group's explanation with the class.

8 Simple Past Versus Past Progressive: Explaining the Mystery of Flight 19

A. Here are some different explanations for the disappearance of Flight 19. Complete the sentences with the verbs from the box. Use the simple past and the past progressive.

1. From the Navy:

   | be | ✓have | hit | disappear | make |

   Flight 19 _had_ a bad compass. Some of the pilots
   (a)

   _____ new and nervous. On that day, they _____
   (b)   (c)

   their first sea flight. They probably _____ a storm and
   (d)

   _____ into the ocean.
   (e)

2. From the movie *Close Encounters of the Third Kind*:

   | take | happen | visit |

   It _____ like this. At that time, some aliens from outer space
   (a)

   _____ the Atlantic Ocean. Their UFOs _____ the
   (b)   (c)

   five planes back to the alien planet.

3. From Charles Berlitz (author of *The Bermuda Triangle*):

   | fly | pull | wait |

   At 4:15, Flight 19 _____ over the Bermuda Triangle—right above
   (a)

   the lost continent of Atlantis. The magnetic crystal from Atlantis

   _____ for them. It quickly _____ the planes to the
   (b)   (c)

   bottom of the sea.

B. What do you think about the mystery of Flight 19? Write at least five sentences. You can agree with one of the explanations in Part A or write your own explanation. Use the simple past and the past progressive.

See the *Grammar Links* Website for a complete model paragraph for this assignment.

9 Simple Past and Past Progressive: Story Writing—It Happened One Night

A. In small groups, complete this mystery story. Write background sentences for paragraphs 1 and 2. Write action sentences for paragraphs 3 and 4. Follow the directions in parentheses. Use your imagination!

1   *One night, I was driving along a country road.*

(Add two sentences. Describe the weather: snow? rain? wind? stars? clouds? Example: *It was raining. . . .*)

2   *Suddenly, someone jumped out in front of me. He looked strange.* (Add two sentences. Describe the person. What was he wearing? What was he doing?)

3   *The strange person pointed to a house at the side of the road.* (Add three sentences. Use verbs with stative meaning. How did the house **look**? What did you **see**? What did you **hear**?)

(See Grammar Briefing 2 in Chapter 3 and Grammar Briefing 3, Grammar Hotspot! in this chapter to review verbs with stative meaning.)

⭕ 4	*I locked my car. I went with the man toward the house.*
	(Add three or four sentences. What happened next? Finish the story.)

B. Share your story with other groups in the class.

GRAMMAR BRIEFING 4

Past Time Clauses with *When* and *While*

FORM

A. Sentences with Time Clauses

1. A time clause has a **time expression** (*when, while*), a **subject**, and a **verb**.

   time expression subject verb
   When   **I**   **shouted**

2. A time clause is not a complete sentence. It must be used with a main clause.

   time clause   main clause
   When I shouted, she ran away.
      NOT: ~~When I shouted~~.

3. A time clause can come before or after a main clause. Use a comma (,) after the time clause when the time clause comes **first**.

   time clause   main clause
   When I shouted, she ran away.

   main clause   time clause
   She ran away when I shouted.

B. *When* and *While*

Use the **simple past** in *when* time clauses. Use the **past progressive** in *while* time clauses.

When I **shouted**, she ran away.

While she **was eating**, her taxi came.

(continued on next page)

A. Overview

Past time sentences with *when* and *while* describe two actions in the past. These actions may happen at the same time or at different times.

Same time: We were swimming while the sun was shining.

Different times: When the bus stopped, we got out.

B. Past Progressive + Past Progressive with *While*

Use the past progressive + past progressive in sentences describing two past actions happening at the same time. Use *while* clauses.

PAST — NOW — FUTURE

was cooking
was talking

While I **was cooking**, she **was talking**.
= She **was talking** while I **was cooking**.

C. Simple Past + Simple Past with *When*

Use the simple past + simple past in sentences describing two past actions—one happening immediately after the other. The action in the *when* clause happened first.

PAST — NOW — FUTURE

shouted   ran
           away

When I **shouted**, she **ran** away. = She **ran** away **when** I **shouted**. (First I shouted; then she ran away.)

D. Past Progressive + Simple Past

The past progressive and the simple past can occur in the same sentence. This means that one action was in progress when the second action interrupted it or happened during it.

PAST — NOW — FUTURE

(taxi) came
was eating

Use *while* + past progressive for the action that started first. Use *when* + simple past for the second action.

While she **was eating**, her taxi **came**.

She **was eating when** her taxi **came**. (First she was eating; then her taxi came.)

Be careful! The *when* + simple past clauses in **C** and **D** above show two different orders of action. With main clauses in the **simple past** (**C**), the *when* clause shows the **first** action. With main clauses in the **past progressive** (**D**), the *when* clause shows the **second action**.

I **left** when the taxi came. (First the taxi came; then I left.)

I **was leaving** when the taxi came. (First I started to leave; then the taxi came.)

GRAMMAR PRACTICE 4

Past Time Clauses with *When* and *While*

10 ***While* Clauses + Past Progressive:** The Way to Go

Last month, Lien and Ida took a trip from Chicago to Denver at the same time. Lien went by train, and Ida went by car. Their trips were very different. Write sentences with *while* and the past progressive. Use the information given.

Lien	**Ida**
1. sit comfortably	drive through heavy traffic

    While Lien was sitting comfortably, Ida was driving through heavy traffic.

2. have lunch in the restaurant car	eat at a fast-food restaurant

_____

_____

3. look at the scenery	stare at the road signs

_____

_____

4. read a mystery story	study her road map

_____

_____

5. listen to soft music	listen to the traffic report

_____

_____

6. talk to the other passengers	pump gas

_____

_____

7. walk around the train	worry about her car

_____

_____

8. take a nap	try to stay awake

_____

_____

11 *When* Clauses + Simple Past: Money, Money, Money

A. Read the pairs of sentences about some lucky people. Which action happened first?
Write *1* above the first action and *2* above the second action.

1. The bus company paid me a lot of money. A bus hit my car.
   ²   ¹

2. Someone left her $100,000. He died.

3. My new book came out. It sold 10,000 copies.

4. We won a lot of money in the casinos. We went to Las Vegas.

5. They looked under the floor of their house. They found a box of jewels.

6. She said yes. He asked a rich woman to marry him.

7. They saw a treasure inside. They looked into the cave.

B. Combine the pairs of sentences in Part A. Use the simple past tense. Write the
clauses in the correct order. Add commas where appropriate.

1. When _a bus hit my car, the bus company paid me a lot of money._____

2. _____

   when _____

3. When _____

   _____

4. _____

   when _____

5. When _____

   _____

6. When _____

   _____

7. _____

   when _____

12 **Simple Past and Past Progressive:** What Happened to Mr. Charles?

A. Read the article. Underline the time clauses.

Where Is Mr. Charles?

Chicago Businessman Disappears Mysteriously

On the morning of July 2, 2004, Mr. Gregory Charles got up very early. He was preparing for an important business meeting in San Francisco. <u>When his wife woke up</u>, he was packing his suitcase. He looked very nervous. While he was eating breakfast, his taxi came. When he got to the station, his train was waiting at the platform. He got on the train from Chicago to San Francisco. When the train arrived in San Francisco, his business client was waiting at the station. But Mr. Charles was not on the train. Later, the police arrested one of the porters on Mr. Charles' train. When they arrested him, he was wearing Mr. Charles' expensive gold watch! The porter said, "I found it while I was checking the bathroom on the train." Mr. Charles' wife is very worried. She has no idea where he is.

---

platform = place where trains stop for passengers. *arrested* = stopped and took to the police station.

B. Look at the article again. For each of the sentences with time clauses, check the action that **started first.**

1. His wife woke up. He packed ✓ his suitcase.

2. He ate some breakfast. His taxi came.

3. He got to the station. His train waited at the platform.

4. The train arrived in San Francisco. His client waited at the station.

5. The police arrested the porter. He wore Mr. Charles' expensive gold watch.

6. I found it. I checked the bathroom on the train.

13 Simple Past and Past Progressive: Mr. Charles' Life Story

The police are looking for Mr. Charles. His life story is very useful to them. Use the information in the file to write sentences with *while* time clauses. Write the clauses in the correct order. Add commas where appropriate.

> **CHARLES, Gregory, Jr.: History**
>
> 1. 1975–1996   Lived in Chicago.   1996: Met his future wife.
> 2. 1996–June 1997   Studied in Germany. May 1997: his father died.
> 3. 1997–June 2004   Managed his father's business. May 2003: Borrowed $100,000.
> 4. June 10–17 2004   Made a business trip. June 12: Stopped in Las Vegas.
> 5. June 12–16 2004   Stayed in Las Vegas. June 13–16: Lost $100,000 in a casino.
> 6. June 17, 12–4 p.m. Flew home to Chicago. 2 p.m.: Called his bank from the airplane.

1. While *he was living in Chicago, he met his future wife.* _____

2. _____
   while _____

3. _____
   while _____

4. While _____
   _____

5. While _____
   _____

6. _____
   while _____

14 *When* and *While* **Clauses:** What the Porter Said

A. Listen to the interview between the police and the porter from Mr. Charles' train. Match the clauses in A with the clauses in B.

A	B
1. He was sitting alone	_____ a. I saw it there.
2. What was he doing	___1___ b. when I came in to check his ticket
3. He disappeared	_____ c. a different man was sitting there.
4. Was his compartment empty	_____ d. while I was talking to him.
5. When I looked in again	_____ e. I was checking the bathroom.
6. He was staring out the window	_____ f. while you were checking it?
7. When the train stopped in Denver	_____ g. while I was checking the other compartments.
8. While I was cleaning the sink	_____ h. when you checked again?

B. On a sheet of paper, write sentences with the clauses you matched in Part A. Add commas where appropriate.

Example: 1. <u>He was sitting alone when I came in to check his ticket.</u>

15 *When* and *While* **Clauses:** Solving the Mystery

A. Work in small groups. Examine the police evidence below, the biography in Exercise 13, page 78, and the porter's story in Exercise 14. Discuss: What happened to Mr. Charles?

B. Did your group guess the answer to the mystery? Find out. Complete the story below with the simple past or the past progressive of the verbs in parentheses.

Chicago Metropolitan Police

Final Report: Disappearance of Charles, Gregory, Jr.

When Mr. Charles _lost_ his money in Las Vegas, he
            1 (lose)

decided to escape. He moved all his money from Chicago to Hamburg,
   2 (decide)

Germany. He _was wearing_ a business suit when he _got_ on
              3 (wear)   4 (get)

the train. But he was carrying old clothes in his suitcase.

While the porter _____ the other compartments, Mr. Charles
                       5 (visit)

quickly _____ his clothes in the bathroom and _____ his
          6 (change)   7 (leave)

watch on the sink. When he _____ out of the bathroom, he
                               8 (come)

_____ his suitcase out the window of the train. When the porter
   9 (push)

_____ (see) him again, Mr. Charles _____ very different.
   10 (see)   11 (look)

Mr. Charles never arrived in San Francisco. He _____ off the train
                                                    12 (jump)

when it _____ in Denver. While he _____ from Denver to
          13 (arrive)   14 (fly)

Germany, the police _____ for him. When he _____ safe
                        15 (look)   16 (feel)

in Germany, he _____ a letter to his wife.
                   17 (send)

C. Discuss in small groups: Was the porter lying when he talked to the police?

Check your progress! Go to the Self-Test for Chapter 5 on the *Grammar Links* Website.

Wrap-up Activities

1 **The Mystery of the *Titanic*:** EDITING

The *Titanic* was a famous ship that went down in the Atlantic Ocean in 1912. Correct the errors in this research report about the *Titanic*. There are 12 errors with the simple past, the past progressive, and past time clauses. The first error is corrected for you.

History 101

The Mystery of the *Titanic*

When the White Star Line built the *Titanic*, the owners ~~feel~~ *felt* very confident. This was the biggest and strongest ship in the world. But on April 15, 1912, the *Titanic* hit a huge iceberg while it went to America.

Why the *Titanic* went down? The iceberg was very big. The ship was travel fast when the accident happened. But perhaps the "accident" was really something else—a curse!

Nearly 3,000 years ago, a woman dies in ancient Egypt. She was a priestess (a female priest) for the sun god, Amon Ra. Priests and priestesses use to be very important in ancient times. So when she died, the Egyptians cover her body with special bandages. In the twentieth century, people taked the mummy to the British Museum in London. While the museum was showing the mummy, many terrible things happened in the building. After that, the British Museum was giving the mummy to a museum in New York.

On April 15, 1912, the *Titanic* carryed this mysterious mummy passenger to New York. She was disappearing forever in the Atlantic Ocean with 1,500 other passengers. Did she destroyed them? The answer is a mystery.

 See the *Grammar Links* Website for more information about the *Titanic*.

2 Life Stories: WRITING/SPEAKING

A. Write your own life story. Mention five important dates and events in your life.

Example:

My Life

Dates	Events
1973–1991	Living in Jakarta, Indonesia
1993	Got married

Memory Book

B. Work with a partner. Find out what he or she was doing during the important dates and events in your life.

Example: A: *What were you doing while I was living in Jakarta?*
B: *I was going to college.*
A: *Where were you living when I got married?*
B: *In Mexico City.*

C. What did you learn about your partner? Write at least five sentences. Use past time clauses with *when* and *while*.

Example: _*While I was growning up in Jakarta, Marisa was going to college.*_

*(She) was living in Mexico when I got married.*

 See the *Grammar Links* Website for a complete model paragraph for this activity.

3 **My Personal Adventure:** WRITING/SPEAKING

A. Write a short story about a strange adventure that happened to you (true or not true). Write at least five sentences. Use time clauses with *when* and *while*, past progressive, and simple past. Answer the questions below to help you.

When did it all happen?

What were you doing when it happened? Where were you living?

What happened first?

What did you do when this happened?

What happened next?

Example: *It all began one morning in 1988. When it happened, I was living at my uncle's house.*

 See the *Grammar Links* Website for a complete model paragraph for this activity.

B. Share your stories in small groups. Ask one another questions. Find out: Are the stories true?

4 Make Sense of Nonsense!: WRITING/SPEAKING

Work in small groups. Explain these strange sentences. Write a story that includes one of the sentences. Write at least four sentences. Use at least one past progressive, one simple past, one time expression, and one time clause with *when* or *while*. Share your story with the class.

The spaghetti disappeared.

She put the fish in her pocket.

We climbed down the telephone pole.

Then they saw the shoe on the bicycle.

Example: Juan invited Olga to dinner last week. He put salad and fish on her plate. But poor Olga hated fish. While Juan was answering the telephone, <u>she put the fish in her pocket.</u> When she left the house, she dropped the fish in the garden.

Future Time

TOPIC FOCUS
Living with Technology

UNIT OBJECTIVES

■ *be going to*
(It*'s going* to *rain.*)

■ *will*
(We *will see* many changes in the future.)

■ choosing between *be going to* and *will*

■ the present progressive and the simple present for future time
(Linda *is flying* to Amsterdam next week. Flight 202 *leaves* at 9:00 tomorrow morning.)

■ future time clauses
(*When he becomes president,* he is going to work hard.)

■ future and factual conditionals
(I *will help* you *if you ask me.* *If you heat water,* it *boils.*)

Grammar in Action

Reading and Listening: Technology in the Twenty First Century

Read and listen.

1   Technology is changing the world we live in and **will continue** to change our lives in the future. What changes **will** technology **bring**?

2   First of all, more and more people **are going to use** the Internet. The Internet is an international network of computers. Right now, many millions of people in hundreds of countries communicate through the Internet. And that number **is going to grow**. Some people say that soon the Internet **is going to connect** all the schools, libraries, businesses, and personal computers in the world. When this happens, we probably **won't need** offices, banks, stores, or schools. We**'ll stay** home and do everything "online," through the Internet. And we **won't need** post offices; we**'ll send** all our letters by electronic mail, or "e-mail."

3   Computer technology **will** also **allow** people to live in a "virtual reality" world. Users of this technology move in an imaginary world. They see and touch virtual objects, and they talk to other people in Internet space. Perhaps, one day, many people **will study** in virtual universities, take virtual vacations, and go to their friends' virtual weddings.

4   Other types of technology **will help** to solve problems. For example, new medical technology **will make** people live longer. They **will work** less; robots, or intelligent machines, **will do** the most difficult and dangerous jobs for them.

5   But technology **will** also **bring** problems. When people live longer, how **are** we **going to find** food for them all? Today, if we need more homes, we build new cities. But if the world's population grows to 9 billion, where **will** everyone **live**? How **will** we **control** our robots if they become too intelligent? **Will** people **spend** too much time on the Internet and forget how to live in the "real" world?

6   Technology brings great hope for this century. But **will** we **learn** to control it before it controls us?

---

network = a group of connections. *virtual reality* = a type of technology that makes computer pictures and sounds seem very real. *imaginary* = not real; in your mind.

Think About Grammar

A. Read the passage again. Look at the **boldfaced** words. Do these words talk

about events in the past, in the present, or in the future? _____

B. Some of the verbs from the passage are in boxes a and b below.
Write the **boldfaced** words that come before these verbs in the passage.

a. (from paragraph 2)   b. (from paragraph 4)

_____ _____ _____ grow			_____ help	
_____ _____ _____ connect			_____ make	

C. The **boldfaced** words in the passage show two ways of talking about future time.
Write the words that show future time.

a. _____

_____

b. _____

D. Look at these two sentences from paragraph 5. Circle the correct answers below.

a. Today, if we need more homes, we build new cities.

b. But if the world's population grows to 9 billion, where will everyone live?

1. Which sentence talks about the future?   a.   b.   a. and b.

2. Which sentence uses the simple present tense after *if*?   a.   b.   a. and b.

Chapter 6

Expressing Future Time

Introductory Task: Education and Information

A. Professor Larsen is making predictions about education in the future. Read them with a partner. In the *You* column, check (✓) the predictions that you both think will come true.

Predictions:	You	Professor Larsen
1. We are going to see a lot of changes in education.	❑	☑
2. School classrooms will look the same as they do now.	❑	❑
3. Students will do all their class work on computers.	❑	❑
4. Students are going to spend a lot of time at home online.	❑	❑
5. Young children will play in virtual reality kindergartens.	❑	❑
6. Professors will fly to many different countries on the same day.	❑	❑
7. Professors will give tele-lectures through videophones.	❑	❑
8. Some students will become technology addicts.	❑	❑

tele-lectures = lectures on TV. *videophones* = telephones that show video pictures of the speakers. *addict* = someone who needs something in an unhealthy way.

B. Did Professor Larsen make the same predictions as you? Listen to the lecture. In the *Professor Larsen* column in Part A, check (✓) the predictions you hear.

Future Time with *Be Going To* I

FORM

A. Affirmative Statements

SUBJECT	PRESENT OF *BE*	*GOING TO*	BASE VERB
I	**am** / **'m**		
You	**are** / **'re**	**going to**	**change.**
We			
They			
He	**is** / **'s**		
She			
It			

B. Negative Statements

SUBJECT	*BE* + *NOT*	*GOING TO*	BASE VERB
I	**am not** / **'m not**		
You	**are not**		
We	**'re not**	**going to**	**change.**
They	**aren't**		
He	**is not**		
She	**'s not**		
It	**isn't**		

FUNCTION

A. Overview

Be going to talks about future events. Common time words and expressions used with *be going to* include *tomorrow*, *next (weekend)*, *this (evening)*, *in (50 years)*, and *soon*.

Tomorrow, Bob**'s going to** see a ball game.

She's **going to** finish **soon.**

B. Predictions and Immediate Expectations

1. *Be going to* makes **predictions** (guesses) about the future.

   Life**'s going to be** different in 50 years.

2. Often, *be going to* talks about the **immediate**, or very near, future. Something happening right now makes us expect something to happen very soon.

   Look out! You**'re going to fall** into that hole. (I can see the hole and the danger right now.)

C. Plans

Be going to expresses plans made before the moment of speaking.

A: What's going to happen now?

B: We**'re going to hear** a lecture. (Someone planned the lecture before now.)

Future Time with *Be Going To* I

1 **Predictions and Future Time Expressions:** Technology and the Future

A. Technology is going to change our lives in many ways. Here are some experts' predictions. Complete the sentences. Use the correct form of *be going to* with the verbs in parentheses.

1. Technology addiction <u>is going to be</u> an international problem.
   (be)

2. Electronic information _____ our lives.
   (control)

3. Books and newspapers _____ from everyday life.
   (disappear)

4. Your child _____ about 40 hours of TV each week.
   (watch)

5. We _____ intelligent life in space.
   (find)

6. You _____ virtual reality vacations in space.
   (take)

7. Intelligent machines, or robots, _____ all our
   (do)

   dangerous jobs.

8. The twenty-first century robot _____ just like a human.
   (think)

9. All college students _____ computer programming.
   (study)

10. I _____ a lot of new friends on the Internet.
    (meet)

See the *Grammar Links* Website for more information about robots of the future.

B. Which predictions in Part A do you believe? When do you think they are going to happen? Write at least five sentences. Use the predictions in Part A or write your own. Add time expressions.

Example: <u>Everyone in this country is going to have a cell phone soon.</u>

 **C.** Work with a partner. Compare your predictions. Were they the same? Discuss any different predictions.

2 Immediate Expectations: What's on TV?

Bill's new TV has a lot of channels. He is checking them out. What is going to happen next in these TV programs? Use the words given and write sentences with *be going to*. Use contractions.

1. He/say, "Marry me!"

   He's going to say, "Marry me!"

2. She/say, "No!"

   _____

3. The spaceship/land

   _____

4. The woman/run away

   _____

5. The short runner/win the race

   _____

6. The tall runner/come in second

   _____

3 Predictions: The Weather Forecast

What does Bill learn from the TV weather channel? Use the words given and write sentences with *be going to*. Use contractions.

1. It/be sunny here in Chicago

   It's going to be sunny here in Chicago.

2. We/have warm temperatures

   _____

3. I/enjoy this beautiful day

   _____

4. It/rain in the East

   _____

5. A storm/move in from the West soon

   _____

6. They/need umbrellas in California, too

   _____

4 Making Plans: Get a Life!

These people are technology addicts, but they are planning to change. Read these journal entries about their present habits. Write sentences about things they are going to do differently. Make negative statements. Then use the words in parentheses to make affirmative statements.

Now		Plans For Change
1. I go online every night.		*I'm not going to go online every night.*
		Tonight *I'm going to read a good book.*
		(read a good book)

Now

2. We talk to friends in a chat room all night.

3. I stay home and work on my computer every weekend.

4. You eat your dinner alone in front of the computer.

5. Your friends worry about you.

6. Paula checks her e-mail many times every afternoon.

7. My children play virtual reality games all weekend.

8. Clara takes her Palm Pilot to class every day.

9. My friend and I read the Internet newsline every day.

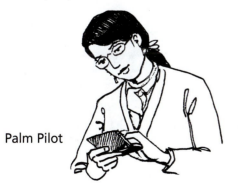

Palm Pilot

Plans for Change

_____

Tonight _____
(do our homework)

_____

This weekend _____
(go for a long bicycle ride)

_____ this evening.
(eat with your family)

_____

_____
(see a big change in you)

_____

_____ this afternoon.
(turn off the computer)

_____

Next weekend _____
(play outside)

_____

_____ tomorrow.
(leave it at home)

_____

Today _____
(buy a newspaper)

chat = friendly, informal conversation.

Future Time with *Be Going To* II

FORM

A. *Yes/No* Questions and Short Answers

QUESTIONS

PRESENT OF *BE*	SUBJECT	*GOING TO*	BASE VERB
Am	I		
Are	you we they	**going to**	**change?**
Is	he she it		

SHORT ANSWERS

YES			NO		
Yes,	I	**am.**	No,	I	**am not. 'm not.**
	you we they	**are.**		you we they	**are not. 're not. aren't.**
	he she it	**is.**		he she it	**is not. 's not. isn't.**

B. *Wh-* Questions and Answers

Wh- Questions About the Subject

QUESTIONS

WH- WORD	PRESENT OF *BE*	*GOING TO*	BASE VERB
Who	**is**	**going to**	**change?**
What			

ANSWERS

My children are.
My life is.

Other Wh- Questions

QUESTIONS

WH- WORD	PRESENT OF *BE*	SUBJECT	*GOING TO*	BASE VERB
Who(m)	**am**	I		**meet?**
What	**is**	he	**going to**	**do?**
How	**are**	we		**pay?**

ANSWERS

The president.
He's going to talk.
With a credit card.

TALKING THE TALK

In speaking, *going to* is often pronounced *gonna*.

WRITING	SPEAKING
They aren't **going to** tell us.	They aren't **gonna** tell us.
What are you **going to** do?	What are you **gonna** do?

Future Time with *Be Going To* II

5 *Yes/No* **Questions and Short Answers:** Surprise, Surprise!

A. Mrs. Baker is telling her middle-school science class about a surprise for next week. Complete the conversation with *yes/no* questions and short answers. Use *be going to* with the words in parentheses.

Annie: <u>Are you going to tell</u> us about the surprise?
1 (you / tell)

Mrs. Baker: Yes, _____. It's about technology.
2

Fred: _____ fun?
3 (it / be)

Mrs. Baker: Yes, _____. Lots of fun.
4

Johnny: _____ us to the video arcade? You know,
5 (you / take)

where they have those great video games?

Mrs. Baker: No, _____.
6

Fred: What? Video games? Wow! _____ free games?
7 (we / get)

Mrs. Baker: No, _____, Fred. You didn't hear me!
8

I said, no video games.

Johnny: What about the kids in the ninth grade class?

_____, too?
9 (they / come)

Mrs. Baker: No, _____. Now, wait, everybody!
10

You're not listening. _____ about this,
11 (I / talk)

or _____ all the time? Okay.
12 (you / shout)

We're going to have a visitor from SETI. SETI means "Search for Extraterrestrial

Intelligence." It's a group of people who are looking for life in space. Our visitor is going

to tell you about SETI's project.

Annie: Great! A visitor! _____ us to the video arcade?
13 (he / take)

Mrs. Baker: No, _____. Oh, you kids! You never listen!
14

---

extraterrestrial = outside the earth.

See the *Grammar Links* Website for more information about SETI.

B. In groups of four, act out the conversation in Part A. Practice using *gonna* wherever possible.

6 *Wh-* Questions: Life in Space?

The visitor from SETI is talking to Mrs. Baker's class. Read his answers to the students' questions. Write the students' *wh-* questions about the boldfaced words in the answers.

1. Students: _What are you going to talk about today?_

    Visitor: I'm going to talk about **the SETI space project**. SETI is an organization of scientists and other people. We're looking for intelligent life in space.

2. Students: How _____

    Visitor: We're going to do that **with telescopes and satellites**. We are building a network of high-power radio telescopes and satellites. We're going to watch the sky with them. We're going to study the stars and planets.

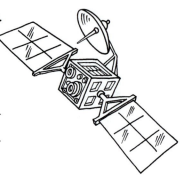

3. Students: Where _____

    _____

    Visitor: Our telescopes are going to be **in our backyards**.

4. Students: How many telescopes _____

    Visitor: We're going to have **5,000 telescopes** around the world.

5. Students: Who _____

    Visitor: **We** are going to pay for this study, but we're also going to ask for help.

6. Students: Who _____

    Visitor: We're going to ask **government agencies** such as NASA, the National Aeronautics and Space Agency.

7. Students: How long _____

    Visitor: The project's going to last **for many years**, I hope—at least until the middle of this century.

8. Students: What _____

    Visitor: **Many exciting things** are going to happen in this century.

9. Students: What _____

    Visitor: We're going to find **extraterrestrial life**.

10. Students: When _____

    Visitor: I don't know, exactly, but we're going to find it **one day**. And with our new technology, I believe it's going to happen soon.

7 *Yes/No* and *Wh-* Questions: Your Future Projects

A. Think of your future life and plans. Are computers going to be very important in your life? Work in groups of three or four. Ask and answer questions with *be going to*. Use the ideas below, or make up your own ideas.

Some uses of computers:

online chat rooms   virtual reality vacations
Internet shopping and banking   Internet college courses
online interviews   Internet newslines

Example: A: How are you going to stay in touch with your classmates?
         B: I'm going to chat with them online.
         C: Are you going to do your shopping on the Internet?

B. Write a paragraph about your future plans. Write at least six sentences. Use *be going to* and time expressions.

See the *Grammar Links* Website for a complete model paragraph for this assignment.

GRAMMAR BRIEFING 3

Future Time with *Will* I

FORM

A. Affirmative Statements		
SUBJECT	*WILL*	BASE VERB
I		
You		
He		
She	**will**	**change.**
It	**'ll**	
We		
They		

B. Negative Statements		
SUBJECT	*WILL + NOT*	BASE VERB
I		
You		
He		
She	**will not**	**change.**
It	**won't**	
We		
They		

(continued on next page)

Predictions

1. Like *be going to, will* is used to make predictions (guesses) about things we expect in the future.	My life **will** be different next year.
2. Uncertain predictions often include *maybe, probably,* and *I think.*	I will **probably** be smarter in 20 years.
3. Certain predictions often include *(almost) certainly* and *definitely.*	I will **definitely** be older in 20 years.

GRAMMAR HOTSPOT!

1. Remember! Use *will* and the base form of the verb.	He **will leave** tomorrow. **NOT:** He will to leave tomorrow. **NOT:** He will leaving tomorrow. **NOT:** He will leaves tomorrow.
2. In statements, *maybe* and *I think* usually go at the beginning of the sentence. *Probably, certainly,* and *definitely* usually go **after** *will* and **before** *won't.*	**I think** I'll be smarter in 20 years. **I'll probably** see you later. I **probably won't** see you tomorrow. **NOT:** I won't probably see you tomorrow.

GRAMMAR PRACTICE 3

Future Time with *Will* I

8 **Predictions with *Will*:** Robots of the Future

Robots are very "smart" machines. Find out about them. Correct the errors in the **boldfaced** words. Use *will* with the verbs given.

Scientists have great plans for the robots of the future. Maybe one day you <u>will seeing</u> a robot that
will see
                                                                                              1

looks like you. Its "eyes" **will to be** small cameras. **It maybe will** hear through microphones.
                          2   3

Minicomputers **making** the "brain." This robot **will speaks** through a sound box in its throat, and
               4   5

it **will have probably** soft plastic "skin." It will look like a human, but it **won't certainly be** human!
      6   7

> *microphone* = an instrument that sends sounds from one place to another.

Future Time with *Will* II

FORM

A. *Yes/No* Questions and Short Answers

QUESTIONS			SHORT ANSWERS				
WILL	SUBJECT	BASE VERB	YES			NO	
	I			I			I	
	you			you			you	
	he			he			he	
Will	she	change?	Yes,	she	will.	No,	she	will not.
	it			it			it	won't.
	we			we			we	
	they			they			they	

B. *Wh-* Questions and Answers

Wh- Questions About the Subject

QUESTIONS			ANSWERS
WH- WORD	*WILL*	BASE VERB	
Who	will	change?	My children will.
What		happen?	Life will change.

Other *Wh-* Questions

QUESTIONS				ANSWERS
WH- WORD	*WILL*	SUBJECT	BASE VERB	
What		it	do?	It will change.
When	will	they	change?	Very soon.
Where		you	go?	Home.

(continued on next page)

More Uses of *Will*

1. Use *will*:

   - To make quick decisions at the moment of speaking.

     > Are you going? Okay, **I'll go** too.

   - To make promises.

     > I **will** always **love** you.

   - To make and refuse requests.

     > *A:* Will you buy me a computer?
     >
     > *B:* No, I **will not buy** you a computer.

   - To make offers and express willingness.

     > Wait! Don't carry that heavy box. **I'll help** you.

2. Time expressions with *will* usually come at the beginning or end of the sentence. *Always* and *never* come between *will* and the main verb.

   > We'll see you **Wednesday**.
   >
   > **Next year** I'll buy you a computer.
   >
   > I'll **never** leave you.

GRAMMAR PRACTICE 4

Future Time with *Will* II

9 *Yes/No* **Questions and Short Answers:** Smart—or Human?

A. Will future robots think like humans? What do you think? Write questions with *will* and the words in parentheses. Then write your answers.

1. (future robots/be intelligent)

   Q: Will future robots be intelligent?

   A: Yes, they will./No, they won't.

2. (they/solve math problems)

   Q: _____

   A: _____

3. (a future robot/feel happy or sad)

   Q: _____

   A: _____

4. (it/understand our feelings)

   Q: _____

   A: _____

5. (we/teach robots to remember people's names and faces)

Q: _____

A: _____

6. (they/make decisions in new situations)

Q: _____

A: _____

7. (robots/have imaginations)

Q: _____

A: _____

B. Work with a partner. Ask each other your questions in Part A.
Are your answers the same? Discuss any answers that are different.

TALKING THE TALK

	WRITING	SPEAKING
1. In speaking and writing, pronouns + contractions of *will* (*'ll*) are common. Only in speaking, nouns + *'ll* are also common.	She**'ll arrive** soon.	She**'ll arrive** soon.
	My wife **will arrive** soon.	My wife**'ll arrive** soon.
2. Only in speaking, *wh-* words + *'ll* are common.	What **will** she do?	What**'ll** she **do**?
	When **will** you come?	When**'ll** you **come**?

---

10 **Contractions with *Will*:** Roboroach

Complete the story with *will* and the verbs given. Use the contracted form of *will* with
pronouns. Use the full form of *will* with nouns.

In the future, we <u>'ll use</u> robots everywhere for difficult and dangerous jobs,
            1 (use)

in places where you and I <u>'ll</u> never <u>travel</u> .
                                    2 (travel)

Right now, for example, the University of Tokyo has a very

useful "pet" robot. It's a cockroach, with an electronic backpack!

Japanese scientists _____, or teach, this
           3 (program)

robot to go through very small spaces. Maybe this "roboroach"

_____ into buildings after earthquakes,
    4 (go)

or maybe it _____ dangerous land mines after wars. Other,
5 (find)

human-size robots _____ for lost planes and ships at the bottom
6 (look)

of the sea. They _____ photographs on faraway planets in space.
7 (take)

They _____ underground mines and nuclear factories for dangerous gases.
8 (test)

Who knows? Perhaps one day your daughter _____ tennis with a robot
9 (play)

"coach"! Or your son _____ a robot tutor for private math lessons at home.
10 (rent)

> *land mines* = small bombs buried in the ground.

🌐 See the *Grammar Links* Website for more information about Roboroach.

11 **Contractions with *Will*: Future Robots: Smart—or Human?**

🎧 **A.** Listen to the interview with Dr. Weber, an expert in robots of the future. Write the words you hear. After pronouns, write contractions of *will* ('ll). After nouns or *wh-* words, write *will*.

Interviewer: Dr. Weber, tell us about the robots of the future. *They'll probably think*
                                                                                    1

like us, right?

Dr. Weber: _____. I think _____
                         2   3

the difference between a robot and a person.

Interviewer: _____?
                                              4

Dr. Weber: Well, even a smart robot _____ happy or sad.
                                                   5

Maybe _____ us smile and learn to smile back
              6

at us, but _____ our feelings. A robot brain
                   7

_____ only one thing at a time, step by step.
         8

And _____ for themselves in new situations.
          9

Interviewer: So _____?
                                        10

Dr. Weber: _____ new languages.
                         11

_____ and dance in movies and shows.
         12

But _____ between right and wrong actions.
          13

Humans _____ their instructions.
               14

12 **More Uses of _Will_: Robots Don't Do This!**

What would you say in these very human situations? Write sentences with _will/won't_.

1. You're at a party, but it's getting late. You decide to leave. Tell your friends.

   I think I'll go home now.

2. You need to mail a letter, but you're busy. Your sister is going to the post office. Make a request.

   Will you mail this letter for me, please?

3. A friend tells you an important secret. Promise never to tell your other friends.

   _____

4. You have a surprise for a friend. She wants to know what it is. Refuse to tell her.

   _____

5. A salesperson wants you and your wife to buy a new car. You both decide to think about it this evening. Tell the salesperson.

   _____

6. Your classmate needs to get to the airport, but she doesn't have a car. Your friend has a car, so he can take her. Make an offer.

   _____

7. You're going to get married! Make a promise to your future husband or wife.

   _____

8. Make a request to your friends: Invite them to your wedding.

   _____

9. Mrs. Cooper found some money in the street. She's a very honest person. Will she decide to keep the money or not? What does she say?

   _____

10. A classmate is sick at home. He needs visitors. Make an offer from yourself and a friend.

   _____

13 *Wh-* Questions and Answers with *Will*: Meeting on the Internet

A. Read this Internet advertisement and answer the questions below.

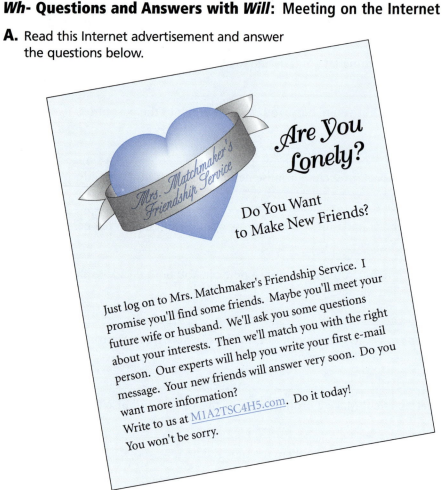

Mrs. Matchmaker's Friendship Service

Are You Lonely?

Do You Want to Make New Friends?

Just log on to Mrs. Matchmaker's Friendship Service. I promise you'll find some friends. Maybe you'll meet your future wife or husband. We'll ask you some questions about your interests. Then we'll match you with the right person. Our experts will help you write your first e-mail message. Your new friends will answer very soon. Do you want more information? Write to us at M1A2TSC4H5.com. Do it today! You won't be sorry.

1. Who(m) will you find through Mrs. Matchmaker's Service?

   A friend.

2. What will they ask you?

   They'll ask you some questions about your interests.

3. What will they do then?

   _____

4. Who will help you with your first e-mail message?

   _____

5. What will happen then?

   _____

6. When will your new friends answer?

   _____

7. How will you get more information?

   _____

8. Where will you write to Mrs. Matchmaker's Service?

   _____

B. You want more information. Write questions for an e-mail message to Mrs. Matchmaker. Use *wh-* questions with *will* and the words in parentheses.

1. <u>How much will the service cost?</u>
   (The service will cost . . .)

2. Who(m) _____
   (I'll send the payment to . . .)

3. What _____
   (I'll say . . . in my e-mail letter.)

4. What _____
   (. . . will happen next.)

5. When _____
   (I'll get an answer to my message . . .)

6. How many _____
   (You'll find . . . friends for me.)

7. Who _____
   (These friends will be . . .)

8. Where _____
   (They'll come from . . .)

C. Work with a partner. Think of two more *wh-* questions for Mrs. Matchmaker. Write them below.

9. _____

10. _____

D. Join another pair of partners. Ask and answer each other's questions in Part C.

GRAMMAR BRIEFING 5

Be Going To Versus *Will*

FUNCTION

A. *Be Going To* and *Will*

Use both *be going to* and *will* for predictions about the future.	My life **is going to be** different next year. My life **will be** different next year.

B. *Be Going To*

1. Use *be going to* for immediate expectations about the very near future, based on something happening now.	Look out! You**'re going to fall** into that hole.
2. Use *be going to* for plans made **before** the moment of speaking.	*A:* What**'s going to happen** now? *B:* We**'re going to hear** a lecture.

(continued on next page)

C. Will

1. Use *will* for quick decisions (plans made **at** the moment of speaking).	Are you going? Okay, **I'll go** too.
2. Use *will* to talk about willingness or non-willingness for promises, offers, requests, and refusals.	I'll always **love** you. Wait. I'll **help** you. **Will** you **buy** me a computer? I **will not buy** you a computer!

GRAMMAR PRACTICE 5

Be Going To Versus *Will*

14 *Be Going To* Versus *Will*: Technical Problems

Complete the conversations. Use *be going to* or *will/won't* and the words in parentheses.

1. A: Hey, Freddie! __Will you stop__ that noisy video game? I'm on the phone!
      a (you / stop)

   B: Sorry, I didn't know. _____ it now, okay?
                                        b (I / stop)

2. A: Where are you putting that message machine?

   B: In a box. _____ it back to the store. It lost all my
                         (I / take)

   messages yesterday!

3. A: Our mechanics are busy right now. What do you want to do with your car?

   B: I think _____ it with you. But I need it back this afternoon!
                    a (I / leave)

   A: No problem. I promise _____ the job today.
                                      b (we / finish)

4. A: Look at that car! Do you see the smoke?

   B: Oh, no! _____.
                    (it / explode)

5. A: Help! My computer isn't working.

   B: Don't worry. _____ at it for you.
                          (I / look)

6. A: I bought this camera for $350 last week. Now it doesn't work. I want my money back!

   B: Sorry, sir. We don't give refunds. But _____ another
                                                        a (you / take)

   camera in exchange?

   A: No. _____ another camera! I want my money back.
               b (I / not take)

7. A: I missed the movie on Channel 6 last night. I really wanted to see it!

   B: Well, _____ it again at eight o'clock tonight.
   　　　　　 a (they / show)

   A: Really? _____ it?
   　　　　　　　 b (you / watch)

   B: Yes. Do you want to come to my house?

   A: Sure. _____ you tonight, then.
   　　　　　 c (I / see)

GRAMMAR BRIEFING 6

Present Progressive and Simple Present for Future Time

FUNCTION

A. Present Progressive

1. The present progressive is sometimes used to describe specific **plans** for the future. A time expression usually shows that the activitity is in the future.

   A: What **are** you **doing tonight**?

   B: **I'm meeting** my uncle for dinner.

2. Use *be going to* (not the present progressive) for **predictions** about the future.

   It **is** probably **going to rain** tomorrow.
   　NOT: It ~~is probably raining~~ tomorrow.

B. Simple Present

1. The simple present is sometimes used to describe future **schedules** that are fixed and regular—for example, in class programs and in timetables for buses, trains, and airplanes. A time expression usually shows that the schedule is in the future.

   My new class **starts next Monday.**

2. Pairs of verbs commonly used with the simple present to express future time include:

   • *Arrive, leave/depart.*

   • *Begin, finish.*

   • *Start, end.*

   • *Open, close.*

   Flight 202 **departs** at 9:00.

   The game **starts** in about three minutes.

Remember! Use *be going to* or the present progressive for **plans** about the future.

> I **am going to visit** Raul tomorrow. OR I **am visiting** Raul tomorrow.

Use only *be going to* for **predictions**.

> It **is going to rain** tomorrow.
> NOT: It ~~is raining~~ tomorrow.

GRAMMAR PRACTICE 6

Present Progressive and Simple Present for Future Time

15 **Future Versus Present Meaning:** My Computer Date

Raul's computer is changing his life! Read Raul's conversation with his friend Jan. Above the **boldfaced** verbs, write **P** if they are talking about present time or **F** if they are talking about future time.

Raul: Why **are** you **running**, Jan?
           P

Jan: I**'m going to be** late for class! It **starts** in a few minutes. But first I **want** to buy
    F

some tickets for the concert. I**'m going** to the ticket office right now.

Raul: Oh, you**'re going** to that laser music concert tonight. **Is** it at 7:30?

Jan: Yes. **Are** you **coming** tonight too? I**'ll get** you a ticket.

Raul: No, thanks. I**'m staying** home this evening. I**'m chatting** to my new girlfriend

online tonight.

Jan: An online date? You**'re joking**!

Raul: No, really. We met through an Internet friendship service. My girlfriend's name

is Linda. She **lives** in Spain. I**'ll tell** you all about her.

Jan: Sure! But not now. The ticket office **closes** in five minutes. And it **doesn't open**

again before the concert.

Raul: Look! There's your class instructor. He**'s coming** this way.

Jan: Uh-oh. I**'m going to go**. I**'ll call** you tonight, okay? After the concert.

16   Present Progressive for Future Time: Making a Date

Jan wants to chat online with Linh, a Taiwanese student in another American city. Work with a partner. Student A looks at Jan's schedule. Student B looks at Linh's schedule. Find a time when they can talk online. Use the present progressive tense. Use time expressions *(on Saturday, at noon, in the morning*, etc.) as appropriate.

Example: A: What is Jan doing next Friday evening?
               B: He's seeing a movie with Bill. Is Linh free on Saturday?
               A: She's visiting her grandmother in the morning.

Jan's Schedule

	Friday	Saturday	Sunday
Morning	go to class		play soccer
Noon		have lunch with Raul	
Afternoon	go to class	attend Suki's wedding	
Evening	see a movie with Bill		study for a test

Linh's Schedule

	Friday	Saturday	Sunday
Morning	go to class	visit my grand-mother	go to church
Noon	see the dentist		eat with my family
Afternoon			
Evening		baby-sit for my sister	

17 Simple Present for Future Time: An Important Trip

A. Raul's new girlfriend, Linda, is coming to meet him in Boston. Write statements about Linda's flight schedule. Use the words given and the simple present tense.

Trip Check   **Flyaway Travel**

□   ⊞ add to calendar

TRIP DETAILS

Travel plans for: Linda

Menu

Trip Tools

Flight Tracking

| **Travel provider** |
| **Print itinerary** |
| **E-mail itinerary** |
| **Add to calendar** |
| **View other itinerary** |

FLIGHT RESERVATION

details ✈ **Wednesday, January 7, 2004**

LV: Madrid, 11:30 a.m., Nonstop, WorldAir 4451

AR: Boston, 1:30 p.m.

AIRFARE: $420 one way

---

1. Linda's flight to Boston/leave

   Linda's flight to Boston leaves on January 7.

2. Linda's flight/not stop in New York

   _____

3. Her flight number/be

   _____

4. The plane/arrive in Boston

   _____

5. The flight/cost

   _____

B. Linda is planning her return trip to Madrid. Work with a partner. Discuss dates, times, and airfares (prices) for the two flights in the advertisement. Which is the better flight for Linda? Write about the schedule you choose. Write sentences like the ones in Part A.

Trip Check   *Flyaway Travel*

🖨 **add to calendar**

Menu

Trip Tools

Flight Tracking

Travel provider

Print itinerary

E-mail itinerary

Add to calendar

View other itinerary

TRIP DETAILS

Travel plans for: Linda

FLIGHT RESERVATION

details ✈ **Tuesday, January 20, 2004**

LV: Boston, 7:35 p.m., Nonstop, WorldAir 3490

AR: Madrid, 7:00 a.m., Wednesday

AIRFARE: $420 one way

details ✈ **Tuesday, January 13, 2004**

LV: Boston, 9:00 p.m., Nonstop, WorldAir 1120

AR: New York, 9:45 p.m.

LV: New York, 1:05 a.m., Wednesday
      Nonstop, SunAir 204

AR: Madrid, 12:30 p.m.

AIRFARE: $400 one way

1. _____

2. _____

3. _____

4. _____

5. _____

C. Can you find a better flight for Linda? Work with a partner. On the Internet, research some airline fares and schedules between Madrid and Boston. Then share your findings with the rest of the class. Who found the best fares and schedules?

18 Present Progressive or Simple Present for Future Time: A Happy Ending

Raul found his future wife on the Internet! Raul and Linda decide to have a virtual wedding and invite their friends to "attend" the wedding online. Complete their electronic wedding invitation. Use the present progressive or the simple present.

From: Raul and Linda
Sent: 3/13/04
To: Everyone
Subject: Come to Our Wedding! Fly with Us to the Moon!

Raul and Linda _____ married on May 20! We _____ a virtual
                       1 (get)   2 (rent)

spaceship, and _____ to the moon for our special day. We _____
                               3 (go)   4 (take)

our friends and families with us. Here's the schedule. Our virtual spaceship _____
                                                                        5 (leave)

at 10:00 in the morning and _____ at 10:15. The wedding _____
                                        6 (land)   7 (be)

at the Crater Chapel, at 11:30. The reception _____ at 2:00 p.m. Our families
                                                          8 (begin)

_____ us a great reception party! They _____ food, drinks, and
        9 (give)   10 (provide)

a mariachi band. _____ you _____ with us? We hope so!
                                          11 (come)

Raul and Linda

19 **Talking About the Future:** Discussion

 In small groups, discuss these questions.

1. Will Raul and Linda have a good future? What will happen after the wedding?

2. What do you think about virtual friendships, dates, and weddings?

3. Are people going to live more and more in a "virtual" world?

4. Is it a good idea to meet new people on the Internet? Is this activity ever dangerous?

Check your progress! Go to the Self-Test for
Chapter 6 on the *Grammar Links* Website.

Chapter 7

Future Time Clauses; Conditionals

Introductory Task: Technology—Friend or Enemy?

 A. Two politicians, Senator O'Leary and Senator Fallows, are discussing technology and the problems of the world. Listen to their discussion. Write the words you hear. Use the correct forms of the verbs in the box.

be	clean	fish	have	✓ need
cause	destroy	✓ go	learn	use
control	(not) find	have	live	

O'Leary: Technology is destroying our environment—the world we live in. Cars and factories

send clouds of smoke into the air. Soon, people __are going to need__ _____
                                                                              1

smog masks when they __go_____ outside. Factories are
                                          2

putting dangerous waste into the water. When we _____
                                                                          3

in the rivers, we _____ anything safe to eat.
                                   4

Technology is also using up the world's natural energy. We are burning forests,

coal, and oil in huge power plants. How _____ we

Coal

_____ in the world after we _____
              5   6

these forms of energy? Technology _____ more and
                                                          7

more problems until we _____ it.
                                      8

Fallows: I disagree. If we _____ technology, we
                                          9

_____ progress. Technology means new discoveries, for
              10

example, in medicine and space research. Technology will help solve the problems of the

environment. For example, the Center for Clean Technology—the CCT—in Los Angeles is

developing new technology to attack pollution. If the CCT _____
                                                                                  11

successful, this technology _____ the waste
                                   12

in our air and water. The CCT is also studying uranium as a form of

energy. If we _____ to control uranium, we
                     13

_____ it for energy and save our forests, and coal and
         14

oil supplies. Yes, Senator O'Leary. Technology will bring good changes for the future.

> *smog masks* = face covers to protect you from bad things in the air. *waste* = useless material. *uranium* = a radioactive element that produces nuclear energy.

B. Work in small groups. Discuss the conversation in Part A. Which statements do you agree with? Which statements do you disagree with? Do you agree more with Senator O'Leary or with Senator Fallows?

GRAMMAR BRIEFING 1

Future Time Clauses

FORM

A. Overview

Some sentences about future time have two clauses: a main clause and a future time clause. The future time clause begins with a time expression. The main clause does not.

time clause	main clause
When the bus stops,	I will get off.

B. Statements

TIME CLAUSE			MAIN CLAUSE			
TIME EXPRESSION	SUBJECT	SIMPLE PRESENT	SUBJECT	*WILL/ BE GOING TO*	BASE VERB	
When	I	know,	I	will	tell	you.
				am going to		
After	he	leaves,	she	won't	stay.	
				isn't going to		

1. The time clause, the main clause, or both clauses can be negative.

> When **I'm not** busy, I'll call you.
> When I finish this project, I **won't be** busy.
> When **I'm not** busy, I **won't be** tired.

2. A time clause can come before or after the main clause. Use a comma (,) after the time clause when the time clause comes first.

> **When I know**, I'm going to tell you.
> I'm going to tell you **when I know**.

(continued on next page)

C. Questions

Questions are formed in the main clause. The time clause does not change.	**Are you going to tell me** when you know? When you know, **what will you tell me?**

FUNCTION

A. Overview

Future time clauses tell the order (first or second) of two actions or situations in the future.	first action second action **When the bus stops**, <u>I will get off</u>.

B. Time Expressions

1. *When, after,* and *as soon as* introduce the action that will happen first. *As soon as* means that the second action will happen i**mmediately** after the first action.	**When** I know, I'm going to tell you. (First I'm going to know; then I'm going to tell you.) **As soon as** I know, I will tell you. (I will tell you right away.)
2. *Before* introduces the action or a situation that will happen second.	**Before** I come, I'm going to call you. (First I'm going to call you; then I'm going to come.)
3. *Until* introduces an action or situation that stops another action. The main clause action starts first and continues to the time of the time clause action.	I'll stay **until** you tell me to leave. (I'll stay; then you'll tell me to leave, and I won't stay anymore.)

GRAMMAR HOTSPOT!

Remember! Use the simple present in the future time clause.	**When I know**, I'll tell you. **NOT:** When I ~~will know~~, I'll tell you.

Future Time Clauses

1 Future Time Clauses: Verb Forms

A. Complete the sentences with the correct form of the verbs in parentheses.
Use *will* when necessary.

1. He __will come__ home as soon as he __finishes__
   (come)   (finish)
   his work.

2. As soon as we _____ him, we _____
                    (see)   (give)
   him your message.

3. I _____ with you until I _____ better.
      (not / stay)   (feel)

4. Before you _____ , I _____ that
               (go)   (get)
   book for you.

5. They _____ you after they _____
          (call)   (arrive)
   in London.

B. Complete the sentences with the correct form of the verbs in parentheses.
Use *be going to* when necessary.

1. She __'s going to be__ rich before she __'s__
        (be)   (be)
   30 years old.

2. After the spacecraft _____ it _____
                         (land)   (send)
   a message back to Earth.

3. Until you _____ "please," I _____
              (say)   (not / give)
   it to you.

4. When we _____ this project, we _____
            (finish)   (have)
   a big party!

5. She _____ very happy when she _____
         (not / be)   (hear)
   the news.

2 Future Time Clauses: Function

Read the underlined sentences. Write *1* above the action that happens first in each one. Then check (✓) the sentence that gives the same information.

1. He's going to eat. Before that, he's going to take a shower.
   $\overset{1}{}$

   a. He's going to eat before he takes a shower. ❏

   b. He's going to take a shower before he eats. ☑

2. They're going to get tired. Until that time, they're going to play.

   a. They're going to get tired until they play. ❏

   b. They're going to play until they get tired. ❏

3. I will tell you the secret. Will you be angry with me after that?

   a. Will you be angry with me after I tell you the secret? ❏

   b. After you are angry with me, will I tell you the secret? ❏

4. I'll clean the kitchen. Then we'll have dinner right away.

   a. As soon as I clean the kitchen, we'll have dinner. ❏

   b. I'll clean the kitchen as soon as we have dinner. ❏

5. She will know him better. Until that time, she won't go out with him.

   a. She won't go out with him until she knows him better. ❏

   b. She won't know him better until she goes out with him. ❏

3 Future Time Clauses and Time Expressions: Presidential Promises

A. Senator O'Leary and Senator Fallows want to be president of their country. They are making promises to the voters. Combine the pairs of sentences below. Write the clauses in the order given. Add commas where necessary.

B. Work in small groups. Look at the promises of each senator in Part A. Discuss their promises. Who do you think will become president? Why?

Senator O'Leary:

1. I'm going to be president. I'm going to protect the environment.

   After _I'm president, I'm going to protect the environment._

2. I won't rest. Our country will use less energy.

   _____

   until _____

3. I'll form my government. We'll pass clean air laws.

   As soon as _____

4. We'll fight big industries. Their factories will destroy nature.

   _____

   _____ when

5. We'll organize free city buses. People won't need so many cars.

   After _____

6. We're going to control technology. Technology is going to control us.

   _____

   _____ before

Senator Fallows:

7. You won't be sorry. You will vote for me.

   You won't be sorry _____

   when _you vote for me._

8. I'm going to work. Our country is going to be a world leader.

   _____

   until _____

9. Other countries will look at us. They'll see great technological progress.

   When _____

10. This progress is going to happen. We're going to develop our medical, space, and energy-production industries.

    _____

    after _____

11. I'm going to support these industries. You're going to make me your president. _____

    as soon as _____

12. I will finish my presidency. I will lead you well into the twenty-first century.

    Before _____

4 Future Time Clauses and Time Expressions: Travel to Mars

Senator Fallows is reading about NASA's plans for future travel to Mars. (NASA is the U.S. National Aeronautics and Space Agency.) Work as a class. Write as many sentences as you can about NASA's schedule. Use future time clauses with *after*, *as soon as*, *before*, *until*, and *when*.

Examples: <u>After Spacecraft 1 goes to Mars, it's going to stay there.</u>

<u>The rocks will stay on Mars until Spacecraft 2 brings them back to Earth.</u>

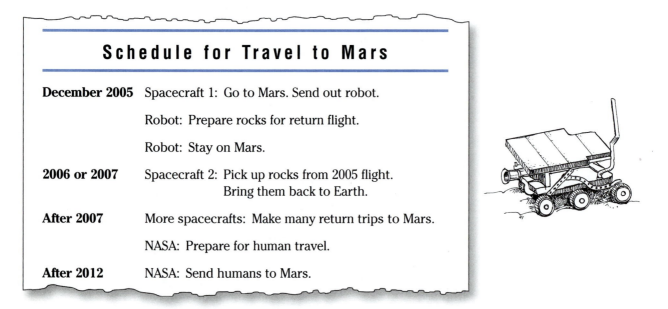

Schedule for Travel to Mars

December 2005	Spacecraft 1: Go to Mars. Send out robot.
	Robot: Prepare rocks for return flight.
	Robot: Stay on Mars.
2006 or 2007	Spacecraft 2: Pick up rocks from 2005 flight. Bring them back to Earth.
After 2007	More spacecrafts: Make many return trips to Mars.
	NASA: Prepare for human travel.
After 2012	NASA: Send humans to Mars.

See the *Grammar Links* Website for more information about NASA.

5 Future Time Clauses—Questions and Answers: Debate

A. Senators O'Leary and Fallows are having a debate (a public discussion) on TV. Senator O'Leary sees many problems with Senator Fallows' ideas about technology. Write Senator O'Leary's questions to Senator Fallows. Combine the sentences below. Replace the **boldfaced** time expressions with *after*, *as soon as*, *before*, *until*, and *when*.

1. Spacecrafts will have accidents in space. What will NASA do **then**?

   <u>When spacecrafts have accidents in space, what will NASA do?</u>

   OR

   <u>What will NASA do when spacecrafts have accidents in space?</u>

2. These accidents will happen. Will NASA send help **right away**?

   <u>Will NASA send help as soon as these accidents happen?</u>

3. We will send people to Mars. Will we solve the problems on Earth **before then**?

   _____

4. We will start to use uranium for energy. Will we learn to control nuclear power **before then**?

_____

5. We will use uranium. Where will we dump the radioactive waste **after that**?

_____

6. All our fish will die. Will submarines dump oil in the oceans **up to that time**?

_____

7. Our children are going to grow up. How will we find the answers to pollution **before then**?

_____

8. Our children will start school. Will they become technology addicts **right away**?

_____

9. Machines are going to take all our jobs. Will scientists keep building robots **up to that time**?

_____

10. Robots are going to make serious mistakes. What will happen **then**?

_____

B. How did Senator Fallows answer Senator O'Leary's questions in Part A? Work in small groups. Ask one another the questions, and think of good answers. If you can't think of an answer, say, "I don't know."

Examples: A: When spacecrafts have accidents in space, what will NASA do?

B: They'll bring the spacecrafts back to Earth.

C: Will NASA send help as soon as these accidents happen?

D: Yes, it will. NASA will have a special ambulance service.

6 Future Time Clauses with *Be Going to* and *Will*: Role-Play

A. Divide into two groups. One group plays the role of Senator O'Leary. You want to fight pollution and control technology. The other group plays the role of Senator Fallows. You want to build technology and use it to solve the world's problems. Write questions to ask the other group. Use future time clauses, *be going to* or *will*, and time expressions. Use the ideas in the Introductory Task and the exercises to help you.

Examples:
(Question for Senator O'Leary): Will you take away our cars as soon as you are president?

(Question for Senator Fallows): What's going to happen to our jobs when you develop all this technology?

B. Role-play the debate between the two senators. Each group asks and answers their questions from Part A.

C. Write about the class debate. In your opinion, which senator has the best promises and answers? Why? Write a paragraph of at least five sentences.

See the *Grammar Links* Website for a complete model paragraph for this assignment.

Factual and Future Conditionals

FORM

A. Factual Conditionals

A factual conditional sentence has a main clause and an *if* clause. Use the **simple present** tense in both clauses.

IF CLAUSE			MAIN CLAUSE		
IF	SUBJECT	SIMPLE PRESENT		SUBJECT	SIMPLE PRESENT
If	you	**heat**	water,	it	**boils**.

B. Future Conditionals

A future conditional sentence also has a main clause and an *if* clause. Use the **simple present** tense in the *if* clause. Use the **future** with *will* or *be going to* in the main clause.

IF CLAUSE			MAIN CLAUSE			
IF	SUBJECT	SIMPLE PRESENT	SUBJECT	*WILL/BE GOING TO*	BASE VERB	
If	you	**leave**,	John	**will/is going to**	**be**	sad.

C. Negative Conditionals

The *if* clause, the main clause, or both clauses can be negative.

If I **don't** work on the weekend, I go out.

If I **don't** work this weekend, I **won't** stay at home.

If I work this weekend, I **won't** go out.

D. Order of Clauses

The *if* clause can come before or after the main clause. Use a comma after an *if* clause at the beginning of a sentence.

If you leave, Jody will cry.

Jody will cry **if you leave**.

(continued on next page)

A. Factual Conditionals

1. A factual conditional tells **what usually or always happens** under certain conditions (situations). The *if* clause describes the condition. The main clause tells the usual result.

   condition — usual result
   If I have time, I walk to work.

   condition — usual result
   If I heat water, it boils.

2. *When* can be used instead of *if* in factual conditionals. The meaning is the same.

   Water boils **if** you heat it. = Water boils **when** you heat it.

B. Future Conditionals

A future conditional predicts **what will happen in the future** under certain conditions. The *if* clause gives the condition. The main clause predicts the result.

condition — predicted result
If it's hot tomorrow, we'll go to the beach.

condition — predicted result
If it's hot tomorrow, we're going to go to the beach.

GRAMMAR **HOT**SPOT!

Remember! Use the simple present in the *if* clause of future conditionals, even though the meaning is future.

We'll go to the beach if it **is** hot tomorrow.
NOT: We'll go the beach if it ~~will be~~ hot tomorrow.

Factual and Future Conditionals

7 **Recognizing Verb Tenses in Factual and Future Conditionals:**
Animal Protection I

 Listen to Senator O'Leary's speech about animal protection. Write the words you hear.

Technology is harming our environment. Without a clean environment, many animals

won't survive. If we ___*continue*___ to pollute the air with our cars and airplanes,
                            1

we _____ many kinds of birds forever. If they _____ clean air,
          2   3

birds suffer and sometimes die. The "noise pollution" we make is also bad for birds.

If there _____ too much noise around them,
                4

birds _____ away and never come back.
           5

Pollution also hurts other animals. The Arctic polar bear is one of

these animals. When we pollute the air, it _____ warmer.
                                                    6

When warm air _____ ice, the ice melts. If ice continues
                     7

to melt in the Arctic, polar bears _____ their home.
                                           8

If this _____, they will not survive.
              9

If you elect me president, I _____ hard for the future of all animals.
                                    10

My government will pass a clean air law. This is a promise I make to you. And if Senator

O'Leary _____ a promise, he _____ it!
               11   12

Polar Bear and Ice

> *survive* = continue to live. *suffer* = feel pain or discomfort.

8 **Conditions and Results in Factual and Future Conditionals:**
Animal Protection II

Look again at Senator O'Leary's speech in Exercise 7.

A. Some of his sentences are factual conditionals. They talk about what usually or always
happens if a condition exists. Write the conditions and results in the columns:

Condition	Result
they don't have clean air	*birds suffer and sometimes die*
_____	_____
_____	_____
_____	_____
_____	_____

B. Some of Senator O'Leary's sentences are future conditionals. They predict what will happen under certain conditions. Write the conditions and his predicted results in the columns:

Condition	Result
we continue to pollute the air	*we will lose many kinds of birds*
_____	_____
_____	_____
_____	_____

9 **Identifying Factual and Future Conditionals:** The Manatee, an Animal in Danger

Read the article. Underline the seven conditional sentences. Label them *Factual* (about usual results) or *Future* (about predicted results).

If you go to a marine zoo in Florida, you will probably see a manatee (a "sea cow"). You will almost certainly see manatees if you look for them at Disney World or Sea World.

Manatees weigh up to 3,000 pounds and grow up to 13 feet long if they reach full size. They are mammals, and they eat only plants.

When they need to protect themselves from boats, manatees dive under water and hold their breath. They can hold their breath for 20 minutes! However, manatees swim slowly. If a boat is moving fast, they don't have time to go under water. Almost all wild manatees have scars from boats.

Manatees are an endangered species. If people don't protect them, they will become extinct. The Save the Manatee Club sends information if you ask for it.

> *marine zoo* = zoo for sea animals. *mammals* = warm-blooded animals that usually have hair or fur. *scar* = mark left on the skin after an injury. *endangered species* = animals in danger of no longer existing.

 Are you interested in protecting endangered species? See the *Grammar Links* Website for more information.

10 Writing Factual Conditional Sentences: Animal Protection III

A. Animals don't wait for humans to protect them. They also protect themselves. Combine the sentences in brackets [ ] to form factual conditionals with *if* or *when*. Use the **boldfaced** sentence for the *if/when* clause. Do not change the order of the clauses. Use commas where necessary.

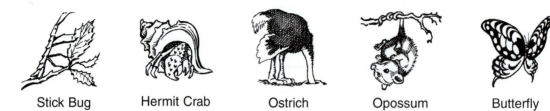

Stick Bug   Hermit Crab   Ostrich   Opossum   Butterfly

1. For protection, the snowshoe rabbit sometimes changes color.
   [**A snowshoe rabbit lives in the northern part of the United States.**
   Its fur turns white in the winter.]

   If a snowshoe rabbit lives in the northern part of the United States, its fur turns white

   in the winter.

2. The stick bug is a long, thin insect.
   [**A stick bug wants to hide.** It stands straight and looks like a stick.]

   _____

   _____

3. The hermit crab is a small sea animal.
   [**A hermit crab doesn't want anyone to see it.** It hides in a big shell.]

   _____

   _____

4. The ostrich is a large bird with a long neck and long legs.
   [An ostrich hides its head in the sand. **It wants to hide from its enemies.**]

   _____

   _____

5. The opossum is an interesting little animal.
   [An opossum lies on the ground and pretends to be dead. **It wants to trick its enemies.**]

   _____

   _____

6. The passionflower butterfly lives in Mexico.
   [**A passionflower butterfly wants to chase away enemies.** It makes a very bad smell.]

   _____

   _____

B. Discuss as a class: Do humans use any protection behaviors similar to those in Part A? Which ones? Use factual conditional sentences.

11 Writing Future Conditional Sentences: Animal Superstitions

We know that human technology affects animals. But some people also believe animals affect us and our behavior, sometimes in very strange ways. Here are some superstitions about the effects of animals on humans.

A. Make future conditional sentences with the words given. Use *if* in the **boldfaced** part of the sentence. Use commas where necessary.

1. **a black cat walk in front of you**/you/have bad luck.

   If a black cat walks in front of you, you will have bad luck.

2. you grow warts (bumps) on your fingers/**you**/**touch a toad.**

   _____

3. **you keep a rabbit's foot in your pocket**/you/be lucky.

   _____

Bat

4. **a bat bite you**/you/become a bat.

   _____

5. you/have good luck/**a cricket visit your house.**

   _____

Cricket

> *superstition* = belief based on magic or chance.

B. Discuss as a class: Have you ever heard any of the superstitions in Part A? Do you believe them? Why or why not?

C. Make up your own superstitions about how animals affect us. Write future conditional sentences.

Worm

Spider

1. If you _____ a worm, _____.

2. _____ if you _____ a spider.

3. If a fish _____, you _____.

4. You _____ if a horse _____.

Add two superstitions of your own. Use superstitions you have heard, or make them up.

5. _____ if you _____
   a _____.

6. _____ if you _____
   a _____.

D. Work in small groups. Discuss the sentences you wrote in Part C. Were any of your sentences similar or the same? Which ones?

12 Negative Conditionals: RoboCat—Pet of the Future

Randy is at a pet shop. Complete his conversation with the salesperson.

Randy: I'm looking for a pet for my mother. If she has a pet, maybe she

_won't be_____ so lonely.
        1 (not / be)

Salesperson: What a wonderful idea. I have the perfect pet for your mother. If you buy this pet,

you _____ sorry.
        2 (not / be)

Randy: That? What is it?

Salesperson: It's RoboCat. Go ahead. Pick it up.

Randy: But . . . it's a machine. And it looks dangerous. If I touch it, it

_____ soft and cuddly. It looks cold and sharp.
        3 (not / be going to be)

Salesperson: Shhh! This RoboCat is very sensitive. If you _____
                                                                4 (not / be)

careful, you will make it feel bad. And it won't hurt you if you

_____ it. This RoboCat is a very
        5 (not / hurt)

gentle, very friendly pet.

Randy: Friendly?

Salesperson: Yes. If you're nice to it, it _____ you.
                                              6 (never / leave)

And if you forget to feed it, it _____ hungry.
                                      7 (not get)

It can live forever without food.

Randy: Okay. But if my mother doesn't like this pet, she _____
                                                              8 (not / want)

to keep it.

Salesperson: If your mother _____ RoboCat, we'll give you back
                                9 (not /like)

your money. But your mother will love it. If she _____
                                                      10 (not / love)

this fine little pet, I'll be very surprised.

13 Editing: Mom's Best Friend

Correct the errors in Randy's note. There are seven errors with factual and future conditionals. The first one is corrected for you.

Dear Mom,

Say hello to your new pet—RoboCat! When I left, she was under the refrigerator. If you ~~will~~ see her, you will love her. She is a wonderful pet. If you don't like her, we are take her back to the pet store. But I think you will like her. And she loves people. When people will be nice to RoboCat, she is nice to people, too. She is also easy to take care of. If you will forget to feed her, she will still be happy. And just like other cats, she makes a noise when she will be happy. When she sounds like a car engine she is happy. Oh—and I think she is going to have babies. If she has babies. You will have about 100 more little RoboCats to keep you company soon!

Love,

Randy

14 Factual and Future Conditionals: Sell That Pet!

 You work in a pet shop. Choose one of these pets. Write an advertisement of at least five sentences for it. Use at least two factual and two future conditionals. Use the picture and the facts about your pet to help you.

 Tarantula

 Flea

 Snake

bites only when you frighten it	likes to do jumping tricks	has a beautiful silver coat
will eat flies and other pests	will be happy living in your rug	will eat mice and other pests
is soft and furry	enjoys the company of cats and dogs	loves to wrap around you and hug you
won't make noise	won't make noise	makes an interesting hissing noise
has eight beautiful deep black eyes	won't take up much space	has two beautiful narrow green eyes

Example:

You'll love this tarantula. If you don't like noise, it's the pet for you. It is very quiet.

If you don't frighten it, it won't bite you.

See the *Grammar Links* Website for a complete model paragraph for this assignment.

Check your progress! Go to the Self-Test for Chapter 7 on the *Grammar Links* Website.

Wrap-up Activities

1 **Technology News:** EDITING

Correct the errors in this advertisement. There are 12 errors with the future tense and with conditionals. The first one is corrected for you. After you finish, guess what the advertisement is talking about. (The answer to the puzzle is on page 132).

INTRODUCING A WONDERFUL INVENTION!

What are you doing next Friday evening?

Are you free?

Come to our demonstration!

*N*ext Friday evening, we are presenting a wonderful piece of information technology. You're going to love it! In fact, you're probably going to buy it as soon as you ~~will~~ see it. This technology will help you with college examinations. It is introducing you to wonderful new worlds. Perhaps it will to teach you a new language. When you'll need to find some information, you'll open a cover at the back, and you'll be see an "index." The index will direct you to the correct information.

You'll save energy if you will use this technology. You won't need batteries or electric wires—just your eyes. If you move your eyes over the information, it will coming straight to you.

It's easy to use—no instructions or programs. It's strong, too—it doesn't break when you will drop it or sit on it. Best of all, it's cheap! After you see the low price, you'll be going to buy two or three.

Our demonstration is at the public library. It starts at 6:00 p.m. and will finishes at 7:30. We'll going to show you this technology and answer your questions. Before you are leaving, you will test several examples. Please come!

What is this advertisement talking about? _____

_____

2 Ideas About the Future: SPEAKING

Step 1 Interview a student in another class. Ask what he or she expects to find in the world 20 years from now. Ask about jobs, nature, homes, and so on. Ask how technology will change the world.

Step 2 Report back to the class and compare the interviews. What did the students from the other classes say about technology?

3 Utopia: SPEAKING

Step 1 Work in small groups. Imagine you have the power to make laws or change anything you want in the world! Make a list of five plans and promises for your "utopia"—your perfect world.

Step 2 Share your ideas with the class. Are there some ideas that you all agree about?

Examples:

When children finish school, we'll send them to live in another country for one year.

We're going to teach everybody in the world to read and write.

We won't spend any more money on space travel.

4 Designing a Pet: SPEAKING/WRITING

Step 1 Draw a picture of your ideal future pet. What will it look like? Will it be alive, or will it be a robot? Or, like Roboroach, will it be half and half?

Step 2 On a different piece of paper, write a paragraph about your new pet. Write at least five sentences. Describe your pet carefully. Use the future tense, and use conditionals in your paragraph.

Example:

My ideal pet of the future will be half dog and half cat. If I need company, it won't run away and hide. . . .

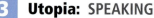 See *the Grammar Links* Website for a complete model paragraph for this activity.

Step 3 Mix up all of the pictures and all of the paragraphs.

Step 4 Match the pictures to the paragraphs. Discuss the ideal animals as a class. Which ones seem the most creative? The funniest? The most interesting? Why?

Answers to Activities
Answer to Wrap-Up Editing Exercise—Unit Three
A book

Nouns, Articles, Quantifiers, and Pronouns

TOPIC FOCUS
Travel and Transportation

UNIT OBJECTIVES

■ **proper and common nouns**
(*Dan Evans* is a *pilot*. He flies *airplanes*.)

■ **count and noncount nouns**
(*Trains* were very popular in the 1800s. *Transportation* by train was fast and convenient.)

■ **articles**
(She bought *a* banana and *an* apple. She took *the* apple on *the* train with her.)

■ **quantifiers**
(*Many* people enjoy walking. They don't need *much* equipment to walk.)

■ **pronouns and possessive adjectives**
(Martin loves to travel. *He* goes all over the world on *his* bicycle.)

Henry Ford in an Early Model Automobile

Grammar in Action

🎧 **Reading and Listening:** Travel Through Time

Read and listen. Write the words you hear.

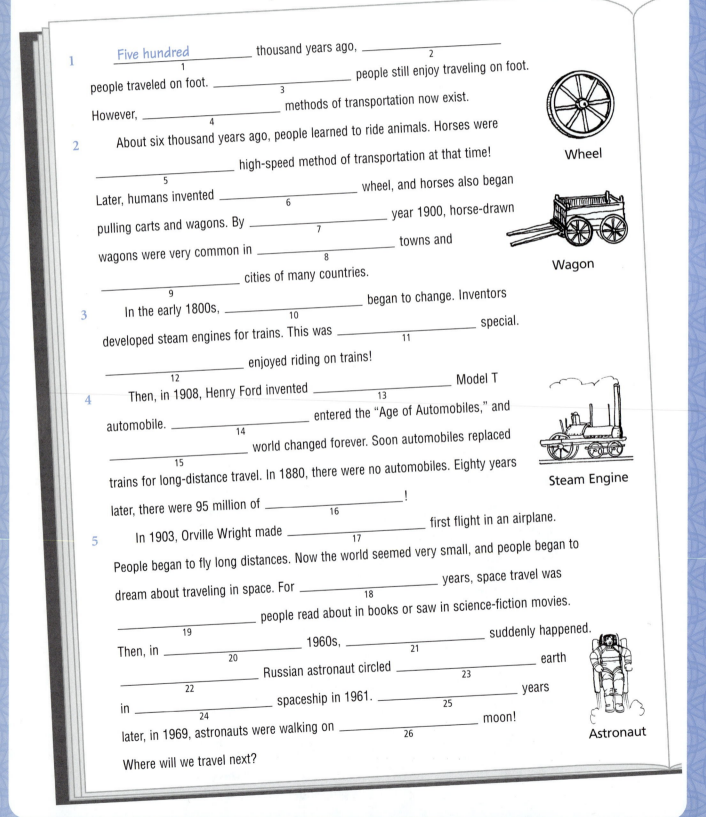

1   <u>Five hundred</u> thousand years ago, _____ people traveled on foot. _____ people still enjoy traveling on foot. However, _____ methods of transportation now exist.

2   About six thousand years ago, people learned to ride animals. Horses were _____ high-speed method of transportation at that time! Later, humans invented _____ wheel, and horses also began pulling carts and wagons. By _____ year 1900, horse-drawn wagons were very common in _____ towns and _____ cities of many countries.

3   In the early 1800s, _____ began to change. Inventors developed steam engines for trains. This was _____ special. _____ enjoyed riding on trains!

4   Then, in 1908, Henry Ford invented _____ Model T automobile. _____ entered the "Age of Automobiles," and _____ world changed forever. Soon automobiles replaced trains for long-distance travel. In 1880, there were no automobiles. Eighty years later, there were 95 million of _____ !

5   In 1903, Orville Wright made _____ first flight in an airplane. People began to fly long distances. Now the world seemed very small, and people began to dream about traveling in space. For _____ years, space travel was _____ people read about in books or saw in science-fiction movies. Then, in _____ 1960s, _____ suddenly happened. _____ Russian astronaut circled _____ earth in _____ spaceship in 1961. _____ years later, in 1969, astronauts were walking on _____ moon!

Where will we travel next?

Wheel

Wagon

Steam Engine

Astronaut

Think About Grammar

A. Look at the words you wrote in paragraph 1. Write them in Column A.

Look at the words you wrote in paragraph 2. Write them in Column B.

Look at the words you wrote in paragraph 3. Write them in Column C.

Look at the words you wrote in paragraph 4. Write them in Column D.

Look at the words you wrote in paragraph 5. Write them in the correct column: A, B, C, or D.

Column A	Column B	Column C	Column D
Quantifiers and Numbers	Articles	Indefinite Pronouns	Pronouns and Possessive Adjectives
Five hundred			

B. Look at the reading and at the words you wrote in Part A. Circle **T** if the statement is true and **F** if the statement is false.

1. Words that come before nouns and tell *how much* or *how many* are quantifiers or numbers.   T   F

2. There are at least two different articles in English.   T   F

3. Pronouns always come just before verbs.   T   F

Chapter 8

Nouns and Articles

Introductory Task: Always Moving Forward!

A. Read this article from a health and fitness magazine. The author is a 78-year-old woman who walks everywhere.

Always Moving Forward!

By Gertrude Jacobs

Walking is the best way to travel. I work at a **bank** three miles from my house. I walk to work every day, and it's very good exercise. It's also a lot of fun because the **children** in my neighborhood sometimes walk with me. We walk and talk together.

You don't need expensive equipment when you walk. I have good shoes, a coat, and an **umbrella** for bad weather. I don't have a **purse**. I carry a **backpack** instead. It holds all the **things** I need: the **keys** to my house, the **wallet** my son gave me, pictures of the **people** in my family, and five or six dollars, in case of an **emergency**. Sometimes I put an **apple** or an **orange** in my backpack, too. When I get hungry on the way home from work, I just stop and have a **snack**!

I never take a **bus** or drive a **car**! The **buses** in this town cause too much pollution, and the **car** I own causes pollution, too. Besides, the **cars** I see on my way to work are standing still in traffic. I never stand still. I'm always moving forward.

---

equipment = things needed for an activity. *purse* = bag for carrying personal items. *backpack* = bag carried on the back. *emergency* = sudden, serious situation. *snack* = food eaten between meals.

See the *Grammar Links* Website for more information about walking and your health.

B. Look at the **boldfaced** words in Part A. They are all nouns.

1. Which of these nouns are singular (only one person, place, or thing)?
   Write them here.

   bank,_____

2. Which of these nouns are plural (more than one person, place, or thing)?
   Write them here.

   children,_____

3. Is this statement true (T) or false (F)? Circle the correct answer.

   All plural nouns in English end in *-s.*   T   F

C. Each **boldfaced** noun has the word *a, an,* or *the* in front of it.

1. Write each **boldfaced** noun in the column that matches the word in front of it.

a	an	the
bank		

2. Are these statements true (T) or false (F)? Circle the correct answer.

   a. The ***a*** column and the ***an*** column have plural nouns in them.   T   F

   b. The ***the*** column has singular nouns and plural nouns in it.   T   F

D. *A* and *an* mean the same thing in English. Look at the nouns in Part C. Some nouns
have *a* in front of them, and some nouns have ***an***. Why do you think this is true?

_____

Proper Nouns and Common Nouns

FORM and FUNCTION

A. Overview

Nouns name people, places, things, or ideas. There are proper nouns and common nouns.	*Proper noun*: **George** *Common noun*: **girl**

B. Proper Nouns

1. Proper nouns are names of **particular** people, places, things, and ideas.	*People*: **Mary Larson** *Places*: **France** *Things and ideas*: **the Empire State Building** (buildings), **Saturday** (days of the week), **May** (months of the year), **Arabic** (languages), **British** (nationalities), **Christmas** (holidays)
2. A proper noun always begins with a capital letter.	**British** NOT: ~~british~~ **Saturday** NOT: ~~saturday~~
3. *A/An* is not usually used with proper nouns. But some proper nouns begin with *the*.	**the** *New York Times* **the Five Spice Restaurant** **the Middle East**

C. Common Nouns

1. All other nouns are common nouns. They do not name particular people, places, things, or ideas.	**girl, cat, car**
2. A common noun does not usually begin with a capital letter unless it is the first word in a sentence.	Henry Ford invented the **automobile**. **Automobiles** are very common today.
3. *A/An* can be used with singular common nouns. *The* can be used with singular and plural common nouns. (See Grammar Briefing 2 in this chapter for more information about singular and plural nouns.)	He invented **a machine**. It was **an invention** with many problems. **The machine** didn't work well. None of **the machines** worked well.

The days of the week and the months of the year are proper nouns. The seasons of the year are common nouns. They do not begin with a capital letter.

He came on a **Sunday** in the **fall**.

NOT: He came on a **Sunday** in the ~~Fall~~.

GRAMMAR PRACTICE 1

Proper Nouns and Common Nouns

1 **Proper and Common Nouns:** Those Magnificent Men and Their Flying Machines

A. Listen to a museum guide talk about the history of flight. He describes six different flying machines. Put these machines in the order in which you hear them: 1 = the first; 6 = the last.

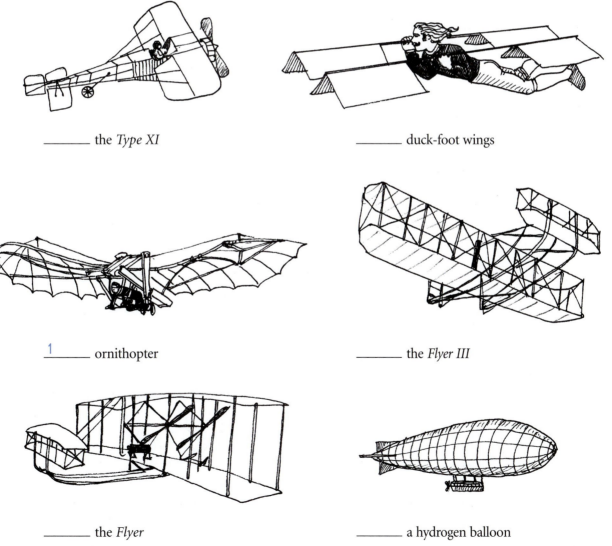

_____ the *Type XI*

_____ duck-foot wings

__1__ ornithopter

_____ the *Flyer III*

_____ the *Flyer*

_____ a hydrogen balloon

B. Look at the chart about some of the inventors from Part A. Correct the errors. There are 20 errors with capital letters. The first two are corrected for you.

Who	When	Where
a ^Ffrench man, ^Bbesnier	1678	France
jacques charles	the Winter of 1783	France
orville and wilbur wright	thursday, december 17, 1903—just before christmas	the united states
the wright brothers	1905	the united states
louis bleriot	1908	the english channel

2 Editing: Proper and Common Nouns—Come Fly with Me

A. An inventor living in New York in 1903 is writing to his girlfriend. Correct the errors in his letter. There are eight errors with common nouns and proper nouns. The first two are corrected for you.

July 14, 1903

Dear a̶ Gloria,

Hello from t̶h̶e̶ New York! I miss you, but I will see you soon. You see, my invention is almost ready. It is a beautiful flying machine. I will name it gloria, for you. It will fly gracefully through the air and take me to the Paris; I will meet you there.

My flying machine has three pairs of Wings. These wings are made of heavy wood. I glued them to a frame. The frame is very strong. I will sit in the center of my flying machine. I will turn a pedals with my Feet and it will move forward. Everyone will know me and my invention. And you and I will spend the Winter together, traveling around in my flying machine. We will be famous.

I can't wait to see you, my darling. Look for me in the sky!

Love,

Dick
Dick

B. Work with a partner. Discuss: Do you think Dick's invention was a success? Why or why not?

Count and Noncount Nouns

FORM and FUNCTION

A. Count Nouns

1. Count nouns are names for people, places, things, and ideas that can be counted. There can be one (singular) or more than one (plural).

   Singular: a **girl**, one **child**

   Plural: two **girls**, five **children**

2. All regular plural count nouns end in -*s*.

   (See Appendix 8 for spelling rules for plural nouns.)

   book**s**, dog**s**, bushe**s**

3. The regular plural ending is pronounced /s/, /z/, or /ɪz/.

   (See Appendix 9 for the pronounciation rules for plural nouns.)

   /**s**/: book**s**

   /**z**/: book**s**

   /**ɪz**/: book**s**

4. Some count nouns have irregular plural forms.

   (See Appendix 10 for a list of common irregular plural nouns.)

SINGULAR	PLURAL
child	**children**
foot	**feet**
woman	**women**
sheep	**sheep**
person	**people**

B. Noncount Nouns

1. Noncount nouns (sometimes called mass nouns or uncountable nouns) are names for people, places, things, and ideas that cannot be counted.

   water, information, air, beauty

2. A noncount noun does not have a plural form.

   homework
     NOT: ~~homeworks~~

   information
     NOT: ~~informations~~

3. Many noncount nouns name groups of things. These groups have individual countable parts.

GROUPS (NONCOUNT NOUNS)	INDIVIDUAL PARTS (COUNT NOUNS)
homework	writing assignments, math problems
jewelry	a bracelet, earrings
luggage	a suitcase, bags
equipment	a hair dryer, computers
clothing	a sweater, socks

(continued on next page)

4. Other categories of noncount nouns include:

LIQUIDS	SOLIDS	PARTICLES	GASES	NATURAL PHENOMENA	ABSTRACT IDEAS	FIELDS OF STUDY
milk	food	sand	air	weather	honesty	journalism
water	hair	sugar	hydrogen	scenery	beauty	mathematics

(See Appendix 11 for a list of common noncount nouns.)

GRAMMAR **HOT**SPOT!

1. Singular count nouns and noncount nouns take singular verbs.

	singular noun	singular verb	
The	**boy**	**is**	tired.

noncount noun	singular verb	
Sugar	**is**	sweet.

2. Plural count nouns take plural verbs.

	plural noun	plural verb	
The	**boys**	**are**	tired.

3. Some noncount nouns end in *-s*. These nouns look plural, but they are not.

   The **news** on television is usually bad.
     NOT: The news on television ~~are~~ usually bad.

   Mathematics is difficult.
     NOT: Mathematics ~~are~~ difficult.

Count and Noncount Nouns

3 Singular and Plural Count Nouns: What Happened to Amelia Earhart?

Imagine it is the year 1937. Listen to the news report about Amelia Earhart, a famous woman pilot. Complete the report with the words you hear. Write the correct form of the nouns in parentheses: singular or plural. See Appendix 8 and Appendix 10 for help.

. . . We interrupt this program to bring you some sad news. Amelia Earhart, world-famous

pilot, is lost. Earhart and her copilot, Fred Noonan, were almost at the end of their _flight_
1 (flight)

around the world. Yesterday, however, they tried to land on Howland Island, a small

_____ in the Pacific Ocean. But something went wrong. The _____
2 (island)   3 (man)

on a nearby _____ lost contact with them early yesterday morning.
4 (ship)

Many _____ are looking for Earhart and Noonan. Even small
5 (person)

_____ from other _____ are helping. Young
6 (child)   7 (island)

_____ from New Guinea are looking in the _____ on Howland
8 (boy)   9 (bush)

Island for airplane _____. We need to find Earhart and Noonan soon. They didn't
10 (part)

have many _____ on their plane. There are _____ in the
11 (supply)   12 (fish)

_____ near Howland Island, and there are wild _____ on the
13 (water)   14 (berry)

island. But these two _____ will not live long without help. Keep your
15 (hero)

_____ tuned to this station for more information.
16 (radio)

---

bush = short treelike plant. *supply* = something (food, water, etc.) people need to survive. *berry* = small juicy fruit. *hero* = person of great courage.

4 Pronunciation of Plural Nouns: More About Amelia Earhart

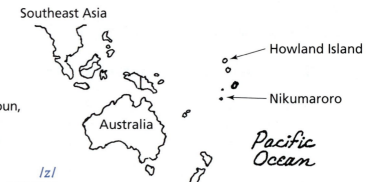

Southeast Asia

Howland Island

Nikumaroro

Australia

Pacific Ocean

A. The year is now 2004. The search for Amelia Earhart continues. Listen to part of a television show about her. Above each **boldfaced** noun, write the plural sound you hear: /s/ (as in *hats*), /z/ (as in *dogs*), or /ɪz/ as in *dishes*.

/z/
Amelia Earhart disappeared almost 70 **years** ago.
1

What happened to Amelia and her airplane, the *Electra*?

Did they fall into the sea near Howland Island? Many **books** are written about this
2

theory. There are, however, other **theories**. Tonight's program is
3

about a new theory.

This year, **researchers** found some interesting **objects** on another island, Nikumaroro
4 5

Island. This island is 350 **miles** from Howland Island. They found **pieces** of **shoes**.
6 7 8

Amelia Earhart wore shoes just like these. In other **places** on Nikumaroro Island,
9

searchers also found old airplane **parts.** Are some of them from the *Electra*?
10

Many people now believe Amelia Earhart landed on Nikumaroro Island. Others

disagree. They tell us airplane **crashes** were very common in 1937. They believe the
11

objects from Nikumaroro probably belonged to someone else. They say Earhart and

Noonan did not have enough fuel in their **tanks** to reach Nikumaroro. Radio **records**
12 13

also tell us the *Electra* was flying very close to Howland Island when it crashed.

So what really happened to Amelia Earhart? In this week's television program, we will

show you **photographs** and **maps.** We will give you more **details.** Then you can decide!
14 15 16

We will be right back. But, first, these **messages** . . .
17

---

theory = belief. *researcher* = person who does careful study. *crash* = accident.
tank = container for holding gasoline. *record* = written account that saves knowledge.

B. Read the news report aloud to a partner. Help each other pronounce the plural nouns correctly.

C. What happened to Amelia Earhart? With your partner, write your own ending to her story. Use one of the theories from Exercise 3 or Exercise 4, or use your imagination! Write at least seven sentences. Read your ending to the class. Be careful about your pronunciation of plurals. See the spelling and pronunciation rules in Appendix 8 and Appendix 9 for help.

See the *Grammar Links* Website for more about the mystery of Amelia Earhart.

5 Regular and Irregular Plural Nouns: Time for a Race

A. How many plural nouns can you think of? Divide into two teams and stand in two lines. The first person in each team writes a different **regular** plural noun on the blackboard and runs to the end of the line. The next person writes a different regular plural noun. Continue the game until one team can't think of any more nouns or for 10 minutes.

B. Now play the same game with **irregular** plural nouns.

6 Singular, Plural, and Noncount Nouns: Modern Airplane Travelers

Read the story. Write each **boldfaced** noun in the correct column of the chart.

Jack and Jill are **students** at the University of Maine, where there is a lot of **snow** during the winter **months**. Jack studies **mathematics**, and Jill studies **journalism**.

Jack and Jill work very hard, and they usually have a lot of **homework** every night. But tonight Jack and Jill are not thinking about homework. They're busy planning a **vacation** instead.

Next **week** is winter vacation week at the University of Maine. Jack and Jill are tired of the cold Maine **weather**, so they're going to take a **trip** to California. They'll visit Jill's **sister**, **brother**, and **cousins** there. While they're in California, Jack and Jill will also go to the **beach**. They'll lie on the **sand**. They'll swim in the warm **water** of the southern Pacific Ocean. They'll breathe the sweet salt **air**. They'll eat **seafood**. They'll watch the **whales** and the **fish** in the sea. They'll enjoy the **beauty** of the landscape. They'll just—relax.

Count and Noncount Nouns		
Singular Count Nouns	Plural Count Nouns	Noncount Nouns
	students	

A. Jack and Jill are deciding what to take on their vacation. They are making lists. Put the items from their lists into the categories in the chart. Some items won't fit any of the categories. Put them in the box marked Other.

Jill's list

gold earrings
bikini
backpack for the beach
journalism assignment
3 cotton dresses
Jack's CD player
shampoo
new watch
makeup
toothbrush

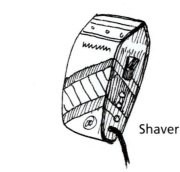
Shaver

Jack's list

large suitcase—for both of us
laptop computer
swimsuit
soap
3 pairs of shorts
electric shaver
math problems
surprise gift for Jill—necklace
toothpaste
toothbrush

Shorts

Bikini

	Groups (Noncount)				
	Homework	Jewelry	Luggage	Electronic Equipment	Clothing
Individual Items (Count)		*gold earrings*			

Other
makeup NC

B. Look at the nouns you put in the *Other* box. Label each noun **SC** (Singular Count), **PC** (Plural Count), or **NC** (Noncount). Not sure whether a noun is count or noncount? Look it up in your dictionary.

8 **Verb Agreement with Count and Noncount Nouns:** Taxi, Please!

Read the passage. Circle the correct verb forms.

The first airplane flight was only about 50 years ago, but people (is / **are**) already flying
                                                                                    1
to the moon! Space travel (is / are) becoming common, but it is difficult, too. Space (has / have)
                          2   3
no gravity. In space, humans (weighs / weight) almost nothing. Weightlessness (makes / make)
                                4   5
it difficult to work and to eat. Food (floats / float) away when you try to eat it, and tools
                                        6
(becomes / become) difficult to use. Nowadays, special new tools (helps / help) astronauts
7   8
work in weightlessness; special food (is / are) also available.
                                      9

Temperature (is / are) another problem in space. Outer space (is / are) very cold
<u>10</u>   <u>11</u>

in some places and very hot in others. Space suits (protects / protect) astronauts from
<u>12</u>

freezing or burning in space.

    Even with these problems, people still (wants / want) to travel in space. In fact, one
<u>13</u>

company (is / are) building space "taxis." These taxis (is / are) waiting to take us to the
<u>14</u>   <u>15</u>

moon someday soon! Are you ready to go? Just pack your space suit and call your local

space taxi for a ride!

---

gravity = the natural force that pulls toward the center of the earth. *weightlessness* = the condition
of having no weight. astronaut = a person who travels in space.

GRAMMAR BRIEFING 3

The Indefinite Article *A/An*

FORM

A. Overview

A/An is the indefinite article. *A/An* comes before singular counts nouns.	**a** boy **an** apple

B. *A* or *An*?

1. Use *a* before consonant sounds. Use *an* before vowel sounds.	**a** baby, **a** class **an** island, **an** orange
2. Vowel letters do not always have vowel sounds.	**an** uncle BUT: **a** university
3. Some words that begin with the consonant letter *h* begin with vowel sounds.	**a** horse BUT: **an** hour

(continued on next page)

Introducing Nouns

1. *A/An* introduces singular count nouns. A noun needs to be introduced when:

Speaker   Listener

- The speaker knows about it but the listener does not.

> *Speaker*: I saw **a** cool car today.

Speaker   Listener

- The listener knows about it but the speaker does not.

> *Speaker*: I hear you bought **a** new car today. What did you buy?

Speaker   Listener

- It is new for both the listener and the speaker.

> *Speaker*: I need **a** new car. What kind should I get?

2. Don't use an article when noncount nouns and plural nouns need to be introduced.

> I'm going to buy **bread** today. (noncount noun)
>
> I need **shoes**. (plural count noun)

The Indefinite Article *A/An*

9 **The Indefinite Article:** A Car for Christine

Christine and Roger are talking on the telephone. Complete their conversation with *a* or *an*. Write **0** when no article is needed.

Christine: I really need _____*a*_____ new car.
1

Roger: Oh, yeah? What kind are you looking for?

Christine: Oh, I don't know. I just need _____ inexpensive, dependable car.
2

Roger: Well, I just bought _____ used car.
3

Christine: What kind did you buy?

Roger: It's _____ orange sports car. It needs _____
4   5

tires, but it's in good shape.

Christine: You're lucky!

Roger: Hey! I saw _____ interesting car the other day. You might like it.
6

Christine: Really? Where?

Roger: It was at _____ house in Williston.
7

Christine: Well, that's pretty far from my apartment . . .

Roger: You have _____ apartment downtown, right?
8

Christine: Yeah. That's right. It's on Spear Street.

Roger: Do you have _____ time right now? Do you want to look at
9

_____ cars?
10

Christine: Well, I guess so. I have _____ homework to do, but—
11

Roger: Great! I'll come and pick you up in my new car.

Christine: Okay. Let's see. You'll probably be here in about _____ hour, right?
12

Roger: Are you kidding? Not in my new beauty! See you in 30 minutes!

Christine: Okay, Roger. But do drive carefully. Roger? Are you there?

The Definite Article *The*

FORM and FUNCTION

A. Overview

The is the definite article. It comes before singular, plural, and noncount nouns.

the boy (singular)

the boys (plural)

the sugar (noncount)

B. When to Use *The*

Use *the* only when the speaker and the listener are thinking about the same noun. Both the speaker and the listener know about the noun. This happens:

- The second time someone mentions a noun.

  I have a car and a truck. **The** car is new. **The** truck is old. (*Car* and *truck* are introduced with *a*; the second time they are mentioned, *the* is used.)

- When the noun is part of or related to something else already introduced.

  I bought a new car yesterday. **The** seats are leather. (We know which seats, since seats are part of the car.)

- When the noun names something unique (one of a kind). There is only one of this person, place, or thing in the world.

  The sun was hot today. (There is only one sun, and everyone knows about it.)

- When the noun is part of the everyday world of the listener and the speaker. It is something or someone that is very familiar to them.

  Mother to son: Did you wash **the** dishes? (The dishes are part of their house; mother and son both know these dishes.)

  Friend to friend: I was listening to **the** news on **the** radio this morning when **the** electricity went off. (The news, the radio, and the electricity are parts of everyday life; it is not necessary to introduce them.)

- When other words in the sentence make the noun known (specific).

  The book **on the table** is mine. (*On the table* tells which book.)

  The second book was the best. (*Second* tells which book.)

- When the listener and speaker can see or hear the noun (or the speaker points to the noun).

  Did you hear **the** thunder? (The speaker and listener hear the thunder.)

  Carol, give me **the** book, please. (The speaker is pointing at the book.)

The Definite Article *The*

10 The Definite Article: The Age of Automobiles

Read this passage from a history book. Above each **boldfaced** phrase, write the
letter of the reason why *the* is used. Choose from the reasons in the box.

> A. The noun has already been introduced.
> B. The noun is part of something else already introduced.
> C. The noun is unique. There is only one of this noun.
> D. Other words in the sentence make the noun known (specific).

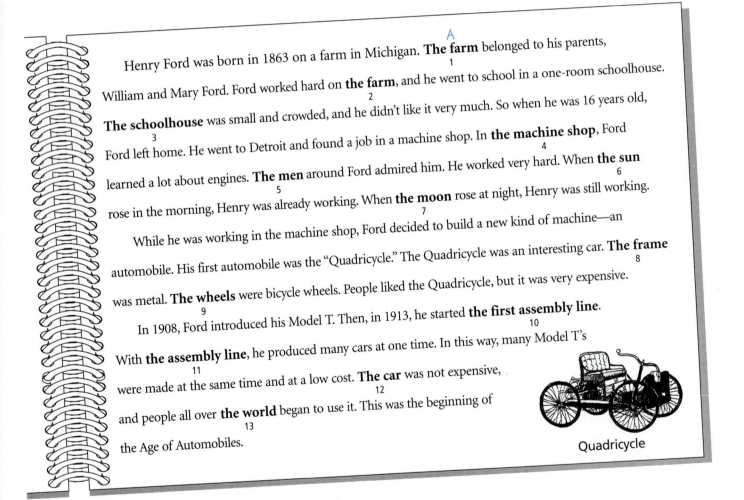

Henry Ford was born in 1863 on a farm in Michigan. **The farm**[A] belonged to his parents,
1

William and Mary Ford. Ford worked hard on **the farm**, and he went to school in a one-room schoolhouse.
2

The schoolhouse was small and crowded, and he didn't like it very much. So when he was 16 years old,
3

Ford left home. He went to Detroit and found a job in a machine shop. In **the machine shop**, Ford
4

learned a lot about engines. **The men** around Ford admired him. He worked very hard. When **the sun**
5   6

rose in the morning, Henry was already working. When **the moon** rose at night, Henry was still working.
7

While he was working in the machine shop, Ford decided to build a new kind of machine—an

automobile. His first automobile was the "Quadricycle." The Quadricycle was an interesting car. **The frame**
                                                        8

was metal. **The wheels** were bicycle wheels. People liked the Quadricycle, but it was very expensive.
9

In 1908, Ford introduced his Model T. Then, in 1913, he started **the first assembly line**.
                                                    10

With **the assembly line**, he produced many cars at one time. In this way, many Model T's
11

were made at the same time and at a low cost. **The car** was not expensive,
                                  12

and people all over **the world** began to use it. This was the beginning of
              13

the Age of Automobiles.

Quadricycle

> *machine shop* = a place where machines are made. *engine* = the part of a car
> that changes energy into motion. *frame* = the inside structure of a car.
> *assembly line* = machines and workers in a factory that work together.

 See the *Grammar Links* Website for more about the history of the automobile.

11 The Definite Article: A Sunday Drive

Henry and Clara are going for a ride in their Model T. Read their conversation. Above each **boldfaced** phrase, write the letter of the reason why *the* is used. Choose from the reasons in the box.

> A. The person, place, or thing is unique. There is only one in the world.
> B. The person, place, or thing is part of Henry and Clara's everyday world.
> C. Henry and Clara can see or hear the person, place, or thing.

Henry: Clara, are you ready? We need to leave soon, or **the sun** will go down.
                                                                          A
                                                                          1

Clara: I'm almost ready. But before we go, we need to feed **the cats**. And did you put
                                                             2

the dog outside?
3

Henry: Yes, I did. Now can we go?

Clara: Well, just a minute. I need to . . . Did you see that? **The lightning** is getting close!
                                                                 4

I heard on **the radio** this morning that **the weather** is going to be bad this afternoon.
            5   6

Henry: But look at **the clouds**. They are very far away. It isn't going to rain here. And
                    7

rain won't bother us anyway. **The car** has a top on it. We won't get wet! I'll go
                              8

outside and get **the car** ready.
                 9

Clara: Well, just in case, I'm going to bring **the umbrella**. Oh, Henry! Did you hear
                                              10

that? **The thunder** is really loud now!
        11

Henry: That wasn't thunder, Clara. The car sometimes makes a little noise when I first

start it. Let's go!

12 Definite and Indefinite Articles: Test Yourself

Complete the sentences with *a, an,* or *the*. If no article is needed, write **0**.

1. We have _a____ black cat, _a____ gray cat, and _an____ orange cat. _The____ black cat and _the____ orange cat are friendly. _The____ gray cat is very independent. We love _0____ cats.

2. Yesterday I bought _____ furniture. I bought _____ new couch and two new armchairs. _____ couch is purple. _____ armchairs are green.

3. Carlos is _____ very nice man. He brought us _____ flowers when he came to visit.

4. Last week Wan met _____ president of his country. It was _____ honor.

5. We need _____ milk. _____ milk in our refrigerator is sour.

6. Andrew and Clarice are cleaning their house this weekend. It will be _____ big job. They want to wash all _____ windows, reorganize all _____ closets, and shampoo all _____ carpets.

7. Answer _____ door, please. _____ doorbell is ringing.

8. There are _____ apples in the bowl. Do you want one?

9. Do you hear _____ rain? It is falling softly on _____ roof.

10. I need _____ information about _____ price of this car.

11. _____ mayor is going to make _____ speech tonight at 9:00. She's going to talk about our city. Let's listen to _____ radio at that time.

12. Karen recently had _____ unpleasant experience. She applied to _____ university in California. There are several universities there, but she applied to only one. _____ university didn't accept her.

13 Understanding Situations: Listening In

A. You are in a crowded airport. You hear the following conversations. Write about the conversations. Make guesses: Who are the two people? What are the people talking about? Use your imagination. Pay special attention to your use of definite and indefinite articles.

1. Two young girls are talking. One says to the other: "Do you think she remembered **the bag**?"

   Example:

   The two girls are sisters. The bag is a bag of toys. They want their mother to bring the bag with the toys on the airplane. OR *The two girls are friends. They are waiting for another girl to join them. She has their concert tickets in a bag.*

2. Two older women are coming out of an airplane. One says to the other: "Did you remember **the oranges**?"

3. A man is greeting a woman. He says to her: "Welcome home! Did you get **the job**?"

4. Two women are walking near you. One says to the other: "I have **the tickets** right here."

5. Two young boys are looking around. One says to the other: "Where's the rest of **the team**?"

6. Two college students sit next to you. One says to the other: "Where's **the computer**?"

B. Exchange papers with a partner. Read your partner's answers. Discuss: Which of your answers are similar? Which are different?

See the *Grammar Links* Website for model answers to this exercise.

Check your progress! Go to the Self-Test for Chapter 8 on the *Grammar Links* Website.

Chapter 9

General Quantifiers; Numbers; Measure Words

Introductory Task: Seeing It All!

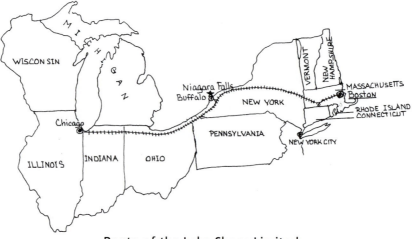

Route of the Lake Shore Limited

🎧 **A.** Kim and Juan are planning a vacation trip together. Listen to their conversation, and write the words you hear.

Kim: Niagara Falls! Boston! New York! I want to see __all__ these places! And I want to visit
1

__some__ small towns and see __some__ scenery, too!
2   3

Juan: Wait. I have an idea. There's a train from Chicago. It goes to Boston and New York.

It's called the Lake Shore Limited. We can buy a ticket to Boston, but we can visit

_____ other places, too. For example, we can stop and visit
4

Niagara Falls. Then, _____ days later, we can get back on the train.
5

The train passes by _____ beautiful scenery, and it stops at
6

_____ small towns, too. What do you think?
7

Kim: Interesting idea. But train travel takes _____ time, and there isn't
8

_____ space on trains.
9

Juan: Well, the Lake Shore Limited is different! It's a fast train. And travel on this train is really

quite comfortable. For example, for _____ extra money, you can
10

get a "sleeper." _____ sleeper is a room with a large bed and
11

_____ windows. _____ sleepers even have
12   13

televisions in them! And _____ passengers in sleepers eat for free
14

in the dining car. _____ food is fresh, and _____
15   16

table has fresh flowers on it.

Kim: That does sound nice! Maybe the train is a good idea, after all. Let's get

_____ information about schedules and prices.
17

See the *Grammar Links* Website for more information about traveling by train in the
United States.

B. Look again at the words you wrote in Part A. These words are general quantifiers.
Write them in the correct columns in the chart. Are you unsure which nouns are
count and which are noncount? See Grammar Briefing 2 in Chapter 8, or look them
up in your dictionary.

Quantifiers used before **singular count** nouns	Quantifiers used before **plural count** nouns	Quantifiers used before **noncount** noun
	all some	

C. Look at the quantifiers you wrote in Part B. Find the ones that are used with both
plural count and noncount nouns. Write them here:

_____

General Quantifiers I

FORM and FUNCTION

A. Overview

General quantifiers express different quantities (amount of something, number of something). Some general quantifiers can be used only with plural count nouns. Others can be used only with noncount nouns. Some can be used with both.

	WITH PLURAL COUNT NOUNS	WITH NONCOUNT NOUNS	WITH BOTH
largest quantity			all
			most
	many	much	a lot (of), lots (of)
	several	a great deal (of)	
			enough, plenty (of)
			some
	a few	a little	
	few	little	
no quantity			none (of the), no

B. *Each* and *Every*

Use *each* and *every* only with singular count nouns. They take singular verbs. They mean "all."

Each/Every train on this route **has** a sleeping car.
= **All** trains on this route **have** sleeping cars.

GRAMMAR PRACTICE 1

General Quantifiers I

1 **General Quantifiers with Count and Noncount Nouns:** Train Talk

Cross out the general quantifiers that *cannot* be used to complete the sentence correctly.

1. This city has _____ train stations.

a few	many
~~a little~~	enough
~~each~~	few
a lot of	lots of
no	plenty of
~~a great deal of~~	

2. Peter has _____ baggage.

a few	many
a little	enough
each	few
a lot of	lots of
no	plenty of
a great deal of	

3. _____ large cities have trains.

Most	Every
Few	Much
Several	Some
Little	A lot of
All	

4. _____ travel by trains takes place during the summer.

Most	Every
Few	Much
Several	Some
Little	A lot of
All	

2 General Quantifiers—Form and Meaning: Railroads

A. Read the passage. Circle the correct quantifiers.

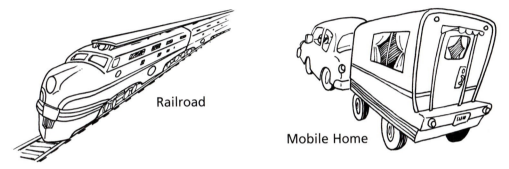

Railroad

Mobile Home

Trains are very common. They are found in almost (no / (every)) country of the
                                                            1
world. Trains roll on tracks. (Each / All) tracks are made of long pieces of steel,
                               2
called rails. When (several / no) rails join together, they make a "road" of rails—
                    3
a railroad. There are more than 14 million miles of railroad in the world. Railroads

carry people and things to (few / many) different places.
                            4
In the 1800s, travel by train was very popular in the United States. (Many / few)
                                                                       5
people traveled by train. In the early 1900s, however, (lots of / much) people began
                                                         6
to buy cars. Train companies began to lose money. (Several / Little) years later, the
                                                    7
mobile home became popular. People pulled these "homes away from home" behind

their cars. (All / A little) mobile homes had beds in them, so they made travel private,
            8
comfortable, and inexpensive.

Finally, airplane travel became inexpensive and more popular. (No / Most) people
                                                                9
preferred air travel over train travel. By the mid-1960s, passenger trains almost

completely disappeared. There were (many / much) other easy ways to travel in
                                    10
the United States.

B. Write the correct quantifiers on the lines.

Today, _____ people are riding trains again. There are now new
            1 (a few / little)

trains with extra services. _____ passenger can now eat and sleep
                                2 (Every / All)

comfortably on the train. _____ long-distance train tries to serve
                              3 (Each / All)

elegant food in its dining car. _____ long-distance trains also have
                                    4 (Most / Much)

sleeping cars with bathrooms and comfortable beds in them. _____
                                                              5 (Some / None)

sleeping cars have television sets and telephones. There are now _____
                                                                    6 (several / a great deal of)

types of tickets for train travelers. There are _____ inexpensive
                                                   7 (few of / plenty of)

tickets on scenic routes. Will passenger trains become popular again? Are there going to be

_____ passengers now? Only time will tell.
8 (enough / a great deal of)

GRAMMAR BRIEFING 2

General Quantifiers II

FORM

A. More About *Much* and *Many*

1. Remember! Use *much* with noncount nouns. Use *many* with count nouns. (See Grammar Briefing 1.)

   We don't have **much** time.
   We don't have **many** books.

2. Use *how much* to ask about noncount nouns. Use *how many* to ask about count nouns.

   How much money do you have?
   How many books do you have?

3. *Many* is common in affirmative and negative statements and in questions.

   I have **many** books.
   I don't have **many** books.
   How **many** books do you have?

4. *Much* is common in questions and negative statements. In affirmative statements, use another quantifier with a similar meaning, such as *lots of* or *a lot of.*

   I don't have **much** free time.
   How **much** free time do you have?
   I have **a lot of/plenty of** free time.
     NOT: I have ~~much~~ free time.

(continued on next page)

B. More About *Some* and *Any*

1. Use *some* in affirmative statements with count and noncount nouns.

   I have **some** cats.

   I have **some** time.

2. Use *any* in most negative statements and questions.

   I don't have **any** dogs.

   Do you have **any** dogs?

FUNCTION

A. *Too Much* and *Too Many*

Too much and *too many* have a negative meaning. They describe a quantity that is more than it should be.

She ate **too much** cake. She was sick.

They bought **too many** new plants. They had no place to put them.

B. *Few* and *Little*; *A Few* and *A Little*

1. *Few* and *little* usually mean "almost no" or "not enough."

   I'm not happy here. I have **few** friends, and I never go out. (not enough friends)

   Hurry! There's very **little** time before the train leaves. (almost no time)

2. *A few* and *a little* mean "a small quantity" or "not a lot, but enough." (*A lot* > *a little*/*a few* > *very little*/*very few* > *none*.)

   I'm happy here. I have **a few** friends, and we go out often. (not a lot of friends, but enough)

   Relax. We have **a little** time before the train leaves. (not a lot of time, but enough)

C. *Enough* and *Plenty* (*Of*)

1. *Enough* and *plenty* (*of*) have similar meanings. *Enough* means "a good quantity, what you need." *Plenty* (*of*) means "enough" or "a little more than enough."

   A: Would you like more dessert?

   B: No, thanks. I've had **enough/plenty of** sweets for one day!

General quantifiers usually occur with nouns. However (except for *no* and *every*), they can also be used alone when their meaning is clear.

Customer: I'd like a ticket, please.

Ticket agent: Sorry. We don't have **any** tickets.
OR Sorry. We don't have **any**.
NOT: Sorry. ~~We have no.~~

GRAMMAR PRACTICE 2

General Quantifiers II

3 *Some* **and** *Any*; *Too Much* **and** *Too Many*; *A Lot of* **and** *Lots of*: Wonder of the World!

Complete Kim's travel journal with the correct quantifiers.

This week we are really having __a lot of__ fun. We're riding the Lake Shore Limited
1 (much / a lot of)

to _____ different places.
2 (lots of / too many)

Our first stop was Niagara Falls. We spent _____ time there because it
3 (lots of / much)

was so beautiful. It is one of the Seven Wonders of the World. _____
4 (Lots of / Much)

water pours over the edge of Niagara Falls—almost 400,000 tons a minute! When the tour guide

told us this, I thought he was wrong. 400,000 tons sounded like _____. But
5 (too much / much)

when I saw Niagara Falls, I changed my mind. The falls are huge! _____ people
6 (Too many / Lots of)

come to see and hear them.

We didn't have _____ trouble with the weather at Niagara Falls.
7 (some / any)

There was _____ sunshine every day. But we got very wet anyway! Why?
8 (some / any)

Well, when the water falls over the edge, it fills the air with _____
9 (much / lots of)

mist. There's also _____ wind near the falls, and the wind blows mist
10 (a lot of / much)

everywhere! _____ people don't like this. They say there is
11 (Some / Any)

_____ mist; but I disagree. I love the mist; it makes beautiful rainbows.
12 (too much / much)

We didn't spend _____ money at Niagara Falls, but I think maybe we
13 (too much / some)

took _____ pictures. Over 100! We won't have _____
14 (many / too many)   15 (some / any)

film left for other things, and we have _____ more places to visit.
16 (some / any)

4 *Few, A Few, Little,* and *A Little*: Riding the Rails

Complete the sentences with *few, a few, little,* or *a little.*

1. Kim and Juan have ___little___ time before their train leaves. They're worried. They might miss it!

2. Kim has _____ extra money. He's happy. He's going to buy another postcard.

3. Kim has very _____ friends in the United States. He hopes to meet new people on the train.

4. Juan has _____ friends in the United States. He'll send them postcards from the next stop.

5. Kim and Juan want to stop for five days in New York at the end of their trip. They can do that because they will have _____ vacation time left.

6. Kim and Juan are planning to visit the mountains of Massachusetts. It is very peaceful in these mountains. There is _____ traffic, and there are _____ crimes.

7. Kim's seat is broken. He says to the conductor, "Excuse me. I'm having _____ problems with my seat."

8. Kim has very _____ money left at the end of the trip. He doesn't buy any gifts.

5 General Quantifiers—Form and Meaning: A Difficult Choice

A. Look at the pictures. What do you think of each vacation? Complete the descriptions with the quantifiers in the box. (More than one answer is possible.)

a lot of/lots of	a few
too many	a little
enough	plenty (of)
too much	no
little	few
a great deal of	

New York

Rustic Retreat

plenty of _____ museums

OR

too many _____ museums

_____ peace and quiet

_____ traffic

_____ nightlife

_____ people

_____ nature hikes

_____ theaters

_____ wild animals

_____ interesting scenery

_no_ _____ museums

_____ peace and quiet

_____ traffic

_____ nightlife

_____ people

_____ nature hikes

_____ theaters

_____ wild animals

_____ interesting scenery

B. Work with a partner. Ask and answer questions about New York and the Rustic Retreat. Use general quantifiers with nouns and general quantifiers without nouns in your answers. Do you and your partner agree? Discuss.

Examples: Question: *How many museums are there in New York?*
Possible Answers: *Too many!* OR *It has too many museums!*
Question: *Does the Rustic Retreat have any museums?*
Possible Answers: *No, it doesn't have any.* OR *No, it doesn't have any museums.* OR *No, none.*

 C. Imagine you are riding the train. You can stop either in New York or at the Rustic Retreat. Which one do you choose? Write a paragraph of at least five sentences about your choice. Use general quantifiers.

Example: *I choose the Rustic Retreat. Every activity there is relaxing. It has a lot of beautiful scenery. . . .*

See the *Grammar Links* Website for a complete model paragraph for this assignment.

6 **General Quantifiers—The Good and the Bad**

A. Choose one of the pairs of topics below. In the chart on page 166, write two sentences about the good things and two sentences about the bad things about your topic. In each sentence, use a general quantifier from the box. Use a different quantifier in each sentence.

1. A. travel on foot
    B. travel by car

2. A. ski vacation
    B. beach vacation

3. A. travel by plane
    B. travel by train

4. A. vacation alone
    B. vacation with friends

all	most
each	(too) much
enough	none
every	plenty (of)
(too) many	some
several	a great deal of

Example:

A. SKI VACATION	
Good	**Bad**
I spend many warm evenings by the fire. There's plenty of snow.	It's cold every day. There isn't much sun.
B. BEACH VACATION	
Good	**Bad**
I have enough time to read a good book. All beach sunsets are beautiful.	Some beaches are dirty. I get too much sand in my hair.

A.	
Good	**Bad**
B.	
Good	**Bad**

B. Discuss your chart in Part A with the rest of the class. Make a class list. What is good and what is bad about each topic?

Numbers and Measure Words

FORM and FUNCTION

A. Numbers

We use definite numbers (*one, two, three, four, five,* etc.) to count people, places, and things. The patterns are:

| **one** book, **two** books, **three** books |

- *One* + singular count noun.
- All other numbers + plural noun.

B. Measure Words

Measure words express specific or exact (not general) amounts. Most measure words follow this pattern:

A/ONE/TWO THREE, ETC.	MEASURE WORD	OF	PLURAL COUNT NOUN
a	box		paper clips
a	cup	of	beans
two	pounds		apples

			NONCOUNT NOUN
a	box		paper
a	cup	of	sugar
two	pounds		meat

C. Special Measure Words

Certain nouns have special measure words. These measure words are used only with a small group of nouns.

a **bunch** of grapes, a **bunch** of bananas

a **clove** of garlic

a **head** of lettuce, a **head** of cauliflower

a **loaf** of bread

1. Do not use *of* after definite numbers.	We live ten miles from town. **NOT:** We live ten ~~of~~ miles from town.
2. Do not add a plural *-s* to definite numbers.	We live ten miles from town. **NOT:** We live ten~~s~~ miles from town.

TALKING THE TALK

In speaking, the *f* sound in the word *of* in quantifiers and measure words is often dropped.

WRITING	SPEAKING
Joe has **a lot of** friends.	Joe has **a lotta** friends.
This recipe needs **four cups of** water.	This recipe needs **four cupsa** water.

GRAMMAR PRACTICE 3

Numbers and Measure Words

7 | **Numbers and Measure Words:** Home Away from Home I

Dick York is a retired English professor. He is giving a talk to other retired people about traveling. Read and listen to the first part of Dick's talk. Circle the numbers and measure words that you hear.

Hello, fellow travelers! As you know, my wife, Helen, and I travel a lot. We used

to travel by train, but then we discovered campers—mobile homes—and we just love

them! We travel (10,000 / 10,000 of) miles a year in our mobile home. Sometimes
        1

we drive (600 / 600 of) miles a day. Sometimes we cover only (60 / 60 of).
        2   3

Today I'm going to talk about traveling in a mobile home. What do you need to

take with you? Of course you'll need (a / one of) good road map, but there are a few
                                         4

other items you need as well. Always take (two / two of) extra tires. It's no fun
                                              5

having a flat tire (50 of / 50) miles from a city. Make sure you also take at least
                      6

(five extra gallons / five extra gallon of) gasoline. I always take (a quart / a quart of) oil, too.
 7   8

You'll also need a good first-aid kit in your mobile home.

Make sure you have (box of / a box of) bandages,
9

(a can / a can of) insect repellent, (a bottle / a bottle of)
10   11

rubbing alcohol, and (a jar / a jar of) first-aid cream.
12

Bandage

First-Aid Cream

8 **Numbers and Measure Words: Home Away from Home II**

 Listen to more advice about mobile home travel. Write the words you hear.
Use the words in the box in this pattern: *a/one/two/three, etc.* + measure word
from the box + *of.*

bag	box	carton	pound	small basket	✓tube
bar	bunch	couple	quart	stick	
bottle	can	head	roll	tin	

1. a tube of _____ toothpaste

2. _____ soap

3. _____ shampoo

4. _____ toilet tissue

5. _____ milk

6. _____ butter

7. _____ eggs

8. _____ lettuce

9. _____ meat

10. _____ beans

11. _____ cereal

12. _____ potato chips

13. _____ tea

14. _____ grapes

15. _____ apples

See the *Grammar Links* Website for more information about mobile home travel
in the United States.

9 Numbers and Measure Words: Chain Game

Play the chain game as a class.

Student 1 says: "I went to the store, and I bought:
measure word/number + a noun beginning with the letter "A."

Student 2 repeats this and adds another *measure word or number + a noun*, this time beginning with the letter *B.* The game continues until someone makes a mistake or forgets.

Example: Student 1: I went to the store, and I bought a bag of apples.
Student 2: I went to the store, and I bought a bag of apples and a box of bandages.
Student 3: I went to the store, and I bought a bag of apples and a box of bandages and two packages of cookies.

10 Numbers and Measure Words: Your Own Creation

Imagine you are going to travel in a mobile home. Write a recipe to take with you on your trip. Be sure to give specific amounts (2 cups, 2½ teaspoons, etc.). Use some of the ingredients below or your own ingredients. Share your recipe with the class.

		Ingredients		
peanut butter	sugar	spaghetti	oranges	peas
bread	bananas	carrots	oil	vinegar
jelly	yogurt	raisins	rice	tortillas
salsa	cabbage	fish	ice cream	pudding
onions	lentils	ketchup	cookies	crackers
marshmallows	chocolate	maple syrup		

Note: Are any of the ingredients above new to you? Find them in your dictionary.

Example: Carmelita's Spaghetti and Peanut Butter
1 cup of peanut butter   4 quarts of water
1 pound of spaghetti   etc.

B. Discuss your recipes. Which ones sound good? Take a vote. Then try them!

11 Numbers and Measure Words: Recipe from Home

A. Bring a real recipe from home to share with the class. Work with a partner. Tell your partner what you need for this recipe and see if she or he can tell it back to you. Correct any mistakes.

B. Work together as a class. Collect all of the recipes. Put them in a class cookbook. Try them!

Check your progress! Go to the Self-Test for Chapter 9 on the *Grammar Links* Website.

Chapter 10

Pronouns and Possessives

Introductory Task: Great Adventure

Photo Safari Adventure

A. Listen to Lizzy talk about a photo. Circle the words you hear.

Hi. My name's Lizzy. I like adventure travel. Here, let (me / my) show you a picture.
₁

Then you'll know what I mean. In the front of the picture are (me / my) friends Frank and
₂

Blake. We all went on a photo safari together in Africa. (We / They) shot lots of photos of
₃

wild animals there. Oh, and that's our guide behind that tree.

He looks a little worried. I'm not sure why. There's (something / nothing) in
₄

the bushes in the background. It's difficult to see. . . . This isn't a very clear picture.

I took (its / it) with Frank's camera. (His / He) doesn't work as well as (mine / my).
₅ ₆ ₇

Anyway, Frank and Blake are a lot of fun. (Everybody / Nobody) really enjoys them. In this
₈

picture, Frank's getting (himself / him) a sandwich from his knapsack. Blake is standing
₉

next to (himself / him).
₁₀

---

adventure = excitement and/or danger. *photo safari* = a trip to take pictures of animals,
especially in Africa. *wild* = living in nature. *guide* = leader; someone who shows the way.

B. Look again at the picture on page 171. Work in small groups. Discuss:

1. Why do you think the guide is standing behind a tree? Why is he worried? What does he see in the bushes? Do Frank and Blake see the same thing?

2. Do you enjoy adventure travel? Are you an adventure traveler? Why or why not?

GRAMMAR BRIEFING 1

Pronouns and Possessive Adjectives I

FORM

PERSONAL PRONOUNS		POSSESSIVES		REFLEXIVE PRONOUNS
SUBJECT PRONOUNS (S)*	OBJECT PRONOUNS (O)*	POSSESSIVE ADJECTIVES (POSS. ADJ.)	POSSESSIVE PRONOUNS (POSS. PRO.)	
I	me	my	mine	myself
you	you	your	yours	yourself
he	him	his	his	himself
she	her	her	hers	herself
it	it	its	—	itself
we	us	our	ours	ourselves
they	them	their	theirs	themselves

*See Appendix 12 for more information about subjects and objects.

Pronouns replace nouns. They include personal, reflexive, and possessive pronouns. Possessive adjectives come before nouns.

          poss.
s   adj.
I like **my** cat.

   s   reflexive
You hurt **yourself**.

poss.
adj.   o
His mother loves **him**.

             poss.
             pro.
Which book is **ours**?

Pronouns and Possessive Adjectives I

1 **Identification of Pronouns and Possessive Adjectives:** Adventure Travel

Above each **boldfaced** word, write **S** (subject pronoun), **O** (object pronoun),
PA (possessive adjective), **PP** (possessive pronoun), or **R** (reflexive pronoun).

                                      S

Adventure travel is becoming quite popular. **It** is a very interesting kind of travel. Adventure

travelers are not just looking for beautiful places to see. **They** are looking for adventure.

Some people think adventure travel is new. But **it** is very old. In the thirteenth

century, Marco Polo traveled thousands of miles, from Europe to China and other

countries in Asia. Sometimes **he** traveled by **himself**. Sometimes **his** uncles traveled

with **him**. **They** loved traveling for adventure.

Once **you** begin adventure travel, **you** cannot stop. Excitement and freedom are

yours, and **you** want more and more adventure. As soon as one adventure vacation ends,

you find **yourself** planning **your** next adventure vacation. **We** owe a lot to the adventure

travelers of the past and of the present. **They** help **us** push **ourselves** forward. **They**

make **us** use **our** imaginations. **They** take **us** into the future.

🌐 See the *Grammar Links* Website for more information about adventure vacations.

Pronouns and Possessive Adjectives II

FORM and FUNCTION

A. Personal Pronouns

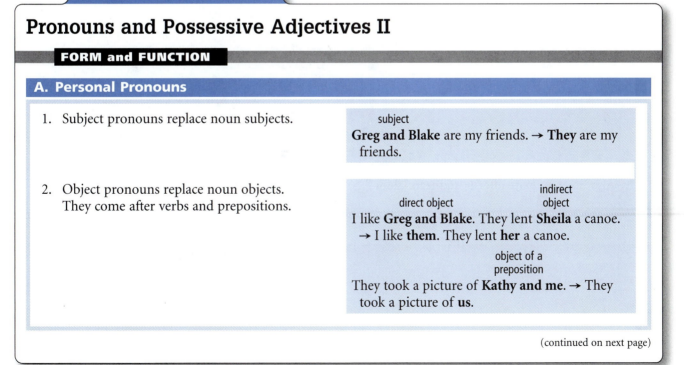

1. Subject pronouns replace noun subjects.	subject **Greg and Blake** are my friends. → **They** are my friends.
2. Object pronouns replace noun objects. They come after verbs and prepositions.	indirect direct object object I like **Greg and Blake**. They lent **Sheila** a canoe. → I like **them**. They lent **her** a canoe. object of a preposition They took a picture of **Kathy and me**. → They took a picture of **us**.

(continued on next page)

B. Possessive Adjectives and Pronouns

1. Possessive adjectives modify nouns and show possession.

> This is **my** camera. (This camera belongs to me; I own it.)

2. Possessive pronouns replace:

   • Possessive adjective + noun.

   > Your camera is good; **her camera** is better.
   > → Your camera is good; **hers** is better.

   • Possessive noun + noun.

   > I lost my camera. I borrowed **John's camera**.
   > → I lost my camera, I borrowed **his**.

3. Use *whose* to ask questions about possessions.

   > Q: **Whose** airplane ticket is this?
   > A: Mine. OR It's mine.

   > Q: **Whose** is this?
   > A: Mine. OR It's mine.

   > Q: **Whose** shoes are in the hallway?
   > A: They're Jane's shoes.

   > Q: **Whose** are these?
   > A: They're hers.

C. Reflexive Pronouns

1. Use a reflexive pronoun when the subject and the object in a sentence are the same.

   >   direct
   > subject   object
   > **Angela** saw **Angela** in the water. → **Angela** saw **herself** in the water.

   >   object of
   > subject   preposition
   > **Angela** likes to talk about **Angela**. → **Angela** likes to talk about **herself**.

   >   indirect
   > subject   object
   > **Angela** bought **Angela** a new bike. → **Angela** bought **herself** a new bike.

2. Also use a reflexive after *by* to mean "alone."

   > He climbed the mountain alone. = He climbed the mountain **by himself**.

1. To form possessive nouns:

   - Add an apostrophe (') to plural nouns that end in -s. | the **babies'** books
   - Add ' or 's to singular nouns that end in -s. | **Charles'** book OR **Charles's** book
   - Add 's to all other nouns. | the **baby's** book
the **children's** book
   - With two or more nouns together, add 's or ' only to the second noun. | **John and Mary's** children
the girls and the boys' teacher

2. Possessive adjectives and pronouns keep the same form before both singular and plural nouns. They do not have special singular or plural forms. | This is **their camera.**
These are not **their cameras.**
   NOT: These are ~~theirs~~ cameras.

TALKING THE TALK

	MOST WRITING AND SPEAKING	VERY FORMAL WRITING
We often use object pronouns after the verb *be*. In very formal writing, we use subject pronouns.	Peter's in the photo. That's **him** in the back.	Peter is in the photograph. That is **he** in the back.

GRAMMAR PRACTICE 2

Pronouns and Possessive Adjectives II

2 **Pronouns and Possessive Adjectives:** Journey to the Center of the Earth

Complete the story with the correct words from the boxes. Use each word only once.

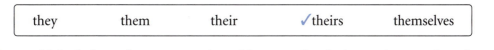

| they | them | their | ✓ theirs | themselves |

Clara and Martin love adventure vacations. Many people take interesting vacations, but

_____theirs_____ are especially exciting. Clara and Martin take all of their adventure
         1

vacations on _____ bicycles. They enjoy _____ very
                    2   3

much on these trips. _____ are planning their next trip now. It will take
                              4

_____ from Cairo, Egypt, across the desert to the Dead Sea.
        5

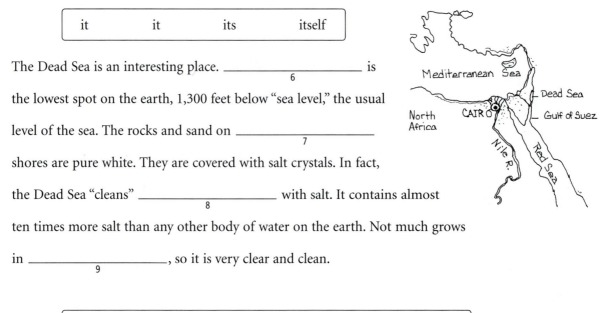

it	it	its	itself

The Dead Sea is an interesting place. _____ is
6

the lowest spot on the earth, 1,300 feet below "sea level," the usual

level of the sea. The rocks and sand on _____
7

shores are pure white. They are covered with salt crystals. In fact,

the Dead Sea "cleans" _____ with salt. It contains almost
8

ten times more salt than any other body of water on the earth. Not much grows

in _____, so it is very clear and clean.
9

she	her	her	hers	herself

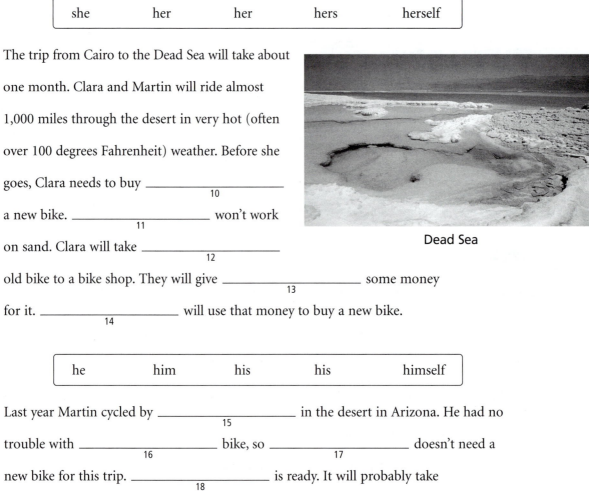

The trip from Cairo to the Dead Sea will take about

one month. Clara and Martin will ride almost

1,000 miles through the desert in very hot (often

over 100 degrees Fahrenheit) weather. Before she

goes, Clara needs to buy _____
10

a new bike. _____ won't work
11

on sand. Clara will take _____
12

old bike to a bike shop. They will give _____ some money
13

for it. _____ will use that money to buy a new bike.
14

Dead Sea

he	him	his	his	himself

Last year Martin cycled by _____ in the desert in Arizona. He had no
15

trouble with _____ bike, so _____ doesn't need a
16   17

new bike for this trip. _____ is ready. It will probably take
18

_____ across the desert with no problems.
19

| you | you | your | yours | yourself |

Why do Martin and Clara want to go to the Dead Sea on bicycles? Does this sound like

a crazy idea to _____? Martin talks about his feelings: "Imagine
                    20

_____ gliding down, down, down off a high hill to the very lowest
        21

spot—the center of the earth. That is a thrilling experience! Then

_____ see this calm shining body of water, with ghostly white shores
        22

all around it. You stick _____ toe in, then your whole body. Your wait
                                23

is over! You finally succeed after 1,000 miles of heat and sand and sun. You drift and float

above the center of the earth. Victory is _____!"
                                              24

| we | us | our | ours | ourselves |

Clara says: "Martin and I have different reasons for our adventure travels, it's true.

But that doesn't matter. Traveling on _____ bikes makes
                                            25

_____ both happy. _____ enjoy
        26   27

_____. _____ is a good life."
        28   29

3 **Pronouns and Possessive Adjectives:** **King of the Mountain!**

Rod is telling his friend Jeff about his adventure vacation to Mount Kilimanjaro in Africa. Listen to their conversation. Write the words you hear.

Rod: Well, here is a photo of Mount Kilimanjaro. __It__ _____ is the highest mountain
1

in Africa. _____ spent five days climbing to the top and back down.
2

Jeff: Wow! _____ really beautiful! And what a great photo! _____
3   4

camera did you use?

Rod: Well, _____ doesn't take very good photos, but _____
5   6

friend Fred came with _____ on the trip. I used _____.
7   8

Here's a picture of Fred. That's _____ on the left.
9

Jeff: And _____ big backpack is that in the photo?
10

Rod: Fred's. He carried it all the way to the top by _____! It was heavy!
11

Jeff: And _____ are the other people in the picture?
12

Rod: We were traveling with three other climbers. _____ were from England.
13

That's _____ on the right.
14

Jeff: You must be pretty proud of _____. I tried mountain climbing
15

_____ once, but I didn't like it very much. I prefer sea level.
16

4 Nouns to Pronouns: An Impossible World!

Change the **boldfaced** nouns to pronouns and possessive adjectives.
Make all the other necessary changes.

?

1. Larry and Charles are talking.

   Larry: Hi, Charles! How was ~~Charles'~~ ^{your} vacation?

   Charles: Oh, hi, Larry. ~~Charles'~~ ^{My} vacation was fine. ~~Charles~~ ^I took ~~Charles'~~ ^{my} family on an adventure vacation. ~~Charles and Charles' family~~ ^{We} had a great time!

?

2. Grace and Alena are talking.

   Grace: Say, Alena, did Lizzy and Kathy give **Alena** back **Alena's** map?

   Alena: No, Grace, **Lizzy and Kathy** didn't. **Lizzy and Kathy** gave **Alena's** map to **Grace**. Where is **the map**?

   Grace: Where is what? What are **Grace and Alena** talking about?

   Grace is confused!

?

3. Rose and Kyle are talking.

   Rose: Jane lost **Jane's** camera on **Jane, Kyle, Rose, Andrea, Peter and Donald's** adventure trip last week. **Does Kyle** know where the camera is?

   Kyle: **Kyle** found **Jane's** camera in **Kyle's** backpack. **Kyle** put **the camera** there by mistake. **Kyle** will bring **the camera** to **Rose** today.

   Rose: Oh, no! Not to **Rose**! Could **Kyle** please take **the camera** to Donald and Peter's house? Jane wants to give **the camera** to **Donald and Peter**. **Donald and Peter** need **the camera** this week. Jane bought **Jane** a new camera. **Jane** doesn't need **Jane's** old camera anymore.

5 Editing: Arctic Adventure

Correct the errors in the story. There are eight errors with pronouns and possessive adjectives. The first error is corrected for you.

Last year my family and I took a wonderful adventure vacation. We gave ~~us~~ *ourselves* a trip to the Canadian Arctic. We traveled across the Ungava Peninsula in dogsleds. We stayed with Inuit families along the way. We slept in they houses, and we ate ours meals

Caribou

with them. Theirs hospitality was wonderful. They served us hot meals—caribou stew and whale blubber. I didn't think I was going to like whale blubber, but its was very tasty!

Everyone in my family learned a lot on this vacation. My parents were quite proud of theirselves and their success. My brother learned a lot, too. He enjoyed hisself very much, but he prefers warm weather. As for me, I had a wonderful time. I am still dreaming about her adventure in the cold, white north.

whale blubber = fat from whales, used as food by the Inuit.

6 Pronouns and Possessive Adjectives: Create an Adventure

A. Choose a method of transportation from Column A and a person or people from Column B. Use them to create an adventure vacation. Write at least five sentences. Use at least one personal pronoun, one possessive pronoun, one possessive adjective, and one reflexive pronoun in your description.

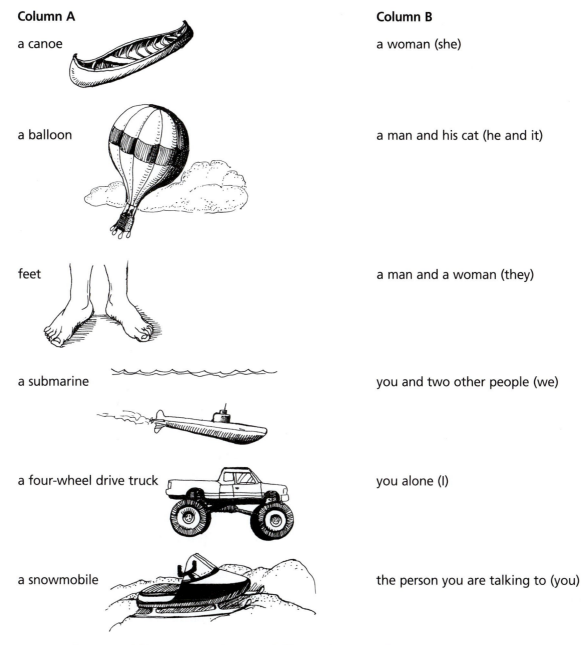

Column A

a canoe

a balloon

feet

a submarine

a four-wheel drive truck

a snowmobile

Column B

a woman (she)

a man and his cat (he and it)

a man and a woman (they)

you and two other people (we)

you alone (I)

the person you are talking to (you)

Example: *A man and his cat are going on a balloon adventure. The man is happy, and he is preparing for his trip. . . .*

See the *Grammar Links* Website for a complete model paragraph for this assignment.

B. Share your description with the rest of the class. Discuss the different vacations. Which ones are the most adventurous? Which one(s) would you most enjoy? Why?

Indefinite Pronouns

FORM and FUNCTION

A. Overview

Indefinite pronouns can be subjects and objects. They can also come after the verb *be*.

> subject
> **Everyone** is here now.
>
> object
> I don't want **anything**.
>
> after *be*
> I heard a noise, but it was **nothing**.

Indefinite pronouns include:

SOME	ANY	NO	EVERY
someone	anyone	no one	everyone
somebody	anybody	nobody	everybody
something	anything	nothing	everything

B. Indefinite Pronouns for People and Things

1. The endings *-one* and *-body* refer to people.

   Someone/Somebody took my camera. (Some person took my camera.)

2. The ending *-thing* refers to things.

   I want **something** for dessert. (I want some kind of dessert.)

3. Indefinite pronouns that begin with *no-* mean "not one person" or "not one thing."

   There was **nobody** in the room. (There was not one person in the room.)

   There was **nothing** on the plate. (There was not one thing on the plate.)

   Don't use *not* and an indefinite pronoun with *no-* in the same sentence.

   I saw **no one**.
   NOT: I ~~didn't see~~ no one.

4. We use indefinite pronouns with *some-* in affirmative sentences. *Any-* replaces *some-* in most negative statements and questions.

   Affirmative: I have **something** for you.

   Negative: I don't have **anything** for you.

   Question: Is there **anything** in this bag?

C. Verb Agreement with Indefinite Pronouns

Indefinite pronoun subjects take singular verbs, even when their meaning is plural.

Everybody **is** here.
  NOT: Everybody ~~are~~ here.

	FORMAL WRITING	SPEAKING AND INFORMAL WRITING
1. Indefinite pronouns are singular. However, we often use the plural pronouns *they*, *them*, and *their* with these words in everyday speaking and writing. In very formal writing, we use singular pronouns.	Someone left **his or her** jacket in the restaurant.	Someone left **their** jacket in the restaurant.
	He or she can pick it up at the counter.	**They** can pick it up at the counter.
	Please tell **him or her** to come and get it.	Please tell **them** to come and get it.
2. We often use contractions of indefinite pronouns with *is* in speaking and informal writing.	**Everyone is** here.	**Everyone's** here.

Indefinite Pronouns

7 **Indefinite Pronouns:** Present and Accounted For!

Read the conversation among hikers returning from a long hike. Circle the correct indefinite pronouns.

Julia: Let's see. Is everybody here? I see only five people. (**Somebody's** / Something's)
1
missing! Who is it? Oh, yes. It's Fred! Where's Fred? Does (anyone / anything) know?
2
Oh, there he is, behind that tree. Okay. Now, does (everybody / everything) have all
3
their belongings?

Rod: I don't have my passport. I asked (everyone / no one), but (nobody / anybody)
4   5
knows where it is! Maybe (someone / anyone) took it!
6

Julia: Let's look around here for it. What's that over there?

Rod: Over where? I don't see (anything / nothing).
7

Julia: Over there on the ground.

Rod: Oh, that's just someone's / no one's) boot. Whose boot is that?
8

Patty: Boot? Oh, thank you for finding it. It's mine. I was looking for it. I want to put it
back on. . . . Wait a minute. There's (something / nothing) inside my boot. . . .
9
Whose passport is this? (Somebody / Something) put their passport in my boot!
10

8 | **Indefinite Pronouns:** Find Someone Who . . .

A. Work with a partner. Take turns interviewing each other. Check the things that are true.

Use questions like: *Do you enjoy . . . ? Do you know what . . . is? Do you want to . . . ?*

My partner:

_____ enjoys trekking

_____ likes camping in the desert

_____ enjoys scuba diving

_____ wants to go on a safari

_____ wants to go to the Arctic Circle

_____ knows what skydiving is

_____ knows how to fly an airplane

_____ knows what spelunking is

_____ enjoys rock climbing

_____ likes camping in the jungle

> *trekking* = making a long trip on foot. *jungle* = tropical forest, such as the forest in the Amazon. *scuba diving* = swimming in deep water with air tanks for breathing.

B. What are the results of the interview? Which of the activities in Part A do students in the class enjoy? One student asks the class questions to find out. Use *anybody* or *anyone* in the questions. Count the number of students for each answer. Write the number on the board.

Example: *Does anyone enjoy trekking?*

Are there questions **everybody** answered "yes"? What are they?

Are there questions **nobody** answered "yes"? What are they?

Discuss: Were you surprised by any of your classmates' answers? If yes, which ones?

9 | **Indefinite Pronouns:** Quick Quiz

Write **C** next to each correct sentence and **I** next to each incorrect sentence. Then rewrite the incorrect sentences, correcting the errors. (Sometimes there is more than one possible way to correct a sentence.

1. __*C*__ Did anyone see Fred? _____

_____

2. __*I*__ Are everybody happy? *Is everybody happy?* _____

_____

3. _____ Nobody didn't lose their boots. _____

_____

4. _____ Everybody climbed that mountain. _____

_____

5. _____ Does everyone have their cameras? _____

_____

6. _____ Julia didn't see no one on the trail. _____

_____

7. _____ Someone forgot their backpack. _____

_____

8. _____ Everyone enjoy adventure vacations. _____

_____

9. _____ Someone left their camera here. They will need it. _____

_____

10. _____ We don't have anything to do tonight. Let's plan our next adventure vacation!

_____

 Check your progress! Go to the Self-Test for Chapter 10 on the *Grammar Links* Website.

Wrap-up Activities

1 Travel in the North: EDITING

Correct the errors in this article. There are 15 errors with nouns, pronouns, possessive adjectives, articles, quantifiers, and numbers. (Sometimes there is more than one possible correction.) The first error is corrected for you.

This vehicle travels up to 70 miles a̶ hour. It travels on the ground, but it doesn't have wheels. And it doesn't have a engine! What is it? It's sled.

People used sleds in ancient times. A first sleds were animal skins. Travelers pulled these sleds behind them. But animal skin sleds were slow. Their didn't slide smoothly. So ancient travelers added runners to they. These runners were long pieces of bone or wood. Travelers put the runners under the animal skins. The runners made their sleds travel faster

and more smoothly, but pulling a sled still took several energy. No one didn't like this very much. So people began training animals to pull their sleds. Then sleds became very fast.

Each years in northern countries, many people gather together for special dogsled races. One famous race, the Iditarod, takes place in the early Spring in northern alaska. In this race, teams of dogs and humans travel from Anchorage to Nome— over 1,000 miles of difficult land. There are much challenges: deep snow, unpredictable weather, and wild animals. Dogs often wear boots to protect theirselves from ice. Approximately 75 team compete each year. Some teams don't finish the long trek. But everybody have a great adventure!

🌐 See the *Grammar Links* Website for more information about the Iditarod dogsled race.

2 **Journey to the Bottom of the Sea:** SPEAKING/LISTENING

Imagine you are going "camping" at the bottom of the sea! You will live in a "sea bubble" for three days. The bubble has lots of glass on the outside, so you can see all of the interesting fish and plants living in the sea.

Step 1 Read the information in this brochure about your adventure.

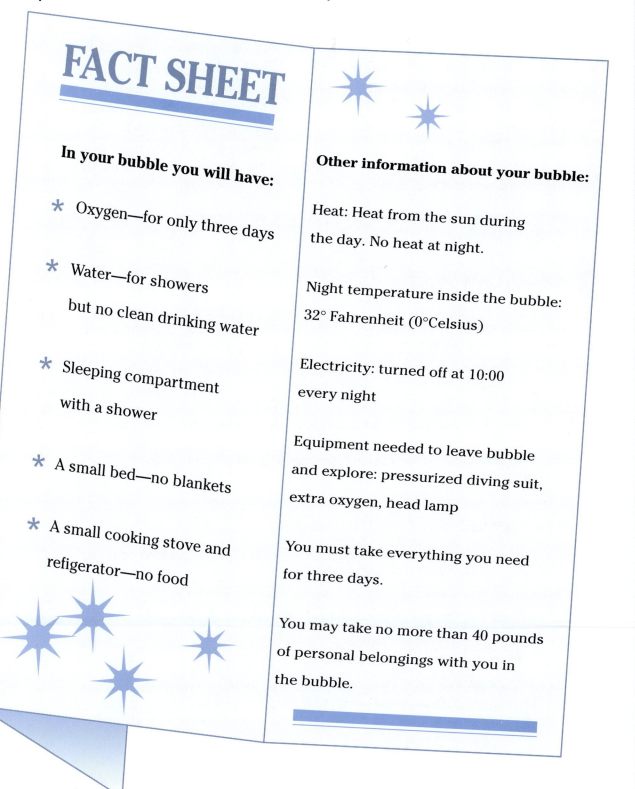

FACT SHEET

In your bubble you will have:

* Oxygen—for only three days

* Water—for showers but no clean drinking water

* Sleeping compartment with a shower

* A small bed—no blankets

* A small cooking stove and refrigerator—no food

Other information about your bubble:

Heat: Heat from the sun during the day. No heat at night.

Night temperature inside the bubble: 32° Fahrenheit (0°Celsius)

Electricity: turned off at 10:00 every night

Equipment needed to leave bubble and explore: pressurized diving suit, extra oxygen, head lamp

You must take everything you need for three days.

You may take no more than 40 pounds of personal belongings with you in the bubble.

Step 2 Look at the list below. As a group, decide what one person will need for three days. Give exact amounts, and add up the weight. Remember! Don't pack more than 40 pounds. (Note: 16 ounces = 1 pound.)

beans (1 can = 1 pound)

rice (1 bag = 1 pound)

apples (1 apple = 4 ounces)

cereal (1 box = 1 pound)

milk (1 quart = 1 pound)

coffee (1 can = 1 pound)

drinking water (1 gallon = 8 pounds)

pressurized diving suit (10 pounds)

towel (1 pound)

soap (1 bar = 4 ounces)

warm coat (5 pounds)

1 camera (1 pound)

film for the camera (4 ounces)

book to read (8 ounces)

journal to write in (8 ounces)

headlamp (1 pound)

toothpaste (1 tube = 4 ounces)

toothbrush (4 ounces)

shampoo (1 bottle = 8 ounces)

extra oxygen (10 pounds)

battery-operated reading light (1 pound)

1 warm sleeping bag (5 pounds)

clean clothes (5 pounds)

battery-operated heater (10 pounds)

batteries for the heater (8 ounces)

Step 3 Present your list to the rest of the class. Discuss: Did everyone agree on the most important items?

3 **A Place I Love:** WRITING/SPEAKING

Step 1 Bring to class a picture of a city or country place you love to visit. Write at least five sentences about this place. Concentrate on using articles, quantifiers, and pronouns in your description.

Example: Here is a picture of a place I love to visit. It is a small town in the
Rocky Mountains. The people there are very friendly. . . .

See the *Grammar Links* Website for a complete model paragraph for this activity.

Step 2 Read your description to your classmates. Show them your photo. Compare and discuss places.

4 **Whose Is What?** SPEAKING/LISTENING

Step 1 Bring to class an object that you like very much and that someone gave you. DON'T LET THE CLASS SEE IT AHEAD OF TIME!

Step 2 Student 1: Put all the objects in a bag.
Student 2: Pick out an object and ask: "Whose _____

is this?" or "Whose _____ are these?"
Whole class: Guess who the owner is.

Step 3 When the class guesses your object, say, "Yes, it's mine." Then explain why you like your object. Describe the person who gave it to you. Use pronouns and quantifiers in your description. Try to talk for 30 seconds without stopping!

Example: This watch is mine. I like it a lot. It always keeps good time. I also like its
color and shape. My aunt Flora gave it to me. Everybody loves my aunt Flora.
She is my mother's sister. She lives in Montana with the rest of my family.

Adverbs and Prepositions

TOPIC FOCUS
Care of Body and Mind

UNIT OBJECTIVES

- **adverbs**
  (Cook the beans *slowly.*)

- **prepositions and prepositional phrases**
  (Pour the water *over the tea.*)

- **phrasal verbs**
  (When did you *give up* smoking?)

- **verb + preposition combinations**
  (We were *thinking about* you.)

- **three-word verbs**
  (I'm finally *getting down to* my homework.)

Grammar in Action

Reading and Listening: Food and Exercise—
The Body-Mind Connection

Read and listen.

1   In some ways, our bodies are like cars. They work **well** when we give them the right fuel and use them **carefully**. They work **badly** when we **never** take them **outside** or don't use them **enough**. But our bodies are also **very** different from machines. They **usually** work **closely** with our minds. Exercise and food affect both our bodies and our minds in very interesting ways.

2   Ancient people knew these things. For example, the ancient Greeks understood the psychology of exercise. When they started the Olympic Games in 776 BC, they made **up** a plan to produce "strong bodies and minds." The Games taught people to work their problems **out** peacefully—at least for one month! Every four years, the cities around Athens signed people **up** for the Games. They also stopped their wars. They didn't give them **up** forever; they just called them **off** during the Games.

3   Other ancient people understood the psychology of food. The Ayurvedic people **in** India used to say, "You are what you eat": In other words, different foods affect your personality. In many cultures, magic power came **from** foods. **In** the "Odyssey" story, Ulysses and his sailors found some delicious magic flowers **on** an island. The sailors ate the flowers **for** several days. **After** that, they became very relaxed and happy. They wanted to stay. When Ulysses tried to lead his men **off** the island, they said no!

4   Today, we still care **about** the Olympic Games. We still believe **in** exercise and think **of** it as a way to build a strong body and mind. We also talk **about** foods that change our feelings "magically," and we look **for** them in health-food stores. Modern science and psychology help us to understand that the human body is a wonderful machine, but it cannot work alone. It depends **on** its driver—the mind.

> *fuel* = something that produces energy when you use it, such as food or gasoline.
> *affect* = make something change in some way.

Think About Grammar

A. Look at the **boldfaced** words in the passage. The **boldfaced** words in paragraphs 1 and 2 are **adverbs**. The **boldfaced** words in paragraphs 3 and 4 are **prepositions**. Read the statements below. Do they describe adverbs, prepositions, or both? Check your answers.

	Adverbs	Prepositions
1. These words sometimes go at the end of a sentence.	☑	❏
2. These words sometimes go after verbs (and their objects).	❏	❏
3. These words always go before nouns or pronouns (including article + noun/quantifier + noun).	❏	❏

B. Look again at paragraph 2. Match the verb + adverb combinations with their meanings below.

Verb	Meaning
1. make up	a. cancel a plan _4_
2. work out	b. invent or form _____
3. give up	c. solve (or find an answer) _____
4. call off	d. stop (an activity) _____

Chapter 11

Adverbs and Prepositions

Introductory Task: Fact or Fiction?
Ideas About Food

Work with a partner. Complete the questionnaire. (You will learn the correct answers as you read this chapter.)

1. Doctors give this advice for a healthy diet:
   a. Eat beans with red meat and rice with white meat.
   b. Eat rice and beans together.

2. Chocolate
   a. often makes people feel relaxed and comfortable.
   b. seldom helps people feel relaxed and comfortable.

3. When you eat chocolate,
   a. special chemicals travel fast to your brain.
   b. your brain works more slowly.

4. Tea
   a. possibly started the American Revolution.
   b. definitely ended the American Revolution.

5. Sunshine
   a. is full of healthy nutrients (or food) for your body.
   b. is bad for you.

6. Some people become psychologically ill
   a. when the sunlight isn't bright enough.
   b. when the sun is too bright.

7. When your feet are tired, this helps them:
   a. putting hot green tea in your bath water.
   b. putting ice on your feet.

Adverbs I

FORM and FUNCTION

A. Overview

Adverbs modify (tell more about) verbs, adjectives,* other adverbs, quantifiers, and whole sentences. They answer questions like *How? When? Where?*

*See Chapter 13 for more information about adjectives.

Q: Where do you work?

A: I work **here**.

B. Adverbs of Manner (*How?*)

Adverbs of manner tell **how** something happens. They include *fast, slowly, well, badly, carefully,* and *right*.

Position:

- After the main verb when there is no object.

- After the verb + object.

I eat **fast**.

verb adverb
I eat **slowly**.

verb object adverb
I read the menu **slowly**.

(See Appendix 13 for spelling rules and irregular forms of adverbs of manner.)

C. Adverbs of Place (*Where?*)

Adverbs of place tell **where** something is or where it happens (location). They also express where something or someone is going (direction). Adverbs of place include *here, there, up, out, away, back, inside, together,* and *home*.

Position:

- Location adverbs: after the main verb when there is no object, or after verb + object.

- Direction adverbs: after the main verb, or before or after a noun object.

Be careful! Direction adverbs always come **after** a pronoun object.

The manager works **here**.

Pour the water **out**.

verb object
We left our money **there**.

verb object
We took the money **back**. OR
verb object
We took **back** the money.

pronoun
We took it **back**.
NOT: We took ~~back it~~.

(continued on next page)

Adverbs of time tell **when** something happens. They include *yesterday, tomorrow, afterward(s), now, then, early,* and *late.*	**Yesterday** I didn't feel well.
Position:	
• Most adverbs of time go at the beginning or end of the clause.	I didn't feel well **yesterday**.
• *Early* and *late* go at the end of the clause.	I went home **early**.

Adverbs I

1 **Identifying Adverbs of Manner, Place, and Time:** Healthy Eating

Label the **boldfaced** adverbs *M* (Manner), *P* (Place), or *T* (Time).

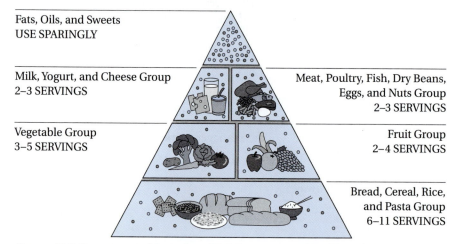

Fats, Oils, and Sweets
USE SPARINGLY

Milk, Yogurt, and Cheese Group
2–3 SERVINGS

Meat, Poultry, Fish, Dry Beans,
Eggs, and Nuts Group
2–3 SERVINGS

Vegetable Group
3–5 SERVINGS

Fruit Group
2–4 SERVINGS

Bread, Cereal, Rice,
and Pasta Group
6–11 SERVINGS

Source: U. S. Department of Agriculture /U. S. Department of Health and Human Services

M
1. Nutritionists **strongly** recommend the "pyramid diet."

2. This diet came from Asia, but **now** it is famous all over the world.

3. Nutritionists say the pyramid diet helps us eat **right**.

4. The pyramid starts at the bottom with grains (like rice and bread) and goes **up** to meats.

5. This means: Eat plenty of grains and vegetables, but choose meats and fats **carefully**.

6. Nutritionists believe that, in a good diet, several different flavors come **together** on your plate—for example, sweet, salty, and spicy.

Spicy

Sweet

Salty

7. If your meals don't balance these flavors **well**, perhaps you'll look for them in unnatural, or "junk," foods.

8. For example, you don't have anything sweet in your lunch, so you want a big chocolate bar **afterward**!

9. Nutritionists have another suggestion: Look at the ingredients on food packages. What do you see **there**? Are the ingredients healthy or unhealthy?

---

nutritionist = a professional who advises us about healthy food.

---

2 Adverbs of Manner—Regular and Irregular Forms: We Are What We Eat

A. A reporter for a health magazine is interviewing a diet expert from India. Complete the interview with the correct form of the words in parentheses. (Note: See Appendix 13 for information about regular and irregular adverb forms.)

Interviewer: Dr. Patel, tell us about Ayurvedic eating. What is it?

Dr. Patel: It's an ancient health plan from my country. We believe the Ayurvedic diet helps us

eat <u>safely</u> and live _____.
    1 (safe)   2 (happy)

Interviewer: You say, "We are what we eat." What does that mean?

Dr. Patel: Our bodies and minds work together very _____. Different personalities
    3 (direct)

need different kinds of food. For example, people with "Vata" personalities have lots of

energy. They move _____. They talk _____. For Vata
    4 (fast)   5 (quick)

types, warm vegetables with salty and sour tastes work _____. But beans
    6 (good)

make them nervous! People with "Pitta" personalities are strong and confident. They

work _____ and eat a lot. They need sweet fruits, like bananas, and bitter
    7 (hard)

vegetables, like broccoli. But when they eat too much sour food, like yogurt, they

sometimes feel angry and behave _____.
    8 (bad)

Interviewer: But how do you know your personality type?

Dr. Patel: Our bodies and minds tell us! When we don't eat _____, we feel
    9 (right)

uncomfortable or unhappy.

B. Discuss as a class: Do you agree with Dr. Patel's ideas? Are you a Vata, a Pitta type, or neither?

See the *Grammar Links* Website for more about foods and your personality.

3 Adverbs of Place and Time: A Dangerous Diet

Read the famous story about a little girl and a wolf with a dangerous diet. Complete the story with adverbs of place and time from the boxes. Follow the instructions under the blanks. Use each adverb only once.

Place		Time
away there		before
back up		✓ early
here inside		then
		today

One morning, the Big Bad Wolf met Little Red Riding Hood in the forest.

"Good morning, little girl," he said. "Where are you going so $\underline{\text{early}}$ in the
1 (time)

morning?"

"I'm going to visit my grandmother," answered Little Red Riding Hood.

"Oh," said the wolf. "Does she live _____? In this forest?"
2 (place)

"Yes. Do you know that little house near the river? She lives _____."
3 (place)

"Ah," said the wolf. "Well, goodbye."

The Big Bad Wolf ran to Grandmother's house. He wanted to eat her! But Grandmother

saw him coming and hid in the closet. The wolf opened Grandmother's bedroom window and

jumped _____. He didn't find Grandmother, so he got into the bed and waited.
4 (place)

Soon, Little Red Riding Hood arrived.

"Grandmother," she said. "Are you all right _____? Your eyes are so big!"
5 (time)

"Yes," said the wolf. "I want to see you, my dear!"

"And your teeth are so white! They didn't look so white _____."
6 (time)

"Yes. I want to smile at you, my dear!"

"But, Grandmother, your teeth are so sharp!"

"Yes," said the wolf. "I want to EAT you, my dear!"

_____ the Big Bad Wolf jumped _____ from the bed.
　　　7 (time)　　　　　　　　　　　　　　　　　　8 (place)

Little Red Riding Hood shouted, "Help!" Grandmother jumped out of the closet, and

they both hit the wolf hard on the nose. He ran _____, rubbing his nose.
　　　　　　　　　　　　　　　　　　　　　　　　　　9 (place)

He didn't look _____. After that, the Big Bad Wolf changed his diet.
　　　　　　　10 (place)

He never tried to eat grandmothers again.

4 **Position of Adverbs—Editing: Comfort Food**

Correct the errors in this story. Move the underlined adverbs to the correct position
in the clause.

　　　When I'm sad or nervous, I look for "comfort foods" to help me feel better. I **crave**

　　　　　　　　　　　　　　　　　　　　　　　　　badly

these foods—in other words, badly I want them ∧, and I right away want them!
　　　　　　　　　　　　　　1　　　　　　　　　　　　2

　　　For example, I was worrying about yesterday my job. I late worked and felt tired.
　　　　　　　　　　　　　　　　　　　3　　　　　　　　4

I came to my dark apartment home and opened the refrigerator. inside I looked. I
　　　　　　　　　　　　　　　5　　　　　　　　　　　　　　6

there saw the salad and fresh fruit, but I didn't take out them. I took the pizza and ice
7　　　　　　　　　　　　　　　　　　　　　　8

cream instead out. I sat at the kitchen table down and fast ate it! Of course, I afterward
　　　　　　9　　　　　　　　　　　　　9　　　10　　　　　　　　　　　11

felt bad.

Adverbs II

FORM and FUNCTION

A. Adverbs of Frequency (*How often?*)

Adverbs of frequency tell **how often** something happens:

100% of the time	always
	usually
	often
	sometimes
	seldom
0% of the time	never

Position:

- After the subject and *be*.

> She is **always** hungry.

- Before other main verbs.

> verb
> She **always** <u>eats</u> at five o'clock.
>
> verb
> She doesn't **usually** <u>eat</u> breakfast.

(See Chapter 1, Grammar Briefing 3, for more adverbs of frequency.)

B. Adverbs of Possibility (*How sure?*)

Adverbs of possibility modify the whole sentence. They tell **how sure** we are about something:

100% possible	certainly, definitely
	probably
	perhaps, maybe
	possibly

0% possible

Position:

- *Perhaps* and *maybe* go at the beginning of the sentence.

> **Perhaps** we should eat out tonight.
> **Maybe** she doesn't like me.

- Other adverbs of possibility usually go **after** the subject and (main verb) *be* but **before** other main verbs.

> This is **definitely** a good idea.
> I **certainly** want to meet the chef.

(continued on next page)

C. Adverbs of Degree (Intensifiers)

Intensifiers modify verbs, adjectives, other adverbs, or quantifiers. They make the word they modify stronger or weaker in meaning.

(See Chapter 9 for more information about quantifiers.)

strong	**extremely**
	too, **very**, **so**, **really**
	quite
	enough
weak	**almost**, **hardly**

Position:

- Most intensifiers go **before** the word they modify.

> adverb
> You work **too** <u>hard</u>!
>
> quantifier
> I like you **very** <u>much</u>.
>
> verb
> They **almost** <u>missed</u> the plane.

- *Enough* comes **after** the word it modifies.

> adverb
> You don't work <u>hard</u> **enough**.

GRAMMAR **HOT**SPOT!

Don't confuse the following pairs of words:

- *Hard* is an adverb of manner. *Hardly* is an intensifier. *Hardly* has a negative meaning ("almost not").

> He works **hard**. = He works a lot.
> He **hardly** works. = He almost doesn't work.

- *Very* means "a lot." *Too* means "more than you want." *Enough* means "a good quantity— what you need."

> I love these oranges. They're **very** sweet.
> I don't like these oranges. They're **too** sweet.
> These oranges are perfect: not too sweet, but sweet **enough**.

- The quantifier *enough* comes **before** a noun. The intensifier *enough* comes **after** the word it modifies.

> quantifier   noun
> Do you have **enough** <u>oranges</u>?
>
> verb   intensifier
> You're not working <u>enough</u>.

Adverbs II

5 **Adverbs of Frequency:** More About Comfort Food

A. Add the adverbs in parentheses to the underlined clauses.

                    seldom
Comfort food is ˰healthy food like vegetables, fruit, or beans. When we look
              1 (seldom)

for comfort food, <u>we look for foods like chocolate, french fries, pizza, or ice cream</u>.
                                    2 (usually)

<u>And we "crave" these foods</u> even when we aren't really hungry.
          3 (sometimes)

Why do we crave comfort foods? Well, foods like chocolate and pizza

send special messages to the brain, which makes chemicals like serotonin

or endorphins. <u>These chemicals make us feel relaxed and comfortable</u>.
                                              4 (often)

<u>We think about brain signals and chemicals</u> when we eat comfort foods.
          5 (never)

<u>We're too hungry</u>!
      6 (always)

---

chemicals = elements that work together and cause changes.

B. What is your favorite comfort food? When do you usually eat it? Write five or
six sentences. Use at least four adverbs of frequency. Read your paper to the class.

Example:

My favorite comfort food is chips. I usually crave them when I'm watching TV. . . .

See the *Grammar Links* Website for a complete model paragraph for this assignment.

6 **Adverbs of Possibility:** The World's Best Diet?

Complete these sentences. Use the words in parentheses in the correct order.

1. What is the best diet in the world?

    <u>Perhaps the answer will surprise</u> _____ you.
    (will surprise / perhaps / the answer)

2. Rice and beans _____.
    (possibly / the perfect diet / make)

3. _____ this combination in many countries
    (find / you / certainly)

    around the world.

4. And _____
    (combine / definitely / rice and beans)

    the three important food groups: carbohydrates, protein, and fat.

5. There are thousands of types of rice and many types of beans, and every country

    _____.
    (its favorite recipe / possibly / has)

6. _____.
    (enjoy / maybe / spicy food / you)

7. Then _____ for you.
    (is / "frijoles" / probably / right)

    This is a Mexican dish with rice, beans, and chilies.

8. _____.
    (love / you / maybe / Italian food)

    Cannellini combines white beans and rice with cheese and garlic in a delicious tomato sauce.

9. And here's the great news: _____.
    (inexpensive / are / rice and beans / certainly)

7 Choosing Intensifiers: The Love of Chocolate

Read the questionnaire for chocolate lovers. Circle the correct form of the words in parentheses.

① **When do you eat chocolate?**

a. When I'm thinking (hard / hardly).

b. When the other food in my diet isn't (sweet enough / enough sweet).

c. All the time.

② **What's your favorite type of chocolate?**

a. I like bitter chocolate, with (hard / hardly) any sugar.

b. I love milk chocolate. It's (very / too) sweet and creamy.

c. ALL chocolate.

③ **Does chocolate help you lose weight?**

a. Yes. When I eat chocolate, I need (almost / hardly) no lunch or dinner.

b. Yes. It makes me exercise. I can never get my chocolate

(fast enough / so fast), so I'm always running to the store.

c. No.

④ **Some nutritionists say chocolate is unhealthy. What do you say?**

a. They don't know (very much / hardly much) about chocolate.

b. Those nutritionists worry (too / very) much. Give them some

chocolate!

c. I don't care.

⑤ **Do you share your chocolate with your friends?**

a. Yes, when I like them (enough / too much).

b. Yes, but only if they eat (very / too) little.

c. I don't need friends. I have my chocolate.

⑥ **Why do you like chocolate?**

a. It tastes (almost / very) delicious.

b. It's (quite / too) relaxing.

c. You ask (extremely silly / silly extremely) questions!

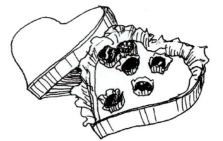

1. *So* is less formal than *very*. It expresses a strong personal feeling about the word it modifies.	This is **so** delicious!
2. *Really* is less formal than *very*.	This chili is **really** spicy.

3. *Pretty* is less formal than *quite*. *Kind of* (pronounced *kinda*) is used only in speaking.

FORMAL	INFORMAL
It is **quite** hot today.	It's **pretty** hot today.
	It's **kinda** hot. (speaking)

8 Intensifiers: Breakfast in America

A. Listen to the conversation between Ghazi and Richard. Circle **T** if the statement is true and **F** if the statement is false.

1.	Ghazi really enjoys American food.	T	F
2.	Ghazi misses his mother's cooking very much.	T	F
3.	He eats hardly anything.	T	F
4.	Ghazi hardly ever ate comfort foods in his country.	T	F
5.	Ghazi hardly studies.	T	F
6.	Sometimes he feels quite nervous.	T	F
7.	He never has enough homework.	T	F
8.	Ghazi is too busy for meals at home.	T	F
9.	He thinks American breakfasts are quite sweet.	T	F
10.	Richard thinks cereal with no sugar is too healthy.	T	F

B. Read the words below. Then listen again to the conversation. Is this a formal or an informal conversation? Circle the words that give you the answer.

extremely	pretty	really	very
kind of	quite	so	

C. Discuss as a class: What do you think about American food? Do you agree with Ghazi?

9 **Using Adverbs: Listen Carefully!**

Work as a class.

Step 1 Stand in a circle. Student A says a sentence containing an adverb.

Step 2 If the adverb is used correctly, everybody repeats it and sits down.

Step 3 If the adverb is not used correctly, everybody stays standing until Student A uses it correctly.

Step 4 Student A then chooses another student until everyone takes a turn.

Use adverbs of manner, time, place, frequency, possibility, and degree (intensifiers).

GRAMMAR BRIEFING 3

Prepositions and Prepositional Phrases

FORM and FUNCTION

A. Overview

1. Prepositions are words such as *in* and *at* that take noun or pronoun objects. The preposition plus its object is called a prepositional phrase.

	PREPOSITIONAL PHRASE	
	PREPOSITION	OBJECT
I'll come	**in**	**the evening**.

2. Very common prepositions include *about, at, by, for, from, in, like, of, on, to,* and *with.*

   Most prepositions can express many different meanings. The most common meanings are about time and place.

   Time: I'll come **at** four o'clock.
   Place: He is **at** school.
   Time: We worked **from** morning **to** evening.
   Place: They moved **from** California **to** New York.

B. Prepositions of Time

1. Prepositions of time include *at, in, for, before, after, during* (= inside a time period), and *until* (= continuing up to a certain time).

   I'll see you **at** ten o'clock **in** the morning.
   We talked **for** a long time **after** dinner.

2. Position: Prepositional phrases of time go at the beginning or end of a sentence.

   During the summer, it stays light.
   It stays light **until nine o'clock**.

(continued on next page)

C. Prepositions of Place (Location and Direction)

1. Prepositions of location include *at, in, on, under, near, in (the) front of,* and *on top of.*

   I'll wait for you **at** the station **in front of** Gate 1 **under** the clock.

2. Prepositions of direction include *to, from, into, onto, out of, up, down, over, off, through,* and *around.*

   The cat jumped **out of** the box and ran **down** the stairs **into** the street.

3. Position: Prepositional phrases of place go after the main verb when there is no object, or after verb + object.

   I sat **in the cafeteria**.

   object
   Pour the tea **into the teapot**.

D. Adjective + Preposition Combinations

Some adjectives are often followed by certain prepositions.

(See Appendix 14 for a list of adjective + preposition combinations.)

Fruit is **good for** you.

My house is **similar to** yours.

I'm **afraid of** mice.

GRAMMAR PRACTICE 3

Prepositions and Prepositional Phrases

10 **Identifying Prepositional Phrases:** The Story of Tea

Label the **boldfaced** prepositional phrases: *T* (Time) or *P* (Place).

The story of tea started thousands of years ago. For example, we know that a teacher

wrote about it **in ancient China**. **For hundreds of years**, traders sailed **around the world**,

             P   T
1   2   3

buying tea in Asia and selling it in Europe. **During the seventeenth century**, the

        4

East India Tea Company imported tea **to Britain**, but it was a

    5

dangerous business. Tea was expensive **at that time**, so thieves

    6

often tried to steal it. Highwaymen **on horseback** used to ride

    7

through the English countryside, steal tea, and sell it secretly.

  8

Women used to hide it **under their floors** **at home**.

    9   10

Highwayman

Some people say that tea caused the American Revolution. **Until 1773**, the British

government made the Americans pay an extra price, or tax, when they imported tea.

Finally, some angry Americans threw 342 tea boxes **into the sea** **near Boston**. **After that**,

the American Revolution began.

---

thieves = people who steal, or take things that are not theirs.

---

11 **Prepositions of Time:** Tea Time!

Complete the sentences with the prepositions in the box. Use the information
from the picture about the history of tea. Use each preposition only once.

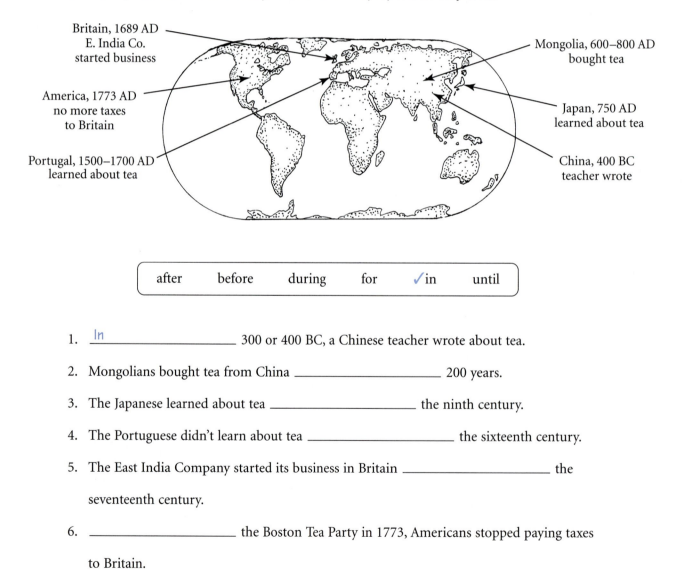

Britain, 1689 AD
E. India Co.
started business

America, 1773 AD
no more taxes
to Britain

Portugal, 1500–1700 AD
learned about tea

Mongolia, 600–800 AD
bought tea

Japan, 750 AD
learned about tea

China, 400 BC
teacher wrote

| after | before | during | for | ✓in | until |

1. _In_____ 300 or 400 BC, a Chinese teacher wrote about tea.

2. Mongolians bought tea from China _____ 200 years.

3. The Japanese learned about tea _____ the ninth century.

4. The Portuguese didn't learn about tea _____ the sixteenth century.

5. The East India Company started its business in Britain _____ the

    seventeenth century.

6. _____ the Boston Tea Party in 1773, Americans stopped paying taxes

    to Britain.

12 Prepositional Phrases of Place: The Psychology of Chili

A reporter for a health magazine is interviewing Señor Lopez at the Fiery Foods Show in Albuquerque, New Mexico. The reporter makes several mistakes in her notes. Listen to the interview and correct the underlined phrases with the correct prepositional phrases.

Fiery Foods Show

Chili is interesting because it has many tastes.

1. Some chili hits the nerves in your teeth.
   in the front of your mouth

2. Some chili burns under your tongue.

3. Some chili hits right on the top of your tongue.

4. The pain goes down your nose and makes you sweat.

People like the chili "burn" because it's exciting. Excitement feels good.

5. When you are excited, your brain sends adrenalin into your mouth.

Chili is healthy. It's used as a medicine and a pain killer.

6. The chili experts work near the National Chili Institute in Las Cruces.

7. Las Cruces is on the Mexican border.

8. In countries like Mexico, Thailand, and India, food goes bad very quickly in the refrigerator.

nerves = threads, or fibers, that carry messages (including pain) between your brain and the rest of your body. *sweat* = produce water (perspiration) from your skin when you are very hot.

13 **Using Prepositional Phrases of Time and Place:** Is Tea Unhealthy?

A. Complete the conversation with prepositional phrases of time and place from the boxes. Follow the instructions under the blanks. Use each prepositional phrase only once.

Time	Place
during the day ✓ until tomorrow at six o'clock in the morning	in my eye out of the cup near my face at the kitchen table into the sugar bowl around the house in your tea

Fred: I'm so tired! <u>During the day</u> _____, I work really hard.
1 (time)

Then I come home and I can't relax.

Jenny: Have a nice cup of tea! It's very relaxing.

Fred: No, I used to drink tea every evening _____.
2 (time)

But it hurt my eye!

Jenny: That's strange. How did it hurt your eye?

Fred: I don't know. I used to drink my tea sitting _____.
3 (place)

Or I sometimes walked _____.
4 (place)

It didn't matter. It always hurt when I picked up the cup and held it

_____. I suddenly felt this sharp pain
5 (place)

_____!
6 (place)

Jenny: Tell me: Do you like sugar _____?
7 (place)

Fred: Yes. Why?

Jenny: Listen. Don't drink any tea this evening. Wait _____.
8 (time)

_____, make a nice cup of tea, and add
9 (time)

your sugar. Then take the teaspoon _____.
10 (place)

Put the teaspoon back _____. I think the
11 (place)

pain will go away!

B. Work with a partner. Discuss: Why did Fred's eye hurt? Share your answer with the class. Do you all agree?

14 **Adjective + Preposition Combinations: Sunlight—A Dangerous Food?**

A. Complete the passage below with the correct adjectives. Use the expressions in the box to help you. Use each expression only once.

afraid of	✓ fond of	responsible for
bad for	full of	sad about
familiar with	good for	sure about

Many people are _fond_____ of sunshine. And they're right: Sunshine is healthy;
                         1

it's _____ for you. Sunshine is an important food for your body and mind.
          2

It is _____ of vitamin D, which makes your bones strong. Sunshine helps
         3

you feel good too. That's why, in dark winter months, people often seem unhappy. They feel

_____ about everything. Doctors are _____ with this
          4   5

psychological problem. They call it "Seasonal Affective Disorder," or SAD.

However, other people are _____ of sunshine. They're
                                   6

also right; too much sunshine is definitely _____ for you.
                                                    7

Sunshine contains a lot of ultraviolet (UV) rays—a part of sunlight. UV rays are

_____ for skin cancer. Some scientists believe that vitamin C is
          8

a good sunscreen for some UV rays. Vitamin C is in oranges and green vegetables. Scientists

will not feel _____ about this until they have more information, but I like
                    9

the idea. Next time I go out in the sun, I'm going to put some orange juice on my face!

> *responsible for* = causing. *sunscreen* = something that blocks the rays of the sun
> and protects your skin.

See the *Grammar Links* Website for more about how sunshine affects you.

B. Think of a food that you like or dislike very much. Write five or six sentences.
Describe the food, but don't name it. Use at least three adjective + preposition
combinations from Appendix 14.

Example:

This food is famous for its wonderful taste. Sometimes it's full of sugar and milk. . . .
(Answer: chocolate)

See the *Grammar Links* Website for a complete model paragraph for this assignment.

C. Share your description with the class. Can your classmates guess the name of
your food?

1. Some common prepositional phrases occur with no article. They usually talk about everyday activities.

   > Larry goes **to church** every Sunday.
   >
   > Larry's **at school**. He's studying.

AT (LOCATION)	TO (DIRECTION)	IN (LOCATION)
school	school	bed
church	church	
lunch	lunch	
work	work	
home	bed	

2. However, when we talk about a specific location (like the building itself), we use the article.

   > Larry's wedding is **at the church** on Main Street.
   >
   > The wedding reception is **at the school** next door.

3. Common prepositional phrases about transportation also occur with no article.

   > I went **by bus**, but she went **on foot**.

BY		ON
plane	boat	foot (= walking)
bus	train	
car		

15 **Common Prepositional Phrases:** Solving Problems

A. Circle the correct prepositional phrase in the sentences.

1. My friend is cooking a special lunch tomorrow. All our friends are going

   (to lunch / (to the lunch)). Some of them like spicy food, and some of them don't.

2. I often work late and eat dinner just before I go (to bed / at bed).

   Then I don't sleep well.

3. Last night, I invited my new girlfriend (to dinner / to the dinner)

   in a restaurant. But I forgot my credit card. She paid for dinner.

   Now I feel bad.

4. I travel a lot (in plane / by plane). I sit for a long time

   and eat heavy airline meals. Then I feel uncomfortable.

5. I'm a postal worker. I go everywhere (by the foot / on foot).

   By the evening, my feet hurt.

U. S.
POST
OFFICE

6. My wife goes (to work / to the work) very early during the week. She needs to rest on the weekend, but she always gets up and makes breakfast for the family.

7. My office (at work / to work) has no windows. When I'm there, I feel sad and sleepy.

8. I eat breakfast (in school / in the school) cafeteria. They serve too much sweet, unhealthy food.

B. Complete these solutions to the problems in Part A. Add the correct prepositions and articles (*the* or *a*) where necessary. Write the number of the problem in Part A beside the solution.

Solution	Problem Number
1. Eat a light meal, like fruit or cereal, before you go _to_ bed.	2
2. Travel _____ train. Then you can stand up and walk around during the trip.	_____
3. Go outside and get some sunshine. When you come back _____ office, you'll work better.	_____
4. Bring your lunch _____ school.	_____
5. Invite her _____ special dinner, in a nice restaurant. And pay!	_____
6. Take a bottle of chili sauce _____ lunch at your friend's house, and leave it on the table.	_____
7. Get up early—before your wife. Bring her breakfast _____ bed.	_____
8. This evening, _____ home, I'll put my feet into a nice bath of hot green tea. It's very relaxing!	_____

16 **Using Prepositional Phrases:** Discussion

 Share your ideas in small groups. How do you use food for your mind and body? How do you make your favorite healthy food? Talk about these ideas, using prepositional phrases of time and place (location and direction).

Examples: I always drink at least five glasses of water during the day. Here is my favorite health drink: Put some ice and milk into a blender with strawberries or any other fruit. Mix everything at a low speed. . . .

17 **Adverbs and Prepositions:** What Did You Learn?

Work with a partner. Go back to the introductory task for this chapter, page 192. This chapter contains all the information you need to complete that task. Can you find the information? (If not, see the bottom of this page for the answers.)

Check your progress! Go to the Self-Test for Chapter 11 on the *Grammar Links* Website.

1.b, 2.a, 3.a, 4.a, 5.a, 6.a, 7.a

Phrasal Verbs and Verb + Preposition Combinations

Introductory Task: Fitness Freak or Couch Potato?

A. Read the passage.

1   Perhaps you're an exercise addict. You **show up** every morning at the gym, **turn up** the music, and **work out**. Or you **build up** your muscles through sports. You're always **pointing out** the benefits of exercise: "It's good for your mind and body," you say. You're a fitness freak.

← muscle

Fitness Freak

2   Or maybe you're more like me. Yes, I know the benefits of exercise, but I can't **figure out** how to enjoy it! Maybe I go to a gym class one morning and **try** it **out**. But the next morning, when I hear the alarm clock, I **turn** it **off** and go back to sleep. Sometimes I plan a volleyball game with my friends. But the night before, I **make up** excuses: "I'm too busy! … I have a headache!" And I **call** the game **off**. Another friend invites me to go swimming, but I **turn down** the invitation. I have a better idea: I'll **take** the afternoon **off**, **pick up** a big pizza, and **settle down** in front of the TV. I'm a couch potato.

Couch Potato

3   We couch potatoes **know about** exercise, but we don't want to **hear about** it or **think about** it every day! When we **think of** exercise, we think of pain. When we **look at** fitness freaks in the gym, we think, "All that huffing and puffing? Not me!" When fitness freaks **talk to** us about sports training, we **listen to** them politely, but we want to say, "**Forget about** all that! Come and have ice cream with us!"

B. Look at the passage again. The **boldfaced** groups of words in paragraphs 1 and 2 are phrasal verbs. The **boldfaced** groups of words in paragraph 3 are verb + preposition combinations. Answer the questions.

1. Which words are often used in phrasal verbs? Circle the words.

   about   at   down   of   off   out   to   up

2. Which words are used in verb + preposition combinations? Circle the words.

   about   at · down   of   off   out   to   up

C. Phrasal verbs usually have special meanings. Look again at paragraphs 1 and 2. Some of the phrasal verbs are repeated in the box below. Match the phrasal verbs with their meanings.

Paragraph 1		Paragraph 2	
Verb	Meaning	Verb	Meaning
1. show up	a. tell __4__	1. figure out	a. make (time) free ____
2. turn up	b. exercise ____	2. try out	b. stop (it) from working __3__
3. work out	c. appear ____	3. turn off	c. test ____
4. point out	d. make louder ____	4. make up	d. invent ____
		5. call off	e. become comfortable ____
		6. turn down	f. cancel (a plan) ____
		7. take off	g. discover an answer ____
		8. pick up	h. get; collect ____
		9. settle down	i. say no to (an invitation) ____

D. Discuss as a class: Are most people in the class fitness freaks, couch potatoes, or something in between?

Phrasal Verbs

FORM

A. Overview

1. Phrasal verbs (sometimes called two-word verbs) consists of a verb plus an adverb. The adverb is called a particle.

   The most common particles in phrasal verbs are *up* and *out*. Down and *off* are also quite common.

   (See Appendix 15 for a list of common phrasal verbs.)

   verb particle
   She **made up** a story.

   verb particle
   Turn off the music.

2. Some phrasal verbs take objects. Other phrasal verbs do not.

   phrasal verb object
   She **made up** a story.

   phrasal verb
   My energy is **running out**.

B. Phrasal Verbs with Objects

1. If the object of the phrasal verb is a noun, it can go **before** or **after** the particle.

   object
   She made **up a story**. OR

   object
   She made **a story up**.

2. If the object is a pronoun, it must go **before** the particle.

   pronoun
   She made **it up**.
   NOT: She made ~~up it~~.

(continued on next page)

C. Function

1. Phrasal verbs usually have a special meaning, which is not the same as the verb meaning plus the particle meaning.	**make up** = invent (a story) **run out** = come to the end
2. Different particles give different meanings to the same verb.	**turn down** = (an offer) say no **turn up** = (the music) make louder **turn off** (the music) = make it stop
3. The same phrasal verb may have more than one meaning.	She **made up** a story. (= invented) She **made up** the time she lost. (= replaced; compensated)

GRAMMAR PRACTICE 1

Phrasal Verbs

1 **Identifying Phrasal Verbs:** Sports, Exercise, and Human Nature

A. Underline the phrasal verbs in the **boldfaced** clauses below. Circle the object if there is one.

Sports Monthly

Why do people love sports? **Biologists point out two important needs**, or instincts,
¹

for humans: the need to fight and the need to work together in groups.

Long ago, **when their food ran out**, ancient people hunted animals for meat.
²
When strangers turned up near their homes, they fought them. Strength and speed
³

were important skills. This was the beginning of competition—the need to fight and win.

Soon **humans figured out a way to protect their homes**: They formed tribes.
⁴
Tribe members worked, hunted, and brought up their children together.
⁵

This was the beginning of teamwork: working as a group.

Now, with technology and city life, **our physical lives are slowing down**.
⁶

We don't need to hunt every day. But we still respect competition and

teamwork. In sports, **we make up different ways to practice these ancient skills**. We love
⁷

to watch teamwork in ball games on TV, and **we look up sports scores** in the newspaper.
⁸

Our love of sports is just our human instinct!

---

skill = ability to do something well. *tribe* = a social group of several families who
are related in some way. *scores* = results of a competition.

B. Work with a partner. Complete these phrasal verbs from the reading in Part A. Write them beside their meanings in the box. Then check your answers as a class.

1. _bring_ up = educate a child
2. _____ out = discover (an answer)
3. _____ up = find written facts about
4. _____ up = invent

5. _____ out = come to the end
6. _____ down = get slower
7. _____ up = come; visit unexpectedly

C. Discuss in small groups: Do you agree with the biologists' ideas? Are sports a part of human nature?

2 **Using Phrasal Verbs:** Excuses for Couch Potatoes

Here are some excuses to use when you don't want to exercise! Complete the sentences with the phrasal verbs in the box.

YOU'RE AT A PARTY, AND YOU DON'T WANT TO DANCE!

give up = stop doing (an activity)
pick up = get; collect

✓ turn down = make (something) quieter
turn up = make (it) louder

1. Excuse me. I'm going next door to _turn down_ the music.
2. I can't dance when the music is so loud! Why did you _____ it _____?
3. The doctor said dancing is bad for my knee. He told me to _____ it _____.
4. I'm waiting for my friend. She went to _____ some food _____ for us.

YOU DON'T WANT TO GO TO YOUR AEROBICS CLASS THIS EVENING!

catch up = reach the same place	make up = replace; compensate
let down = disappoint; not keep a promise	work out = solve a problem

5. I'm working this evening. I missed two work days and I'm _____ them

   _____ .

6. I need to stay home with the children. My babysitter _____ me _____ .

7. I missed the first three classes, so I don't know the steps! It's too late to _____

   _____ now.

8. We're having problems here at the office. I need to stay and _____ them

   _____ .

---

3 **Pronoun Object Placement:** Preparing for a Trip

Steve and Louise are almost ready to leave on a bicycling trip, but Steve is worrying about everything. Complete the dialogue with Louise's answers to Steve's questions. Change noun objects to pronouns.

Steve:

1. Did we turn off the lights?

2. Did you look up the address of the campsite?

3. Did I pick up the map?

4. Did you check out the weather report?

5. Did you figure out the directions?

6. Did you try out your new bicycle seat?

7. Oh, no—I forgot! That big cycling race is on TV tonight. What are we going to do— call off the trip?

Louise:

Yes, _we turned them off._____

Yes, I _____

Yes, you _____

Yes, I _____

Yes, I _____

Yes, I _____

No, we're not going to _____

_____. We're not going to be

couch potatoes tonight!

4 Phrasal Verbs with and Without Objects; Noun Object Placement: Women in Sports

Rewrite the underlined clauses that have noun or pronoun objects. Place the object between the verb and the particle.

Sports Monthly

1. In the past, we never saw many women in professional or Olympic sports. We saw young girls in gymnastics and ice-skating competitions, but only <u>until they grew up</u>.

2. Then <u>they gave up competitions</u>.
   gave competitions up

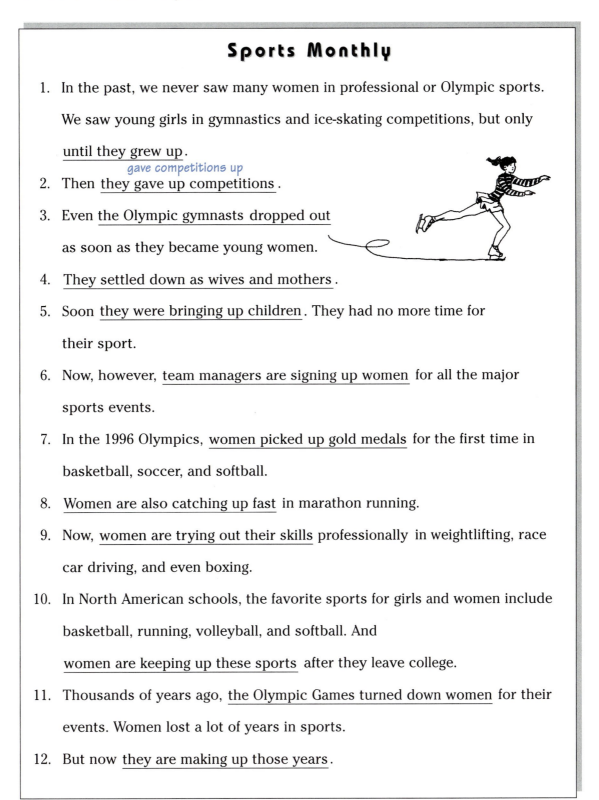

3. Even <u>the Olympic gymnasts dropped out</u> as soon as they became young women.

4. <u>They settled down as wives and mothers</u>.

5. Soon <u>they were bringing up children</u>. They had no more time for their sport.

6. Now, however, <u>team managers are signing up women</u> for all the major sports events.

7. In the 1996 Olympics, <u>women picked up gold medals</u> for the first time in basketball, soccer, and softball.

8. <u>Women are also catching up fast</u> in marathon running.

9. Now, <u>women are trying out their skills</u> professionally in weightlifting, race car driving, and even boxing.

10. In North American schools, the favorite sports for girls and women include basketball, running, volleyball, and softball. And <u>women are keeping up these sports</u> after they leave college.

11. Thousands of years ago, <u>the Olympic Games turned down women</u> for their events. Women lost a lot of years in sports.

12. But now <u>they are making up those years</u>.

---

5 Phrasal Verbs: A Dictionary

A. Make your own dictionary of the phrasal verbs in this chapter. Use the lists in the Introductory Task and Exercises 1–4, or use Appendix 15. Write the phrasal verbs beside their meanings. (Note: The phrasal verbs are listed in alphabetical order.)

Phrasal Verbs Without Objects		
catch	up	reach the same place
drop	out	leave an activity or group
____	____	become adult
____	____	come to the end
____	____	become comfortable
____	____	appear
____	____	become slower
____	____	come; visit unexpectedly
____	____	exercise

Phrasal Verbs With Objects		
bring	up	educate (a child)
____	____	cancel (a plan)
____	____	find information about
____	____	discover (an answer)
____	____	stop doing (an activity)
____	____	continue
____	____	disappoint; not keep a promise
____	____	find written facts about
____	____	1. invent
____	____	2. replace; compensate
____	____	get; collect
____	____	tell
____	____	register; add (a name) to a list
____	____	make (time) free
____	____	test
____	____	1. make quieter
____	____	2. say no to (an invitation)
____	____	stop from working
____	____	make louder
____	____	solve (a problem)

B. Work with a partner. Compare your dictionary lists and correct your work.

6 Choosing Phrasal Verbs; Object Placement: Women and Sports Heroes

A. A reporter is interviewing a sports psychologist. Replace the verbs in parentheses with phrasal verbs from your dictionary in Exercise 5. Use the objects in parentheses. Use a different phrasal verb each time.

Sports Monthly

Interviewer: Why are women's sports important?

Psychologist: Sports are important psychologically, especially for children. Teamwork helps children

work their problems out/work out their problems
_____
1 (solve / their problems)

together. Children also need heroes, and girls didn't use to have many sports heroes.

But now, adult women

_____
2 (are appearing)

in professional soccer and basketball games. Women sports stars

_____
3 (are exercising)

beside men in gyms.

Interviewer: Do women sports stars want to be heroes?

Psychologist: Yes, many want to help young girls. Sometimes, they

_____
4 (make free time / a few hours)

from their busy schedules and visit schools.

They _____
5 (visit unexpectedly)

at girls' clubs. They talk about self-confidence and hard work.

Interviewer: What do they say?

Psychologist: They _____
6 (tell / important ideas)

—for example, patience. They say, "Heroes need time to grow. Take your time

and _____.
7 (become slower)

Then you'll work better." They talk about education, too. They say, "What about your

school work?

_____?
8 (Are you continuing / it)

That's very important."

B. Write about a sports hero or any other hero in your life. What did you learn from this person? Why is he or she a hero for you? Write at least six sentences. Try to use at least four phrasal verbs from your dictionary in Exercise 5.

Example: When I was growing up, my hero was the mail carrier. He used to show up early every morning. . . .

See the *Grammar Links* Website for a complete model paragraph for this assignment.

7 Using Phrasal Verbs: Charades

Work in small groups.

Step 1 Write the particles to make phrasal verbs with each verb below. Use Appendix 15 to help you.

Step 2 Write sentences that use the phrasal verbs.

Step 3 Act out your sentences for the rest of the class. Can they guess your phrasal verbs?

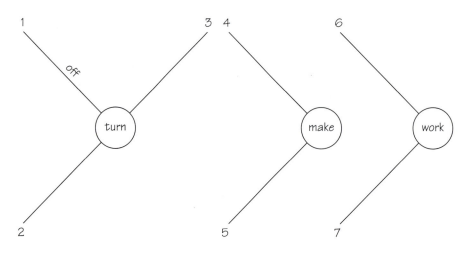

Example: Sentence: I'm turning off the light.
　　　　　　Actions: (Pretend to get up from a sofa, look sleepy, walk to the door, and click something on the wall.)

Verb + Preposition Combinations

FORM and FUNCTION

A. Overview

Verbs and prepositions sometimes go together as a fixed unit. Like phrasal verbs, these combinations are sometimes called two-word verbs.

The most common prepositions in these combinations include *about, for, in, on,* and *to. After, at, of,* and *from* are also quite common.

The preposition forms a prepositional phrase with its object.

		PREPOSITIONAL PHRASE	
	VERB	PREPOSITION	OBJECT
I'm	**thinking**	**about**	my dinner.
I don't	**care**	**for**	spaghetti.
Please	**look**	**after**	her.
She's	**looking**	**at**	you.

(See Chapter 11, Grammar Briefing 3, for more information on prepositional phrases. See Appendix 16 for a list of verb + preposition combinations.)

B. Meaning of Verb + Preposition Combinations

Verb + preposition combinations often include verbs of thinking, speaking, sensing, or feeling.

He **thought of** a good idea. (= thinking)

Let's **talk to** him. (= speaking)

Please **look after** her. (= sensing)

I don't **care for** spaghetti. (= feeling)

GRAMMAR HOTSPOT!

Verb + preposition combinations are different from phrasal verbs:

- *Up, out, off,* and *down* are used only in phrasal verbs.

  I **turned off** the light. (*turned off* = phrasal verb, not verb + preposition combination)

- In phrasal verbs, pronoun objects come **before** particles.

  She **made** it **up.**
  NOT: She made ~~up it.~~

- In verb + preposition combinations, all objects come after their prepositions.

  Please **look after** her.
  NOT: Please look ~~her after.~~

Verb + Preposition Combinations

8 Identifying Verb + Preposition Combinations: Politeness

Read this conversation between an American and a very polite Englishman at a tennis match. Find and underline the verb + preposition combinations in the box. Circle the prepositional phrases.

belong to	forget about	pay for
care about	happen to	think about
care for	look at	wait for
✓ concentrate on	look for	✓ worry about

American: Oh, I'm so sorry! I hit you! (1) I wasn't <u>concentrating</u> (on my game.)

Englishman: (2) Don't <u>worry</u> (about it.) I'm fine.

American: But your eye! It's all black! (3) I'm going to look for a doctor.

Englishman: No, no. That's only dirt. (4) Don't think about it anymore.

American: Can you stand? Here, let me help you. (5) Oh, no! Look at your leg!

             Did you break it?

Englishman: No problem. (6) I don't care about this leg. I have another one!

American: But how will you walk home? (7) I want to pay for your taxi.

Englishman: (8) I'll wait for my wife. She has a car.

American: Oh, look— there's a pair of glasses.

             (9) Do they belong to you? I think you

             lost them when the tennis ball hit you.

Englishman: Ah, but you found them again.

             Thank you so much.

American: You're really very kind. But I feel terrible.

             (10) I'm so sorry this happened to you.

Englishman: (11) Forget about it, my dear friend.

             Now, would you (12) care for another

             game of tennis?

9 Using Verb + Preposition Combinations: A Quiet Fitness

Add verbs before the prepositional phrases in the passage. Use the verb + preposition combinations in the box to help you. Use each verb only once, in the correct form.

believe in	hear about	live on (= use for food)	talk to
come from	know about	look after	✓ think of
depend on (= need)	listen to	recover from (= get well after)	

When we hear the word *exercise*, we often ___think_____
                                                    1
of sports and fitness activities such as tennis or aerobics. But many people

_____ in slow, quiet ways to keep fit, like fishing or walking.
            2
Gardening is one of these quiet fitness activities.

Gardening is very good exercise. You bend and walk and pull weeds. But you don't

get tired when you're breathing fresh air and _____ to the
                                                          3
songs of the birds in the trees.

Gardening gives you food for the body and mind. Gardeners often

_____ on the vegetables from their gardens—they never eat
            4
supermarket vegetables. And many natural medicines _____
                                                              5
from plants. We often _____ about "healing gardens"
                              6
in hospitals. Some hospitals grow flowers like foxglove for medicine.

Other flowers help patients meditate, or quiet their minds. Some patients even

_____ to plants. Doctors say this helps their patients
            7
_____from illnesses faster.
            8

All over the world, doctors _____ about these benefits
                                          9
and _____ on plants for a lot of their work. When you
            10
_____ after a garden, you are helping nature, but nature is
            11
also helping you.

Foxglove

weeds = plants that you don't want to keep.

10 Verb + Preposition Combinations: A Dictionary

Make your own dictionary of verb + preposition combinations in this chapter. Use the lists in Exercises 8 and 9. Write the appropriate prepositions after the verbs.

worry _____

wait _____

think _____

think _____

talk _____

recover _____

pay _____

look _____

look _____

look _____

live _____

listen _____

know _____

hear _____

happen _____

forget _____

depend _____

concentrate _____

come _____

care _____

care _____

belong _to_____

believe _in_____

Verb + Preposition Combinations

11 **Using Verb + Preposition Combinations:** Health from the Inside Out

Complete these sentences with verb + preposition combinations and the objects given.
Use the verbs in parentheses and appropriate prepositions.

1. What is the most important exercise in our lives? We do it more than 1,000 times every hour.

   Did you _think of the right answer_____?
   (think / the right answer)

   The answer is: *breathing*.

2. We don't _____ very often.
   (think / this exercise)

3. However, our life and health _____.
   (depend / it)

   Breathing brings oxygen into our body.

4. Breathing exercises are relaxation, too. When we are _____,
   (worrying / something)

   people tell us "Take some deep breaths!"

5. You _____ in a meditation
   (hear / all these things)

   or yoga class.

6. Meditation and yoga _____.
   (come / India)

   They are part of the Hindu and Buddhist religions.

7. However, most religions _____.
   (know / meditation)

   Sometimes they call it *prayer*.

8. Many people don't _____.
   (care / religious meditation)

9. But they _____. Some find it in yoga.
   (look / mental relaxation)

10. In yoga exercises, people _____.
    (listen / their breathing)

11. Sometimes they _____.
    (look / a picture)

12. Sometimes they _____.
    (concentrate / a special word)

12 Choosing Verb + Preposition Combinations: My Kind of Activity

Do you like "fast" or "quiet" activities? Write at least six sentences about your favorite activities. Use the list below, or choose your own activities. Use verb + preposition combinations from your dictionary in Exercise 10.

"Fast" Activities

rollerblading, skateboarding, ice skating, soccer, tennis

"Quiet" Activities

fishing, gardening, karate, golf, walking

Example: I don't care for very fast sports, but I like karate. I know about karate because I'm Japanese. . . .

See the *Grammar Links* Website for a complete model paragraph for this assignment.

13 Phrasal Verbs Versus Verb + Preposition Combinations: Sleep

Look closely at the underlined parts of these sentences. Replace the **boldfaced** noun objects with pronouns. Write the pronouns in the correct position.

1. During the day, we look after our minds and bodies. We also look after **our minds**
   look after them

   and bodies at night, when we sleep.

2. Sleep helps us with our problems. We work out our **problems** in our dreams.
   work them out

3. We use a lot of energy during the day. We build up **our energy** again when we sleep.

4. Sometimes we have a hard day. Sleep helps us recover from **the hard day**.

5. What happens during sleep? Researchers don't really know the answer. They

   look for **the answer** in sleep experiments.

6. Researchers examine the sleeping brain's activity. They check out **the brain's activity**

   with electronic machines.

7. We need two kinds of sleep: REM (rapid eye movement) and non-REM. In REM

   sleep, our eyes and body move. REM activity happens many times each night.

   We keep up **REM activity** for about ten minutes each time.

8. People stay in non-REM sleep for one or two hours each time. Interesting things

   happen to **people** during non-REM.

9. People dream, walk, and talk during non-REM sleep. These activities are

   unconscious—people don't know about **these activities** while they are sleeping.

10. Sometimes people are so busy that they don't get enough sleep. They **give up sleep** for several days.

11. When people get too tired, they forget simple things. Their memory <u>lets down</u> **people**.

12. In some countries, people sleep fewer hours at night but <u>make up</u> **the hours** in the afternoon. Spanish speakers call this afternoon sleep a "siesta." English speakers call it a "nap."

See the *Grammar Links* Website for more information about REM and non-REM sleep.

Three-Word Verbs

FORM

A. Phrasal Verbs with Prepositions

Three-word verbs combine a phrasal verb (a verb + particle) with a preposition:

	THREE-WORD VERB		
	PHRASAL VERB	PREPOSITION	
I	**met up**	**with**	Fred.
Let's	**get down**	**to**	work.

(See Appendix 17 for a list of three-word verbs.)

TALKING THE TALK

Particles in phrasal verbs are often stressed. Prepositions in verb + preposition combinations or in three-word verbs are not usually stressed.

particle
She **made** it **úp**.

preposition
I thoúght **about** it.

particle preposition
Let's get **dówn** **to** it.

Three-Word Verbs

14 **Three-Word Verbs:** Those Healthy Hills

A. Read the magazine article about hiking. Underline the three-word verbs in the article. Use Appendix 17 to help you.

Hiker's Digest

Why do people love to walk or run up hills and mountains?

Here are some readers' answers:

It's good exercise!

1. When I get through with a run in the hills, I feel great. (*Amy, AK*)

It's good for the mind!

2. Sometimes I can't concentrate. After I enjoy the fresh mountain air, I get down to my work quickly. (*Reyna, Mexico*)

3. When I get to the top of a mountain, I feel confident. I know I can face up to my problems. (*Fred, CA*)

4. I always come up with good ideas when I'm looking at the scenery. (*Mitsuko, Japan*)

It's social!

5. I often meet up with old friends on the top of a mountain! It's such a nice surprise. (*Susan, Great Britain*)

6. It's a way to meet new people. Then if I get along with them really well, we become friends. (*Sergio, Brazil*)

7. It's great for children. They can run and shout in the mountains, and the adults put up with them! (*Young Soo, Korea*)

It's natural and easy!

8. It's not like sports. I walk at my natural speed. I don't always keep up with other people, but that's fine. (*Imad, Jordan*)

9. I don't need any special equipment— just water. I never cut down on water. (*Melita, Bosnia*)

10. You don't need any preparation. Yesterday, a friend dropped in on me unexpectedly, so we just decided to go for a walk. (*Dimitri, Russia*)

scenery = the view of nature in a beautiful place.

B. Look at the verbs you underlined in Part A. Write them beside their meanings in the box.

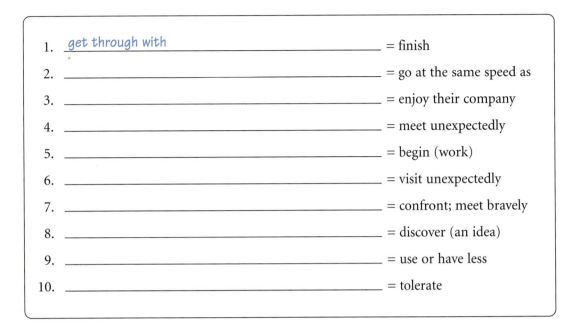

1. <u>get through with</u> _____ = finish

2. _____ = go at the same speed as

3. _____ = enjoy their company

4. _____ = meet unexpectedly

5. _____ = begin (work)

6. _____ = visit unexpectedly

7. _____ = confront; meet bravely

8. _____ = discover (an idea)

9. _____ = use or have less

10. _____ = tolerate

C. Work in small groups. Interview the other people in your group. Who likes hiking? Who does not like hiking? Why or why not? Compare your answers with those of the rest of the class.

15 Three-Word Verbs: Game

Work as a class.

Step 1 Form three groups, one for each circle below. Each person chooses at least one word from their circle. Use all the words in your circle.

Step 2 Walk around the class. Share your word(s). Find two people with the words you need to make a three-word verb. Then make up a sentence together using your three-word verb.

Step 3 With your two new partners, share your sentence with the class.

Example: Your three-word verb = meet up with
         Your sentence = Yesterday, I met up with a classmate in the mall.

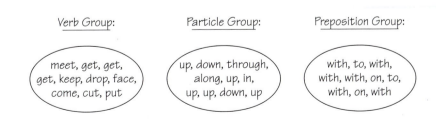

Verb Group:
meet, get, get, get, keep, drop, face, come, cut, put

Particle Group:
up, down, through, along, up, in, up, up, down, up

Preposition Group:
with, to, with, with, with, on, to, with, on, with

16 Stress Placement for Particles and Prepositions: Staying Fit

A. Two middle-aged men meet after several years. Read their conversation and look at the **boldfaced** words. Then listen to the conversation and underline the stressed word in each group of words.

Jack: Bob, you look great. How do you keep so fit?

Bob: It's simple. Exercise.

Jack: Exercise? (1) **I never thought you cared for it.** You used to start, (2) **but then you always gave it up.**

Bob: Well, in those days, (3) **I never really got down to it.** But then I found a great way to exercise and save one dollar every day.

Jack: How?

Bob: I run to work. Every morning, (4) **I wait for the bus.** Then I run behind it and save the bus fare. It's a great idea. (5) **Check it out!**

Jack: Oh, that's not such a great idea. I save five dollars every day!

Bob: Okay, tell me. (6) **I'm listening to you.**

Jack: Bus fare is only a dollar. But taxi fare is about five dollars. I know, (7) **because I looked it up.** So every day, (8) **I look for a taxi**, and I run behind the taxi!

B. Discuss as a class: Does Jack really save more money than Bob? Explain your answer.

Wrap-up Activities

1 **Kings of the Hills:** EDITING

Correct the errors in this article. There are 13 errors with adverbs, prepositions, phrasal verbs, verb + preposition combinations, and three-word verbs. The first error is corrected for you.

Geographic Monthly

The Tarahumara Indians are probably the most famous marathon runners in the world. They come ~~for~~ *from* the mountains of northern Mexico. About 50,000 Tarahumara people live in the Copper Canyon in the Sierra Madre mountains. Most of them hardly never go outside the canyon.

Every day, the Tarahumara develop their running and hill-walking skills. They work very hardly, and they go everywhere on the foot. They grow corn on the sides of the canyon, so they climb up and down every day. They also hunt animals, so they learn to run too fast. Sometimes 40- and 50-year-old men can run after a deer for hours and keep it up with. At the summer, when the weather is extreme hot, they stay at the top the canyon. When the weather is enough cool, they go down again for the winter.

In 1993, Victorio Churra, a Tarahumara, won a 100-mile race in Leadville, Colorado. The mountains in Leadville are very high, but Churra ran them up easily. He was wearing old sandals on his feet! People heard this about, and they invited the Tarahumara people to more races in the United States.

Now several runners come every year to a big race in California. They use their prize money to help their families at the home.

marathon = a running race, just over 26 miles. *sandals* = simple shoes with open toes. *prize* = money you win in a competition.

 See the *Grammar Links* Website for more information about the Tarahumara.

2 Diet Budget: SPEAKING/WRITING

Work in small groups.

Step 1 Plan a healthy and interesting diet (= eating plan) for one week.
Use the ideas from Chapter 11.

Step 2 You have $100 to spend on your diet.
❑ Go to the supermarket.
❑ Check food prices.
❑ Make your shopping list and budget
   (= spending plan) for the week.

Step 3 Share your diet budget with the whole class. Explain why it's a great plan.
Is it healthy enough? Did you spend carefully? Use adverbs, prepositions, phrasal verbs,
and verb + preposition combinations.

Step 4 Vote as a class on the best diet budget. Give reasons. Use the same structures
as in Step 3.

Example: You have hardly any vegetables in this diet. The diet has too much chocolate.
You didn't think about tea.

3 Phrasal Verb Tag: SPEAKING

Work as two teams. Use Appendix 15 or your phrasal verb dictionary from Exercise 5.

Team A, Student 1: Choose a phrasal verb and call on a student from Team B.
Team B, Student 1: Make up a sentence using that phrasal verb. Then choose another
                     phrasal verb and call on another student from Team A.

Every phrasal verb that is used correctly wins a point for the team. Continue for
15 minutes or until everyone takes a turn.

4 Lifestyle Log: WRITING

A. Keep a log, or a record, every night
for five nights before you go to sleep.
Answer these questions:

How did I care for my health today?
What did I eat for breakfast/lunch/dinner?
What kind of exercise did I do?

B. Write a paragraph explaining your health habits for the week. Use the information
in the log. If you don't want to tell the truth, make up an interesting story! Write
at least six sentences. Use adverbs, prepositions, phrasal verbs, verb + preposition
combinations, and three-word verbs.

Example: Last week, I didn't have time to care for my health. I got down to work for
my exam. . . .

See the *Grammar Links* Website for a complete model paragraph for this activity.

 **Check your progress! Go to the Self-Test for
Chapter 12 on the *Grammar Links* Website.**

Adjectives; Comparison with Adjectives and Adverbs

TOPIC FOCUS
The Wild West

UNIT OBJECTIVES

- **adjectives**
  (It's a *valuable* gift. The gift is *valuable*.)

- **nouns used as adjectives**
  (She took a *train* ride.)

- **adjectives ending in *-ing* and *-ed***
  (Student life is *interesting*. I'm *interested* in this life.)

- ***as . . . as* with adjectives and adverbs**
  (Spiders are *as dangerous as* snakes. I run *as fast as* you.)

- **comparative adjectives and adverbs**
  (California is *bigger than* Nevada. It rains *less frequently* in Nevada.)

- **superlative adjectives and adverbs**
  (Alaska is *the biggest state* in the United States. The Amazon flows *the most slowly* of all rivers.)

Grammar in Action

Read and listen.

Travel Today:
The Adventure of the West

1 For many young people, the North American West means adventure: wild country, wide spaces, and wonderful views.

2 The West has a fascinating history. Thousands of years ago, the Native Americans came here from Siberia. They were interested in the big, new hunting lands. Much later, the Spanish came after they heard amazing stories about cities of gold. In the nineteenth century, many more Europeans came and then African Americans. They were excited about building new lives in the wild, empty West.

3 In the twentieth century, Route 66, the road from Chicago to California, became a name that meant adventure. Jack Kerouac described it in *On the Road*, a travel book for the 1950s generation. Then, in the 1960s, San Francisco in California became a center for the hippy generation. The San Francisco "flower children" dreamed of making the world a better place.

4 The modern West is not **as wild as** the nineteenth century West. Life isn't **as uncomfortable** or dangerous. The new West isn't **as empty as** the old West, either. For example, California is one of **the most crowded** states in the United States and has **the largest** population now. It also has some of **the most comfortable** homes in the United States.

5 But you can still find adventure in the West—for example, in the national parks. Western parks are much **larger than** Eastern parks, with higher mountains and deeper canyons. Wild animals move **more freely** because Western parks are **less crowded than** Eastern parks. So if you are looking for adventure, I can still say to you, "Go West!"

---

wild = free, natural, and not controlled by humans. *fascinating* = holding your attention and interest. *Native Americans* = the people who lived first in North America. *generation* = people who are all born around the same time.

Think About Grammar

A. Look at the words in the lists below. They are adjectives; they modify, or tell you about, nouns (or the pronouns that replace nouns). Find the adjectives in the passage. Underline the adjectives and the words they modify. The first one is done for you in the passage.

Adjectives	*-Ing/-ed* Adjectives	Nouns as Adjectives
(Paragraph 1)	(Paragraph 2)	(Paragraph 3)
young	fascinating	travel
wild	interested	1950s
wide	amazing	hippy
wonderful	excited	flower

B. Write the **boldfaced** phrases from paragraphs 4 and 5 in the chart.

As . . . (as) (4)	**Comparatives** (5)	**Superlatives** (4)
as wild as	larger than	the most crowded

C. Look again at the passage and at the phrases you wrote in Part B. Answer the questions.

1. *As . . . as* talks about two things that are similar or not similar. Paragraph 4 talks about which two things? _____

2. Comparatives talk about two things that are different. Paragraph 5 talks about which two things? _____

3. Superlatives compare one thing to all other things in a group. Paragraph 4 compares California to which other places? _____

Adjectives

Introductory Task: Cowboys, Pioneers, and Native Americans

A. Form three groups. The first group reads about cowboys, the second group reads about pioneers, and the third group reads about Plains Indians. Read only your group's paragraph and questions. Cover up the others. After you read, discuss the information in the map and answer the questions.

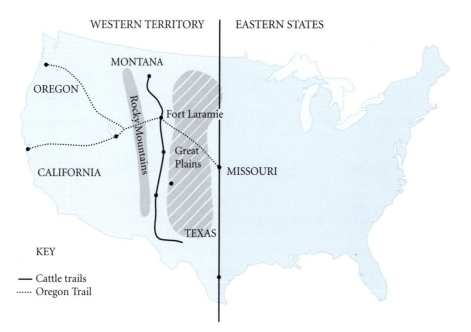

pioneers = the first people who travel to a new place. *Plains Indians* = the Native American tribes who lived on the Great Plains, the huge grasslands in the central part of North America.

Pioneers

The pioneers were mostly families from eastern states in the United States. Some of them were rich and educated. In the 1850s and 1860s, they traveled west to Oregon or California on the Oregon Trail. The trail was tiring and dangerous. The pioneers were always hungry and worried about food. Sometimes they met the Plains Indians on the trail. When the Indians had extra buffalo meat, they sold it to the pioneers and bought valuable guns from them.

1. Who were the pioneers and what were they like?
2. What was the Oregon Trail like?
3. What were the pioneers worried about?
4. What did they buy and sell?

Plains Indians

The Plains Indians included the Cheyenne, Arapahoe, Kiowa, and Comanche tribes. They were buffalo hunters and wonderful horse riders. They lived on the Great Plains. Buffalo hunting was tiring and extremely dangerous, so the Indians needed horses and guns. From the 1840s to the 1860s, they stole fast horses from the cowboys and bought powerful guns from the pioneers. But the Plains tribes were worried about all the new people on their hunting grounds, and more were coming every day!

1. Who were the Plains Indians and what were they like?
2. What was buffalo hunting like?
3. What did the Plains Indians steal or buy?
4. What were they worried about?

Cowboys

The cowboys were mostly young men from Texas or eastern states in the United States. Most of them were poor and not very educated. They worked on Texas ranches. In the 1860s and 1870s, cowboys took their cows north on trails from Texas to Montana. The trails were tiring and dangerous. Sometimes the Plains Indians stole the cowboys' valuable horses. The cowboys were always worried about storms or stampedes, when the cows ran away.

1. Who were the cowboys and what were they like?
2. What were the cattle trails like?
3. What sometimes happened to the cowboys' valuable horses?
4. What were the cowboys worried about?

ranches = big horse or cow farms. *trails* = paths or narrow roads. *stampedes* = accidents where many big animals suddenly run wild together.

B. Form three new groups. Each group includes at least one person from the *Cowboys*, the *Pioneers*, and the *Plains Indians* groups. Share the information you found in Part A, including the map, and answer the following questions.

1. How were the cowboys, pioneers, and Plains Indians different?

2. How was life similar for all three groups?

3. Did the three groups meet each other? How do you know?

4. Were the three groups worried about the same things? Explain.

C. Work as a class. Share your answers to Part B. Did each group get the same answers?

GRAMMAR BRIEFING 1

Adjectives

FORM and FUNCTION

A. Adjectives

1. Adjectives modify nouns (or the pronouns that replace nouns).

   He's a **happy person**. (*happy* modifies *person*)

2. Adjectives usually come before the nouns they modify.

   adjective   noun
   She gave me a **wonderful gift**.

3. Adjectives can also come after the nouns or pronouns they modify when they follow *be* and other linking verbs (for example, *become, feel, look, seem, smell, sound, taste*).

   The gift **was wonderful**.
   You **look sad**.

B. Nouns Used as Adjectives

Nouns sometimes function as adjectives—to modify other nouns.

(See Chapter 8 for more about nouns.)

modifier noun
Their **home life** was quiet.

modifier noun
I am a **science student**.

(continued on next page)

C. Word Order of Adjectives

Sometimes more than one adjective is used with a noun. Follow this order:

	ADJECTIVES					NOUN
	QUALITY	SIZE	AGE	COLOR	NOUN AS ADJECTIVE	
an			old	white	stone	house
some	dangerous	little			desert	animals

- After *be* or linking verbs, place *and* before the last adjective in a list.

  The house is **old and white**.

- Place commas between adjectives in a list.

  The children are **happy, small, and young**.

  On **cold, dark** nights, I love to build a fire.

- Do not place a comma before a noun used as an adjective.

  On cold, **dark December** nights . . .

  NOT: On cold, dark, December nights . . .

GRAMMAR HOTSPOT!

1. Use adjectives, not adverbs, after verbs with stative meaning.

   (For more on stative meanings, see Chapter 3, Grammar Briefing 2.)

   active verb   adverb
   She **spoke seriously** about the problem.

   stative verb   adjective
   The problem **sounded   serious**.
     NOT: The problem sounded ~~seriously~~.

2. Some adjectives and adverbs have the same form.

   adjective   adverb
   You're **early**. Cowboys get up **early**.

   adjective   adverb
   You're **late**. I worked **late**.

3. Remember: *Hard* is an adjective or adverb. *Hardly* is an intensifier meaning "almost not at all."

   (For more information about adverbs and intensifiers, including *hardly*, see Chapter 11, Grammar Briefing 2.)

   adjective   adverb
   Your work is **hard**. You **hardly** work.

4. *Good* is an adjective. The adverbial form of *good* is *well*.

   adjective
   This is a **good** lesson.

   adverb
   This isn't working **well**.

   But:

   Well is often used as an adjective to describe health.

   adjective
   I'm very **well**, thank you.

Adjectives

1 Identifying Adjectives: Life on the Oregon Trail

A pioneer wrote this letter to her sister in Illinois. Underline the adjectives in her letter. Circle the words they modify. There are 28 adjectives. The first two are underlined and circled for you.

July 1, 1854

Dear Sister,

We arrived at Fort Laramie last Sunday afternoon. Now we can buy fresh food and wash our dirty clothes. They smell so bad!

We had a difficult time after we left Missouri in May. Ten of our pioneer families became sick in Nebraska, but now we are all safe and well. However, many others have died on this sad trail. We read their names on stone signs beside the road.

Soon we will leave Fort Laramie and cross the Rockies. They look lovely this evening. The evening sun is going down behind them, and the mountain snow seems warm under the red sky. But those mountains are difficult and dangerous. We are going to leave our furniture here. Our animals can't pull heavy wagons over the high mountains. Some of our friends will leave us soon. They will take the southern trail to California. It crosses a huge, dry salt lake.

Goodbye for now, Sister. I feel lonely when I think back to our happy home life in Illinois.

Love,

Margaret

Wagon

2 Adjective Versus Adverb Forms: The End of the Trail

Read the passage. Circle the correct words.

When the first pioneers said goodbye in Independence, Missouri, they said it (serious / *seriously*) because they were leaving the
1
United States! Until the 1840s, the land west of Nebraska was still "Indian territory" with no government. But then, in the (late / lately) 1840s,
2
Oregon became a state, and people discovered gold in California. In 1850 alone, 55,000 people crossed Indian territory. This land was becoming (important / importantly), and the U.S.
3

government decided to buy it from the Plains Indians. At first, the Indians seemed (happy / happily). The Kiowa tribe, for example, sold millions of acres of land
4
(peaceful / peacefully). But their buffalo and hunting lands were disappearing
5
(quick / quickly). Also, the pioneers brought (new / newly) diseases to the West. Many
6   7
Cheyenne people died (painful / painfully) from these diseases, and others were not
8
(good / well). Soon everything looked (different / differently) to the Indians. By the late
9   10
nineteenth century, the U.S. government was trying (hard / hardly) to take more lands,
11
but the Plains Indians were not going to give them up (easy / easily). The (final / finally)
12   13
solution was (painful / painfully). (Final / Finally), Indian territory became part of the
14   15
United States, and the Indians received special pieces of land called "reservations." Many tribes still live on reservations today.

3 **Word Order of Adjectives:** The Buffalo Story

Complete the sentences with the words in parentheses. Write the words in the correct order to modify the **boldfaced** nouns. Add commas or *and* where necessary.

1. Yellowstone National Park is a __wonderful, huge park__ in Wyoming.
   (park / wonderful / huge)

   This tourist **area** __is very famous and popular__.
   (very famous / is / popular)

2. In Yellowstone Park, you will see a large herd of buffalo.

   These _____ are fairly safe now.
   (dark / animals / huge)

3. But their **history** _____.
   (long / is / sad)

4. In the early nineteenth century, there were more than 50 million

   _____.
   (Plains / buffalo / wild)

5. Native American hunters used to sell buffalo meat to _____
   (hungry / families / pioneer)

   on the Oregon Trail.

6. But after the 1840s, hunters with _____
   (guns / new / big / powerful)

   killed more than 100,000 animals every year.

7. By the early twentieth century, only a few hundred buffalo were still alive in

   North America. Most of them lived in zoos.

   These city **zoos** _____.
   (uncomfortable / were / noisy / small)

8. After 1940, the government brought the buffalo back to special grasslands such as Yellowstone

   Park. There, the buffalo's **lives** _____.
   (are / free / comfortable)

9. Now you can see thousands of buffalo in the West. But don't get too close for your

   _____. These wild animals are still dangerous!
   (photographs / beautiful / buffalo)

> *herd* = a group of big animals.

4 Using Adjectives: The Marriage Market

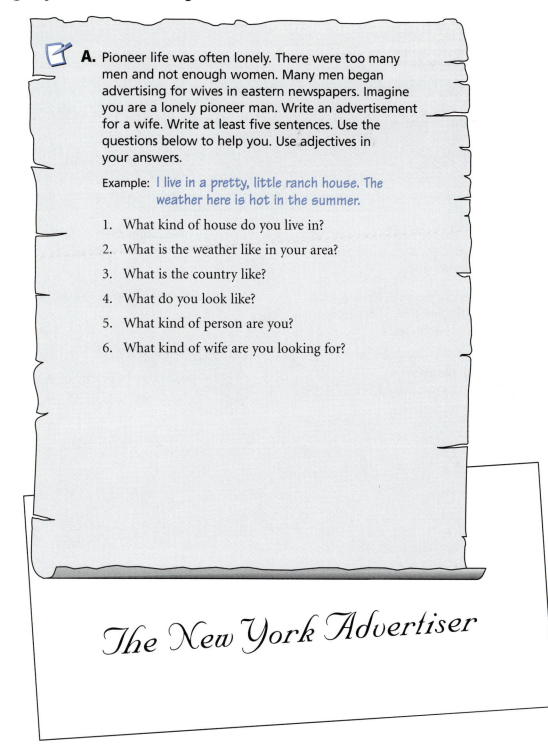

A. Pioneer life was often lonely. There were too many men and not enough women. Many men began advertising for wives in eastern newspapers. Imagine you are a lonely pioneer man. Write an advertisement for a wife. Write at least five sentences. Use the questions below to help you. Use adjectives in your answers.

Example: I live in a pretty, little ranch house. The weather here is hot in the summer.

1. What kind of house do you live in?

2. What is the weather like in your area?

3. What is the country like?

4. What do you look like?

5. What kind of person are you?

6. What kind of wife are you looking for?

The New York Advertiser

See the *Grammar Links* Website for a complete model paragraph for this assignment.

B. Read your advertisement to the class. Discuss: How are your advertisements similar or different?

Adjectives Ending in *-ing* and *-ed*

FORM and FUNCTION

A. Overview

Verb forms ending in *-ing* or *-ed* often function as adjectives to modify nouns or pronouns. They often express emotions or feelings.	This is a **boring** class. I'm **frightened** of snakes.

B. *-ing* or *-ed*?

1. The *-ing* adjective modifies the word that causes the emotion. It describes what the noun or pronoun **does**.	It was an **interesting** show. (The show interested me.)
2. The *-ed* adjective modifies the word that experiences the emotion. It describes what the noun or pronoun **feels**.	We were **interested**. (We felt interest.)
-ed forms are often followed by prepositional phrases. (See Appendix 18 for a list of *-ing/-ed* forms and of prepositions following *-ed* forms.)	I'm **interested** in travel. She was **amazed** at the beauty of the park. Many people are **frightened** of snakes.

GRAMMAR **HOT**SPOT!

Remember! *-ing* and *-ed* adjectives have different meanings. If something is *-ing* to a person, the person is *-ed*.	The news was **surprising** to me. I was **surprised**.

Adjectives Ending in *-ing* and *-ed*

5 Meaning of *-ing/-ed* Adjectives: Home on the Range

Listen to the lecture about cowboys' lives in the nineteenth century. Write the words you hear, using the correct forms from the box.

boring/bored	exhausting/exhausted	✓ inspiring/inspired
confused/confusing	fascinating/fascinated	terrifying/terrified
exciting/excited	frightening/frightened	tiring/tired

In the nineteenth century, many young men from the East felt __*inspired*_____
₁

after they read about cowboy adventures in popular magazines. These magazines told

_____ stories about life on the Western cattle trails. The young men
₂

came to Texas, looking for the same _____ adventures. Other cowboys
₃

had been soldiers in the Civil War from 1861 to 1865 and came West to escape from its

_____ memories.
₄

In fact, life on the trail was sometimes very _____. The cowboys were
₅

always very _____ by the end of the day. On the cattle trails, cowboys often
₆

worked for 16 _____ hours every day.
₇

In the early morning roundup, cowboys gathered their cows together for the cattle drive along

the trail. Cattle needed a lot of attention. Sometimes locoweed, a bad grass, made the cows

crazy and _____. Sometimes loud storms upset them, and the
₈

_____ animals ran away. Occasionally, thousands ran away in a
₉

stampede. This meant more work for the _____ cowboys.
₁₀

But most days were long and quiet, with time

to think.

inspired = filled with energy; moved to act.

Roundup

6 Using -*ed* Adjectives with Prepositional Phrases:
Buffalo Bill and the Wild West Show

Complete the sentences with correct prepositions.
More than one preposition may be possible.
Use Appendix 18 to help you.

1. William F. Cody was a buffalo hunter. But after a few
   years, he became tired __*of*_____ this job.
   He found a way to make much more money.

2. In the 1880s, people all over North America were very
   interested _____ stories about "cowboys
   and Indians." So Cody changed his name to "Buffalo
   Bill" and started his Wild West Show.

3. Bill and other cowboy actors showed off their
   horse-riding skills. City audiences were amazed
   _____ these skills.

4. One big star was Annie Oakley, a cowgirl from Ohio.
   Everyone was fascinated _____ her use
   of guns.

5. Another star was Chief Sitting Bull, a Native American from the Sioux tribe of Dakota.
   People were frightened _____ him. They knew he had attacked the U.S. army
   at the Battle of the Little Bighorn in 1876.

6. People loved to see this battle on stage. When Sitting Bull galloped in with his Indian actors,
   people became wildly excited _____ the story.

7. However, Chief Sitting Bull was almost certainly not satisfied _____ his new life
   as an actor.

8. He was probably worried _____ his tribe back in Dakota. His people were losing
   their lands and going to live on reservations.

9. But Buffalo Bill was never disappointed _____ his Wild West Show. It traveled to
   Europe and made cowboys and Indians famous forever.

---

battle = an important fight in a war. *gallop* = ride a horse very fast.

See the *Grammar Links* Website for more information and pictures about Buffalo Bill's
Wild West Show.

7 **Using -ing and -ed Adjectives:** The Black Cowboy Hall of Fame

Complete the sentences with the -ing or -ed form of the words in parentheses.

1. Until recently, African Americans didn't have a place

    in stories about the West. For Paul Stewart, this idea

    was <u>depressing</u>.
    (depress)

2. As a child, Paul Stewart had always been

    _____ in cowboys.
    (interest)

3. But he was _____ when he
    (disappoint)

    tried to play with other children. They used to say,

    "You can't be a cowboy. You're black!"

4. However, in 1960, Stewart went to Denver, Colorado,

    and heard some _____ information:
    (surprise)

    Almost half the cowboys in the nineteenth century

    West were African American!

5. Stewart decided to change people's ideas of the Wild

    West. He was _____. He
    (inspire)

    moved to Denver and opened a museum about African-American cowboys.

6. At first, the Black Cowboy Hall of Fame was not very _____.
    (excite)

    The museum contained only a few hats, guns, and clothes from African-American cowboys.

7. But now, when you go to the museum, you will see a _____ collection
    (fascinate)

    of thousands of objects.

8. You can read about African Americans like the soldiers at San Juan Hill. Theodore Roosevelt (the

    twenty-sixth president of the United States) was _____ with these
    (please)

    soldiers. They helped him win a very important battle.

9. The Black Cowboy Hall of Fame will never be as famous as Buffalo Bill's Wild West Show.

    But it is very _____. And these stories are all true!
    (interest)

 See the *Grammar Links* Website for more information about the Black Cowboy
Hall of Fame.

8 Using Adjectives: Heroes or Villains?

A. Billy the Kid and the James brothers were famous gunfighters. Many Western movies have shown them as heroes, but some people say they were villains. What do you think? Work in small groups. Read the information below. Discuss: Was Billy the Kid a hero or a villain? What about the James brothers?

> *gunfighter* = someone who lives by fighting with guns. *villain* = a bad person; the opposite of a hero.

Example: A: I think Billy the Kid was a villain. He killed a lot of people.
B: Yes, but he had a good reason.

Billy the Kid

Billy the Kid was 15 years old when he first went to prison in New Mexico. He escaped from prison several times. He killed 21 people before he died in 1881 at the age of 21. His troubles began after some bad people killed his best friend, Tunstall. Billy never rested until he killed all these villains. But Billy loved his friends, and he always stayed near home. He spoke respectfully to everyone, especially women. Everyone who knew him loved him and thought he was a hero—even Pat Garrett. Garrett was the sheriff who finally killed Billy, his old friend. Garrett said about Billy, "His face always wore a smile. He ate and laughed, talked and laughed—and killed and laughed."

The James Brothers

The James brothers came from Missouri. Frank James loved to study books. Jesse James cared a lot about religion. Both brothers were soldiers and heroes in the Civil War. But after the war, they became the first famous bank robbers. Between 1866 and 1881, they stole about half a million dollars from banks and trains, mostly in the state of Missouri. At this time, many people in Missouri were very poor. They did not like bankers because these rich people did not help them to keep their farms after the war. The James brothers also came from a poor farm. So for many Missourians, the James brothers were heroes.

> *sheriff* = a type of police officer. *robber* = someone who steals.

B. Write a paragraph about either Billy the Kid or the James brothers. Write at least five sentences. Describe the gunfighter(s) and your opinion about them. Use words from the lists below to modify nouns in your sentences.

Adjectives	Nouns as Adjectives	*-Ing/-ed* Forms
happy	bank	amazing/amazed
religious	war	disgusting/disgusted
friendly	train	interested/interesting
serious	farm	depressing/depressed
intelligent	New Mexico	fascinating/fascinated
popular	town	shocking/shocked
polite		
excellent		
dangerous		

Example: Billy the Kid was a popular New Mexico gunman. He did some shocking things. I think he was a villain. . . .
OR
The James brothers were war heroes and excellent soldiers. . . .

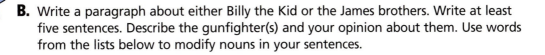 See the *Grammar Links* Website for a complete model paragraph for this assignment.

See the *Grammar Links* Website for more information and pictures about Billy the Kid, Jesse James, and other famous gunfighters of the West.

9 Using Adjectives: A Special Place

A. Think of a perfect place—wild or peaceful—that you like very much. Write six sentences to describe this place. Use adjectives to modify nouns.

Example: I'm thinking of a very large, exciting place. Sometimes it looks dark blue under the sun. . . .

See the *Grammar Links* Website for a complete model description for this assignment.

 B. Share your description with the class. Can your classmates guess where your place is?

> **Check your progress! Go to the Self-Test for Chapter 13 on the *Grammar Links* Website.**

14

Comparison with Adjectives and Adverbs

Introductory Task: Do You Believe?

Many people believe these "facts" about animals in the American Southwest. Some are true, some are partly true, and some are false.

A. Work with a partner. Circle the number of each sentence you both believe.(You will find the correct answers later in Exercise 1.)

Jackelope and Antelope

1. Jackelopes have horns like antelopes. They are as big as horses.

2. Tourists see jackelopes less frequently than cowboys do.

3. Cowboys ride jackelopes as easily as they ride horses.

Coyote

4. Coyotes are bigger than some dogs.

5. Coyotes are much less friendly than dogs.

6. Coyotes sing to the moon as sadly as a cowboy in love.

7. The roadrunner doesn't fly as fast as other birds.

8. The roadrunner isn't as strong as a rattlesnake.

Rattlesnake and Roadrunner

9. Rattlesnakes are more dangerous than other snakes.

10. The gila monster smells worse than bad meat and is much more dangerous!

B. Discuss as a class: In your opinion, which Southwestern animal in Part A is the strangest? Which is the most attractive? Which is the least attractive?

Gila Monster

As . . . as with Adjectives and Adverbs

FORM and FUNCTION

A. Overview

1. *As . . . as* is used to make comparisons—to show how two ideas are similar.

   I'm driving **as fast as** you are.

   Not as . . . as shows how two ideas are not similar.

   Dogs are **not as big as** horses.

2. *As . . . as* with adjectives compares two nouns (persons, places, things or ideas).

   noun   noun
   Beth is **as tall as Liz.**
   noun   noun
   Dogs aren't **as big as horses.**

3. *As . . . as* with adverbs compares two verbs (actions or situations).

   verb   verb
   Dogs don't **run as fast as** horses (**run**).

4. Adverbs commonly used with *as . . . as* include *just* and *nearly*. These adverbs emphasize the similarity or nonsimilarity.

   Beth is **just** as tall as you.
   Dogs don't run **nearly** as fast as horses.

B. Comparisons with *as . . . as*

	VERB	(ADVERB)	*AS*		*AS*	
Beth	**is**	(**just**) (**nearly**)	as	**tall**	as	you.
Dogs	**don't run**			**fast**		horses.
She	**speaks**			**clearly**		she writes.

C. *As . . . as* + Verb

1. The part of the comparison that follows *as . . . as* sometimes includes a verb.

   Beth is as tall as you **are.**

2. When the second verb is the same as the first, it may be replaced by an auxiliary verb (for example, *do*).

   Dogs don't run as fast as horses **run.** OR
     Dogs don't run as fast as horses **do.**

   I'm driving as fast as you **are driving.** OR
     I'm driving as fast as you **are.**

(continued on next page)

TALKING THE TALK

In formal English, use subject pronouns after *as . . . as.* In informal English, use object pronouns.	**FORMAL**	**INFORMAL**
	She is as tall as **I.**	She is as tall as **me.**

GRAMMAR PRACTICE 1

As . . . as with Adjectives and Adverbs

1   *As . . . as* with Adjectives and Adverbs: **Tall Tales or Truth?**

A. Tall tales are untrue stories told as jokes. Find out which "facts" are really tall tales in the Introductory Task on page 252. Complete these sentences with *as . . . as* and the words in parentheses.

Jackelope

1. Jackelope stories are tall tales! Jackelopes <u>are not as real as</u>
(not / are / real)

   they seem in the tourist stores.

2. Tourists *think* they _____
   (not / see jackelopes / frequently)

   cowboys do. Cowboys don't see jackelopes, either; jackelopes are not real! Cowboys see them

   in their imagination. Tourists never see them!

3. You can _____ you want in the Southwest.
   (look / hard)

   You won't see a cowboy riding a jackelope. Jackelopes don't exist!

4. Yes, a coyote _____ a medium-size dog.
   (is / big)

5. Coyotes _____ most
   (not / are / nearly / friendly)

   dogs. In fact, they are wild.

6. I don't know if coyotes fall in love! But when they're hungry, they

   _____ any other animal.
   (act / strangely)

7. The roadrunner is very slow. It _____
   (not / fly / nearly / well)

   other birds.

8. Yes, the roadrunner _____ a rattlesnake. It
   (just / strong)

   can eat a rattlesnake.

9. Rattlesnakes are dangerous, but they _____
   (not / kill people / often)

   some other snakes.

10. Yes, the gila monster smells and looks terrible. But smelling a gila monster

    _____ eating bad meat!
    (not / is / nearly / bad)

---

wild = not used to living with or near humans.

B. Work as a class. Look again at the Introductory Task on page 252. Discuss: Which "facts" are tall tales? Which are true? How many did you guess correctly before?

2 Listening to *as . . . as*: Route 66

🎧 Gregory Graystone is a travel expert. Listen to his report and write the words you hear. Write a dash (—) in the blanks where there are no words.

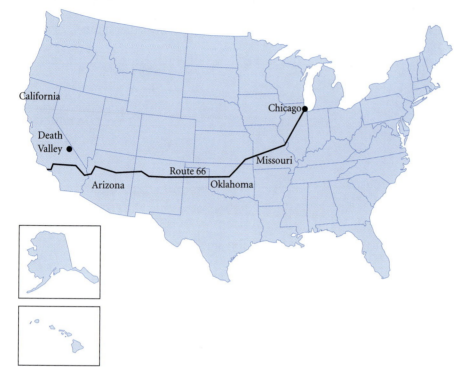

Here we are on Route 66. Come with us along this famous highway from Chicago to California.

When the mapmakers named this highway in 1926, it wasn't as popular _as it is_ today.
                                                                      1

But then people didn't travel nearly as comfortably _____ now, and they certainly didn't
                                                          2

travel as safely _____. The first travelers were poor Oklahoma farmers, escaping the
                       3

terrible dry dust storms of the 1930s. On the road west, they looked for work. But everyone else

needed food and work just as badly _____ did. Some of these "Okies" arrived safely in
                                          4

California. Others weren't as lucky _____. They died along the road.
                                          5

But now Route 66 means freedom and adventure for travelers. The country you see from this road

is as exciting as anyplace in the world _____. Just west of Chicago, the plains are just as
                                              6

flat and wide as a huge pancake _____. If you drive as slowly _____,
                                      7   8

you'll take a long time to cross them! In Missouri, see the Meramec Caverns. The famous James

brothers used to hide there after they robbed banks and trains. Luckily, these caverns aren't as

dangerous now _____. And farther west, in Oklahoma, the land isn't as dry as
                     9

_____ in the 1930s—now, they say, the corn is "as high as an elephant's eye"
     10

_____!
     11

Soon, we reach the mountains. Route 66 doesn't climb as sharply as some other mountain roads

_____, but you will see wonderful desert views here. In Arizona, the Grand Canyon
     12

looks nearly as deep as the center of the earth _____, and in Death Valley, California,
                                                       13

the desert floor is as low as a seabed _____.
                                          14

3 **More Sentences with *as . . . as*:** Jackelopes and Antelopes

 Jackelopes are imaginary animals. They are similar to antelopes in some ways, but they are not similar in others. Read the information below. Write five or six sentences comparing jackelopes and antelopes. Use *as . . . as* with adjectives and adverbs.

Similarities

Both hear very well.
Both are about four feet tall.
Their horns are long and sharp.
Both can jump about 27 feet high.
Both are wild and shy.

Jackelope   Antelope

Differences

The jackelope:	*The antelope:*
eats a lot	doesn't eat much
fights often (when frightened)	hardly ever fights
ears: long	ears: short
vision: sees normally	vision: sees very well
Speed: 30–35 mph	speed: up to 60 mph

Example: The jackelope hears as well as the antelope. But it doesn't see as well.

See the *Grammar Links* Website for a complete model paragraph for this assignment.

See the *Grammar Links* Website for more information about and pictures of jackelopes, antelopes, and other animals.

Comparative Adjectives and Adverbs

FORM and FUNCTION

A. Overview

1. Comparative adjectives describe how two nouns (persons, places, things, or ideas) are different.

   noun   noun
   Dogs are **bigger than cats.**

2. Comparative adverbs describe how two verbs (actions or situations) are different.

   verb   verb
   Dogs **run faster than** cats (**run**).

3. *-Er* and *more* mean "greater in size, amount, or degree." *Less* means "not as great in size, amount, or degree."

   Lions are **more dangerous than** cats.
   I write **less quickly than** I read.

4. To form comparative adjectives and adverbs, add *-er* to short words. Place *more* in front of longer words.

   Lions are **bigger** and **more dangerous** than cats.

   (See Appendix 19 for more information on the use of *-er* and *more*.)
   (See Appendix 19 for spelling rules for *-er* forms.)

B. Comparatives with *-er*

	ADJECTIVE/ADVERB + *-ER*	*THAN*	
Dogs are	**bigger**	**than**	cats.
Dogs run	**faster**		

C. Comparatives with *More/Less*

	MORE/LESS	ADJECTIVE/ADVERB	*THAN*	
Lions are	**more**	**dangerous**	**than**	cats.
I write	**less**	**quickly**		I read.

D. Comparatives + Verb

1. The part of the comparison that follows *than* sometimes includes a verb.

   Dogs are bigger than cats **are.**

2. When the second verb is the same as the first, it may be replaced by an auxiliary verb (for example, *do*).

   Dogs run faster than cats **run.** OR Dogs run faster than cats **do.**

   I'm eating more slowly than you **are eating.** OR I'm eating more slowly than you **are.**

(continued on next page)

E. Quantifiers with Comparative Adjectives and Adverbs

Quantifiers and measure words are often used with comparatives. The intensifier *very* is not used. (See Chapter 9 for more information on quantifiers and measure words.)	She works **much/a lot** faster than he does. **NOT:** She works ~~very~~ faster than he does.

F. Short Form of Comparatives

When the meaning is clear, *than* and the following part of the comparison are optional.	June is shorter than May. It is also warmer **than May.** OR It is also **warmer**. I get up earlier than you. And I go to bed later **than you.** OR And I go to bed **later**.

GRAMMAR **HOT**SPOT!

1. Some adjectives and adverbs have irregular comparative forms.

   The road is **worse** than that road.
   NOT: This road is ~~badder~~ than that road.

ADJECTIVE	ADVERB	COMPARATIVE
good	well	**better**
bad	badly	**worse**
far	far	**farther**

2. Be careful! Form comparatives correctly.

   Asia is **bigger than** Australia.
   NOT: Asia is ~~more~~ bigger than Australia.

   I work **more slowly** at night.
   NOT: I work ~~slowlier~~ at night.

Comparative Adjectives and Adverbs

4 Comparative Adjectives and Adverbs: Form Practice

A. Write the comparative form of the adjectives and adverbs in the correct column. Use Grammar Briefing 2 and Appendix 19 for help.

✓ beautiful	dry	friendly	often	well
✓ clear	easily	high	polite	
closely	far	honest	populated	
crowded	freely	intelligent	quickly	
difficult	frequently	✓ lovely	Spanish	

-ER THAN	*MORE THAN*	*-ER THAN* OR *MORE THAN*
clearer than	more beautiful than	lovelier than OR more lovely than

B. Are there any words in Part A that you don't know? Circle them. Then work with a partner. Find the meanings of the words in a dictionary.

5 Comparative Adjective and Adverb Forms: The Pueblo

Complete the passage with comparative forms of the adjectives and adverbs in parentheses. Use *more* or *-er than* when you see a plus sign (+). Use *less than* when you see a minus sign (–).

Route 66 takes you to northern New Mexico. New Mexico feels <u>more Spanish than</u>

1 (+ Spanish)

other parts of the United States because, in the nineteenth century, Mexico extended

_____ it does now and included this area. *Pueblo* is a Spanish word
2 (+ far)

meaning "village" and also "people." The Pueblo tribes come from the area along the Rio Grande.

Pueblo Building

There, the land is _____ the desert nearby. Many Pueblo still live in

their villages, which are much _____ the towns around them. Pueblo

buildings are also _____ most New Mexico buildings. This is because

the villages used to be _____ they are today, and the people lived

together _____ Americans do now.

    The Pueblo tribes learned about horses from Spanish soldiers, but they rode

_____ their Native American neighbors, the Apache tribe. The Apache

were buffalo hunters and needed horses. With horses, they could travel _____

they could before, and they grew tired _____ the buffalo. In contrast,

the Pueblo were farmers. They stayed in one place, and they met the Spanish

_____ the Apache did. Many Pueblo are still farmers today and speak

Spanish _____ than the Apache.

3 (– dry)
4 (– modern)
5 (+ tall)
6 (+ populated)
7 (+ closely)
8 (– often)
9 (+ freely)
10 (– quickly)
11 (+ frequently)
12 (+ easily)

> *Rio Grande* = a long river (the Spanish name means "big river") that runs from
> Colorado to the Gulf of Mexico.

---

6   Quantifiers and Measure Words with Comparatives: The Grand Canyon

A reporter is interviewing Bob Brown, a Park Service interpreter at the Grand Canyon
National Park. Complete the interview with the words in parentheses. Use *more* or *-er
than* when you see a plus sign (+). Use *less than* when you see a minus sign (–).

Interviewer: How old is the Grand Canyon?

Bob: Well, the rocks are _a few million years older than_ you or me! The top layers are

1 (a few million years / + old)

_____ the bottom ones. As you walk

2 (much / + young)

down through the canyon, you can see rocks from 250 million to two billion years old.

So you can travel through time here _____

3 (a little / + easily)

you can in other places.

Interviewer: Which side of the canyon is more interesting?

Bob: The North Rim is _____ the South Rim.
4 (a lot / – crowded)

But I don't think it's _____ other parts
5 (– beautiful)

of the canyon. It's about _____ the
6 (1,200 feet/ + high)

South Rim. And you can see _____ you
7 (many miles / + far)

can from the other side. Personally, I think it's _____
8 (a little / + lovely)

_____ the South Rim.

Interviewer: Is the northern trail _____ the
9 (much / + difficult)

southern trails?

Bob: Not really. The North Kaibab Trail is about _____
10 (five miles / + long)

the Bright Angel Trail, which is on the south side. But it's easier than the

South Kaibab Trail.

Interviewer: What's it like at the bottom of the canyon?

Bob: Hot! In May, the temperature at the top is about 70 degrees Fahrenheit. At the bottom, it

sometimes gets _____ that. But you can
11 (40 degrees / + high)

always step into the Colorado River. That's always _____
12 (a great deal / + cold)

the land around it.

> *interpreter* = someone who explains things.

TALKING THE TALK

In formal English, use subject pronouns after comparatives. In informal English, use object pronouns.	FORMAL	INFORMAL
	She runs faster than **I**.	She runs faster than **me**.

Listening to Comparatives: Horse Tales

A. Cowboys like to tell tall tales about their horses. Listen to the conversation between two cowboy actors, and write the words you hear. Write a dash (—) in the blanks where there are no words.

Cowboy 1: Hey there, pardner! What are you doing these days?

Cowboy 2: Oh, I just got back from a movie set in Death Valley with my horse, Champion.

It's hotter _than anything_ out there. I used to think the Nevada desert
                  1

was bad, but this is worse _____. How about you?
                              2

Cowboy 1: I'm doing a TV show with my horse, Fury. He's wonderful. Everyone loves him on

the set. Of course, he's friendlier than most people _____.
                                                        3

In fact, he's more polite _____!
                            4

Cowboy 2: How's that?

Cowboy 1: Well, every morning on the set, he nods his head and says good morning to everyone.

Cowboy 2: Oh, Champion's more polite _____! You know, when Champion's
                                        5

standing near a door, he always pushes it open for people.

Cowboy 1: Well, my horse behaves better _____. Why, the other day, Fury
                                          6

picked up a plate of cookies and offered it to all the actors!

Cowboy 2: Okay, but my horse is definitely more intelligent _____. When
                                                              7

other actors forget their lines, he shows them the lines on the page with his nose!

Cowboy 1: Huh. Well, reading's less difficult than writing _____. Fury writes
                                                            8

with a pencil between his teeth. He writes his name more clearly _____.
                                                                   9

Cowboy 2: Oh, any horse can do that. Now, Champion writes his own

checks. He adds up numbers more correctly than my

accountant _____! And he's a lot more
              10

honest _____.
          11

---

set = a place where people make movies.

B. Write your own tall tale about a pet or someone you know (for example, a parent or friend). In your story, write at least five sentences with comparative forms. Use your imagination!

Example: *My sister Sheila is stronger than most men, and she can run faster. She can lift much heavier things than you or I....*

See the *Grammar Links* Website for a complete model paragraph for this assignment.

C. Share your paragraph with the class. Whose tall tale is the craziest?

Superlative Adjectives and Adverbs

FORM and FUNCTION

A. Overview

1. Superlative adjectives and adverbs compare three or more things. They show which is the first or last in a group.

   Mountain Everest is **the highest mountain in the world**. (first)

   The Pacific Ocean is growing **the least quickly of all the oceans**. (last)

2. *-Est* and *most* mean "greater in size, amount, or degree" than all the other members of the group. *Least* means "smaller in size, amount, or degree" than all the other members of the group.

   He drives **the most carefully** of all my friends.

   Airplanes are **the least dangerous** of all forms of travel.

3. To form superlative adjectives and adverbs, add *-est* to short words. Place *most* in front of longer words.

   Mount Everest is the **highest** and **most fascinating** mountain in the world.

   (See Appendix 19 for more information on the use of *-est* and *most/least* and for spelling rules for *-est* forms.)

B. Superlatives with *-est*

	THE	ADJECTIVE/ADVERB + *-EST*	
Mexico City is	the	**largest**	city in the world.
She works		**hardest**	in the company.

(continued on next page)

C. Superlatives with *Most*

	THE	MOST/LEAST	ADJECTIVE/ADVERB	
Humans are	the	most	intelligent	of all animals.
He drives	the	least	carefully	of all my friends.

D. Superlatives and Prepositional Phrases

Prepositional phrases often follow superlative adjectives and adverbs.

Mexico City is the largest city **in the world.**

The prepositional phrase may be omitted when the meaning is clear.

I have three sisters. Melita is **the youngest of my sisters.** OR Melita is **the youngest.**

E. *One of the* + Superlative

One of the often comes before a superlative adjective. *One of the* selects one item from a superlative group.

That was **one of the** happiest days of my life.

GRAMMAR **HOT**SPOT!

1. Some adjectives and adverbs have irregular superlative forms.

   This is **the worst** road in the country.
   NOT: This is ~~the baddest~~ road in the country.

ADJECTIVE	ADVERB	COMPARATIVE	SUPERLATIVE
good	well	better	**best**
bad	badly	worse	**worst**
far	far	farther	**farthest**

2. Be careful! Form superlatives correctly.

   The Nile is **the longest** river.
   NOT: The Nile is the ~~most~~ longest river.

   He works **the most carefully.**
   NOT: He works the ~~carefullest~~.

Superlative Adjectives and Adverbs

8 **Superlative Adjective and Adverb Forms:** Superlative Game

A. Write the superlative form of the adjectives and adverbs in the correct column. Use Grammar Briefing 3 and Appendix 19 for help.

✓ active	early	hot	pretty
amazing	exciting	long	rainy
bad	far	✓ lovely	rapidly
carefully	good	painfully	worried
commonly	✓ high	pleasant	

THE . . . -EST	**THE MOST**	**THE . . . -EST OR THE MOST**
the highest	the most active	the loveliest OR the most lovely

B. Are there any words in Part A that you don't know? Circle them. Then work with a partner. Find the meanings of the words in a dictionary.

C. Play *tic-tac-toe* as a class.

Step 1 In each box in the chart below, write one superlative form from the list in Part A.

Step 2 One student calls out words from the list in Part A. Everyone else matches the words with their superlative forms. Cross out each form that matches. When you have crossed out three words in a row, either up (|), across (—), or diagonally (/), raise your hand. The first person to raise his or her hand wins.

9 **Superlative Adjectives and Adverbs:** Trivia Quiz

Work with a partner. Try to guess the facts. Complete the quiz with the superlative forms of the words in parentheses. Use *the most* or *the . . . -est* when you see a plus sign (+). Use *the least* when you see a minus sign (–). Circle the subject that you think is correct. You can find the answers at the bottom of this page.

1. (California / New York) has <u>the highest</u> population in the United States.
    (+ high)

2. (Hollywood / India) has the _____ film industry in the world.
    (+ active)

3. The (gila monster in Arizona / Komodo dragon in Indonesia)

    smells _____ of all lizards.
    (– pleasant)

4. (California redwoods / Alaskan spruce) grow _____ of
    (– rapidly)

    all trees in the world.

5. The (California bristle cone / African teak) lives _____ of all
    (+ long)

    trees in the world.

6. The (American antelope / African cheetah) runs

    _____ of all   Cheetah
    (+ far)

    high-speed animals.

7. (Death Valley in California / The Atacama in Chile) recorded _____
    (+ hot)

    temperatures of all time in the western hemisphere.

8. Chili peppers from (California / Madras, India) burn _____
    (+ painfully)

    of all spices in the world.

9. A museum in (New Mexico / Perth, Australia) has _____
    (+ large)

    dinosaur in the world.

10. (Summer / Winter) is the _____ season in the southwestern
    (– rainy)

    desert.

1. California 2. India 3. The gila monster 4. Alaskan spruce 5. California bristle cone 6. American antelope 7. Death Valley in California 8. California 9. New Mexico 10. Winter

hemisphere = half the world.

10 Superlative Adjectives and Adverbs with Prepositional Phrases: Trigger, the Superhorse

Read the article. Complete the sentences with the superlative forms of the words in parentheses. Use *the most* or *the -est* when you see a plus sign (+). Use *the least* when you see a minus sign (–). Underline the prepositional phrases that complete the superlatives.

The road between Death Valley and Hollywood isn't __the prettiest__
                                                              1 (+ pretty)
section __of Route 66_____. Maybe it's one of

_____ parts of southern California—except for
        2 (– exciting)
one town: Victorville. Until recently, Victorville was the home of the Roy Rogers Museum.

Roy Rogers was a cowboy actor in the 1930s, during _____
                                                              3 (+ early)
days of Hollywood. His horse, Trigger, is probably _____
                                                              4 (+ popular)
horse of all time. I'm sure Trigger studied his acting parts _____
                                                              5 (– carefully)
of all actors, but he was still one of _____ stars in
                                       6 (+ good)
Hollywood. With his long, white tail and golden body, people thought he was

_____ animal under the Western sun. But Trigger's
        7 (+ lovely)
intelligence was _____ thing about him. He could count up
                     8 (+ amazing)
to 25 by waving his foot in the air. He performed this

_____ of all his tricks.
        9 (+ commonly)
When Trigger died, Roy Rogers put his body in the

Victorville museum. Just recently, the museum moved to

Branson, Missouri. The owners hope to attract more visitors

there, but this will be _____
                          10 (+ bad)
loss for Victorville in a long time. However, Trigger won't

mind where he lives—he's probably _____
                                       11 (– worried)
of anyone!

See the *Grammar Links* Website for more information about and pictures of Trigger, Roy Rogers, and the museum.

Check your progress! Go to the Self-Test for Chapter 14 on the *Grammar Links* Website.

Wrap-up Activities

1 **The Clever Coyote:** EDITING

Correct the errors in this student essay. There are 15 errors with both adjectives and comparisons with adjectives and adverbs. The first error is corrected for you.

The Clever Coyote

Some old Native American stories say coyotes are the ~~most~~ smartest animals in the world. One story says coyotes created humans! Here is the story.

At one time, all the animals made some carefully plans to create humans. These plans seemed quite well, but the coyote was less happier than the others with them. So during the night, he got up and destroyed the plans complete. He made new, more good plans by himself. He gave humans a clever coyote new brain. And so, today, human minds are clever, quick, sharp — in fact, as intelligent than coyote minds!

Ranchers and farmers are often disgusted of coyotes because they kill their animals. However, tourists are fascinating by coyotes. In New Mexico gifts shops, you can buy friendly souvenir coyotes. Cowboys say that coyotes sing to the moon, and you can hear their song the most clearest in the desert late at night: "Yip-yip-yip-ooooohh!" The song sounds sadly and lonely. Perhaps the coyotes remember a happyer time from millions of years ago.

create = make something out of nothing. *souvenir* = an object you can buy as a gift or to remember a place.

2 Definitions: SPEAKING

Work in small groups. Sit in a circle.

Step 1 On a piece of paper, write a word you have used in this unit (for example, *frightened*, *mountain*).

Step 2 Pass your paper to your neighbor.

Step 3 Your neighbor tries to define the word without using the word. The other members of the group guess what the word is. Use adjectives and comparisons with adjectives and adverbs in your definitions.

Examples: It's a feeling—something like excited but much worse. You feel this way when you see something very, very dangerous. (= frightened)

It's a high piece of land you see in states such as New Mexico. (= mountain)

3 A Trip to the West: WRITING/SPEAKING

Step 1 Imagine you have a week's vacation and a free plane ticket to anywhere in the West. Where will you go? How will you travel when you get there? What will you see? How will you spend your time? Use adjectives and comparisons with adjectives and adverbs to describe your vacation. Write at least six sentences.

Example: I'm going to Arizona. I'm going to stay on a vacation ranch and work as hard as the cowboys. . . .

See the *Grammar Links* Website for a complete model paragraph for this activity.

Step 2 Share your description with the whole class. As a class, vote for the most exciting trip and explain why you chose it.

4 A Superlative Group: SPEAKING

Step 1 Work with a partner. Answer these questions together.

1. How tall are you? Who is taller?
2. How often do you travel? Who travels more often?
3. How well do you cook? Who cooks better?
4. Which of you has a more unusual hobby? What is it?
5. What is the strangest thing in your home? Who has a stranger thing?
6. Ask three more questions of your own.

Step 2 Work in small groups of three or more. Compare your answers from Step 1. Make a "Superlative Group" list. Report back to the whole class.

Example: Superlative Group List

Jahan travels the most often in our group. She visits her country three times every year.

Li He has the strangest thing. It's a pet snake!

The Present Perfect

TOPIC FOCUS
Science—Fact and Fiction

UNIT OBJECTIVES

- **the present perfect tense**
  (They *have lived* in Texas for 20 years.)

- **choosing between the present perfect and the simple past**
  (They *have lived* in Texas for 20 years. Before that, they *lived* in California.)

- **the present perfect progressive tense**
  (I *have been reading* all day.)

- **choosing between the present perfect and the present perfect progressive**
  (I *have been reading* all day. I *have read* two books about Mars.)

Grammar in Action

🎧 Reading and Listening: Fact and Fiction

Read and listen.

A fact is something true. Fiction is something that is not true. And we all know the difference between the two. Or do we? For centuries, science-fiction writers **have been telling** stories about fact and fiction. They **have been writing** "odd" and "unbelievable" fiction about the future. But are their stories always really fiction?

In the early 1930s, science-fiction writers predicted the invention of robots. Everyone laughed at this "fiction." But now robots are a part of life; science fiction **has become** science fact.

Sometimes science "fact" **has changed** to science fiction, too! Since ancient times, scientists **have been looking** for facts. They **have been studying** everything in the world around us, and **they have been searching** for facts in the sky above us. Scientific study **has been helping** us learn important facts about ourselves and our world.

But scientists **have** also **made** some mistakes. For thousands of years, they believed an important "fact": The earth was the center of the universe. We now know that this science "fact" is really science fiction. Astronomers **have shown** that the earth is not the center of the universe.

So what are the facts today? And what is fiction? It isn't always easy to know.

universe = the space around us. *astronomer* = a scientist who studies the universe.

Think About Grammar

A. Look at the **boldfaced** verbs in the passage. Circle **T** if the statement is true and **F** if the statement is false.

1. There is a form of *have* in all of these verbs. T   F

2. There is a form of *be* in all of these verbs. T   F

3. Each **boldfaced** main verb ends in *-ing*. T   F

B. Write the boldfaced verbs from the passage in the chart.

have/has + a form of the main verb	*have/has* + *been* + main verb + *-ing*
Present Perfect Tense	Present Perfect Progressive Tense
has become	have been telling

Chapter 15

Present Perfect Tense; Present Perfect Versus Simple Past

Introductory Task: Science-Fiction Stories

A. Read the paragraphs.

1. Space travel **has fascinated** people since ancient times. Science-fiction writers **have written** many stories about space travel. However, space travel isn't science fiction anymore. It **has become** "science fact." Humans **have traveled** in space. We **have** even **lived** in space for months at a time. Our space adventures are just beginning.

2. In the past, people **believed** in dragons. In 1790, Sir Francis Larkin **wrote** a story about a fire-breathing dragon. This dragon **destroyed** several villages before someone **killed** it. In the early 1900s, Otis Kline also **wrote** stories about dragons. In his stories, some dragons **were** good and some **were** evil.

evil = bad; wicked.

B. Look at the **boldfaced** verbs in paragraph 1. Write them here. _____

_____

These verbs are in the **present perfect tense.** They describe things that began in the past, continue in the present, and might continue in the future.

Look at the **boldfaced** verbs in paragraph 2. Write them here. _____

_____

What is the tense of these verbs? _____

Do they describe things that began in the past, continue in the present, and might continue in

the future? _____

C. Discuss as a class: Do you like science fiction? Have you ever read a science-fiction story about space travel? Have you ever watched science-fiction movies? Which ones? Have you ever heard stories about dragons or other strange animals?

GRAMMAR BRIEFING 1

Present Perfect Tense I

FORM

A. Statements

AFFIRMATIVE STATEMENTS

SUBJECT	HAVE/HAS	PAST PARTICIPLE OF MAIN VERB
I		
You	**have**	
We	**'ve**	**traveled.**
They		
He		
She	**has**	**eaten.**
It	**'s**	

NEGATIVE STATEMENTS

SUBJECT	HAVE NOT/ HAS NOT	PAST PARTICIPLE OF MAIN VERB
I		
You	**have not**	
We	**haven't**	**traveled.**
They		
He		
She	**has not**	**eaten.**
It	**hasn't**	

B. Regular and Irregular Verbs

Regular Verbs

The past participle form of regular verbs is the same as the simple past form: base verb + *-ed*.

SIMPLE PAST	PAST PARTICIPLE
travel**ed**	travel**ed**
work**ed**	work**ed**

Irregular Verbs

Many common verbs have irregular past participle forms.

(See Appendix 6 for more irregular verbs.)

eat → **eaten**, begin → **begun**, go → **gone**, put → **put**

GRAMMAR HOTSPOT!

Be careful! The contraction for both *is* and *has* is *'s*. Do not confuse them.

He**'s** here. = He **is** here.

He**'s** been here for five days. = He **has** been here for five days.

Present Perfect Tense I

1 Irregular Past Participles: Verb Forms

A. Write the past participle of these irregular verbs. Use Appendix 6 for help.

1. be _been_____

2. become _____

3. begin _____

4. come _____

5. give _____

6. go _____

7. have _____

8. make _____

9. put _____

10. see _____

11. show _____

12. teach _____

13. think _____

14. write _____

B. Write the base form of these irregular verbs. Use Appendix 6 for help.

1. brought _bring_____

2. built _____

3. chosen _____

4. eaten _____

5. felt _____

6. found _____

7. grown _____

8. known _____

9. proved/proven _____

10. told _____

11. took _____

12. shut _____

13. won _____

14. worn _____

2 Affirmative and Negative Statements: Mars Colony

A. Complete the science-fiction story with the present perfect tense of the verbs in parentheses.

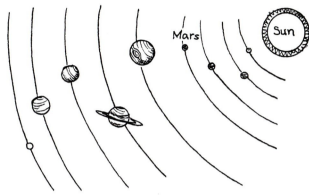

Mars Colony

It is the year 2100. There ___has been___ a human colony on Mars since the year 2050.

1 (be)

Since the colony began, it _____ quickly. It now includes 1,000 scientists

2 (grow)

and their families. David Bow is a child. He lives on Mars. David _____

3 (be)

there since he was born in 2090. David _____ a very interesting life.

4 (have)

He _____ underground all his life. He _____

5 (live)   6 (not / see)

the surface of Mars. He _____ the warmth of the sun.

7 (not / feel)

He _____ the strong Martian wind. But today everything is

8 (not / hear)

going to change. The scientists on Mars _____ the surface of the planet.

9 (change)

They have "terraformed" it—made it like Earth. They _____ Mars

10 (make)

warm enough for humans. They _____ the frozen Martian water. They

11 (melt)

_____ the oxygen in the Martian air. They _____

12 (increase)   13 (build)

sheltered cities. Now, everything is ready. Now David can move to the surface of Mars. Finally, he

will have the chance to see the evening star—Earth—rise and set in the Martian sky.

> *colony* = group of people who settle in a distant place. *surface* = the outside.
> *sheltered* = protected.

B. Discuss as a class: This is a science-fiction story. Or is it? What do you think? Will humans live on Mars? Will this science fiction ever become science fact?

	WRITING	SPEAKING
In speaking, contractions of *have* (*'ve*) and *has* (*'s*) are common.	They **have gone** to school.	They**'ve gone** to school.
	Chuck **has gone** to school.	Chuck**'s gone** to school.
	What has happened?	**What's** happened?

3 **Affirmatives, Negatives, and Contractions:** Science Fiction or Science Fact?

A. Isaac Asimov was a famous science-fiction writer. In the 1900s, he predicted the future. Here are some of his predictions. Have they come true? What do you think? Write an affirmative or a negative sentence for each prediction. Use the present perfect tense.

1. Paper money will begin to disappear.

   Paper money has begun to disappear.

2. Humans will clone other animals.

   _____

3. Everyone will learn the same language.

   _____

4. People will live on the moon.

   _____

5. There will be "bionic" men and women—humans with artificial body parts.

   _____

clone = copy. *artificial* = not natural; mechanical.

B. A scientist of today is talking about Asimov's predictions. Listen and write the full forms of the contractions you hear. (Some contractions are for *is* or *are*. Other contractions are for *has* or *have*.)

Many of Isaac Asimov's predictions about the future _____have come_____ true.

$\underset{1}{}$

Others are still science fiction.

Prediction One: For several years, we _____ electronic banking.

$\underset{2}{}$

It _____ an influence on all of us. What

$\underset{3}{}$

_____? Paper money

$\underset{4}{}$

_____ to disappear.

$\underset{5}{}$

Prediction Two: What _____ you _____ about cloning? Scientists

$\underset{6}{}$

_____ frogs and other small creatures. One scientist

$\underset{7}{}$

_____ good luck with sheep, too! What's next?

$\underset{8}{}$

Prediction Three: Asimov predicted one language for all people. But this prediction

_____ true. Everyone _____

$\underset{9}{}$ $\underset{10}{}$

the same language. At least, not so far!

Prediction Four: We _____ to start colonies on the moon, but we

$\underset{11}{}$

_____ successful. This prediction

$\underset{12}{}$

_____ still science fiction. Will it become fact someday?

$\underset{13}{}$

Prediction Five: And what about bionic men and women? Doctors _____

$\underset{14}{}$

success with this idea. They _____ people artificial

$\underset{15}{}$

arms and legs. At least one patient _____ an artificial

$\underset{16}{}$

heart for a long time, too. Are these people bionic?

Present Perfect Tense II

FORM

A. Yes/No Questions and Short Answers

QUESTIONS

HAVE/HAS	SUBJECT	PAST PARTICIPLE OF MAIN VERB
Have	I you we they	**eaten?**
Has	he she it	**traveled?**

SHORT ANSWERS

YES			NO		
Yes,	I you we they	**have.**	No,	I you we they	**have not.** **haven't.**
	he she it	**has.**		he she it	**has not.** **hasn't.**

B. Wh- Questions and Answers

Wh- Questions About the Subject

QUESTIONS

WH- WORD	HAVE/HAS	PAST PARTICIPLE OF MAIN VERB	
Who	**has**	**gone**	to school?
What	**has**	**happened?**	

ANSWERS

John has.
Nothing.

Other Wh- Questions

QUESTIONS

WH- WORD	HAVE/HAS	SUBJECT	PAST PARTICIPLE OF MAIN VERB	
Who(m)	**have**	you	**talked**	to recently?
How long	**has**	she	**lived**	here?
How often	**have**	they	**been**	to France?

ANSWERS

My mother.
For 20 years.
Several times.

Present Perfect Tense II

4 *Yes/No* **Questions and Short Answers:** Asimov's Predictions

A. Write *yes/no* questions and short answers about the predictions discussed in Exercise 3. Use the present perfect tense and the words in parentheses.

1. (scientists/clone animals)

   Q: Have scientists cloned animals? _____

   A: Yes, they have. _____

2. (paper money/begin to disappear)

   Q: _____

   A: _____

3. (all people/start speaking the same language)

   Q: _____

   A: _____

4. (people/live on the moon)

   Q: _____

   A: _____

5. (doctors/make bionic body parts)

   Q: _____

   A: _____

6. (Isaac Asimov/predict many facts about today)

   Q: _____

   A: _____

B. Discuss as a class: Do you think all people will speak the same language someday? Why or why not? Do you think people will live on the moon someday? Why or why not?

5 *Wh-* Questions and Answers: More About Isaac Asimov

Imagine that the year is 1991, and you are interviewing Isaac Asimov. Write *wh-* questions and answers with the words given. Write complete sentences. Use the present perfect tense.

Issac Asimov

1. Q: You were born in Russia. How long/you/live in the United States?

   How long have you lived in the United States?

   A: I/live/in the United States for 70 years.

   I've lived in the United States for 70 years.

2. Q: What other jobs/you/have? _____

   _____

   A: I/have several other jobs. _____

   _____

3. Q: How often/you/change jobs? _____

   _____

   A: I/change jobs many times. _____

   But now writing is my full-time job.

4. Q: How many books/you/write? _____

   A: I/write/350 books. _____

5. Q: What/help you write so many books? _____

   A: I/love books all my life. _____

6. Q: Who/write books with you? _____

   A: My friend Arthur C. Clarke/write books with me. _____

   _____

7. Q: Who/influence your writing career? _____

   _____

   A: There isn't just one person. Everyone/influence me. _____

   _____

Present Perfect Tense III

FUNCTION

A. Past Continuing to Present

The present perfect often describes actions or states that **began in the past**, **continue into the present**, and **might continue into the future**.

| He **has lived** in Detroit for 10 years. (He began living there in the past and continues to live there now; he might continue to live there in the future.) |

PAST —— NOW ▼ —— FUTURE
has lived

For and *Since* with the Present Perfect

We often use *for* or *since* with the present perfect to express "past continuing to the present." Time expressions with *for* and *since* can come at the beginning or at the end of a sentence:

- *For* tells how long a period of time has lasted.

  He has lived here **for** 20 years. (The period of time = 20 years long.)

- *Since* tells when a period of time began.

  Since 1989, he has lived in Detroit. (He began living there in 1989.)

- *Since* can introduce a time clause. The verb in the time clause is usually in the simple past tense.

  time clause
  I have loved him **since I met** him.

(See Chapters 5 and 7 for more information about time clauses.)

B. The Indefinite Past

1. The present perfect often describes actions or states **completed at an indefinite (unspecified) time** in the past. The exact time is not important or is not known.

   I **have read** that book. (The action is completed; we don't know the specific day or time.)

PAST —— NOW ▼ —— FUTURE
have read

2. Indefinite actions in the present perfect are often **repeated** actions.

   I have eaten at that restaurant **five times**.

PAST —— NOW ▼ —— FUTURE
have eaten

Present Perfect Tense III

6 **Present Perfect Tense-Function:** News from Mars

Mars Probe

A. Read the first sentence. Then check (✓) the sentence that you know is true.

1. For centuries, humans have dreamed about traveling to Mars.

    ☑ a. Humans began dreaming about traveling to Mars centuries ago.

    ❑ b. Humans don't dream about traveling to Mars these days.

2. For many years, scientists have planned to start a human colony on Mars.

    ❑ a. Scientists began planning a human colony on Mars many years ago.

    ❑ b. Scientists are not planning a human colony on Mars.

3. Humans have tried to land on Mars.

    ❑ a. Humans tried to land on Mars, but they won't try again.

    ❑ b. Humans might try to land on Mars again someday in the future.

4. So far, 26 spaceships have traveled near Mars.

    ❑ a. Spaceships will not travel near Mars again.

    ❑ b. More spaceships will possibly travel near Mars in the future.

5. Since the 1970s, several special spaceships, or probes, have gone to Mars. They collect information and send news back to Earth.

    ❑ a. Probes began going to Mars in the 1970s.

    ❑ b. Probes stopped going to Mars in the 1970s.

7 *Since* and *For*: Sailing Through Space

Complete the article with *for* or *since*.

<u>Since</u>

1 1958, the National Aeronautics and Space Administration (NASA) has sent

thousands of spaceships into space. NASA satellites have circled the earth _____

2

decades. _____ 1964, hundreds of NASA probes (information-gathering spaceships)

3

have traveled to distant planets as well.

NASA has also sent humans into space. Two astronauts walked on the moon on July 20, 1969.

_____ then, ten more astronauts have safely gone to the moon and back.

4

_____ the past 20 years,

5

NASA astronauts have stopped traveling

to the moon. _____ they

6

discovered evidence of possible past life

on Mars, they have begun plans to go

there instead. However, today's spaceships

need a lot of heavy fuel to travel in

space—too much for a trip to Mars.

_____ many years, NASA

7

scientists have tried to build lighter

spaceships that need less fuel, but they

have not succeeded.

Walking on the Moon, 1969

Science-fiction writers have written about the problems of space travel _____ a long
₈
time. In 1963, Arthur C. Clarke wrote a story about traveling to Mars in a "solar sailboat." This sailing
spaceship was not heavy. It used only
the sun for power. _____
₉
they read this story, NASA scientists
have thought about building a solar
sailboat. Will Arthur C. Clarke's science
fiction become science fact? What do
you think?

Solar Sailboat

satellite = a machine sent into space. *evidence* = signs or indications.
fuel = something that is burned to make energy. Gasoline is a type of fuel.

See the *Grammar Links* Website for more information about space travel.

8 Questions and Answers with *Since* and *For*: About You

A. Work with a partner. Student A asks questions with *How long* and the words given.
Student B answers each question two ways: once with *for* and once with *since*.
Then switch roles.

1. be a student?

   Student A: How long have you been a student?
   Student B: I've been a student since 1998. I've been a student for several years.

2. live in this city?

3. know the teacher in this class?

4. study English?

5. (Add three questions of your own.)

B. Write about your partner. Use the answers to Part A. Use *for* and *since* in your
sentences. Then tell the class about your partner.

Example: Xio Lee has been a student for several years. . . .

9 Present Perfect Tense—Function: Amazing Creatures

A. Read the passage.

Amazing Creatures

We have all read about mythical unicorns, mermaids and mermen, sea monsters, dragons, and other creatures. But are these creatures really mythical? Some people think they are real. For example, many hikers have seen a huge, apelike monster in the mountains of the northwestern United States. They have named it Bigfoot. Hikers in Tibet have seen a very similar creature. In the United States, hundreds of people have also seen a giant sea monster. In Scotland, people have seen a similar monster. How can this be? Are these monsters real? What are the facts and what is fiction?

Loch Ness Monster

Bigfoot

Mermaid

Dragon

Unicorn

mythical = imaginary. *monster* = an imaginary creature, usually a frightening one.

B. Circle **T** if the statement is true and **F** if the statement is false.

The passage tells us these things:

1. exactly when hikers saw Bigfoot.   T   F

2. people will never see Bigfoot again in the future.   T   F

3. people saw giant sea monsters in the past.   T   F

4. people do not see sea monsters now.   T   F

Time Expressions with the Present Perfect

FORM and FUNCTION

A. *Already* and *Yet*

Already and *yet* mean "at some time before now."	I have **already** eaten.
	I have eaten **already**.
Use *yet* in negative statements and questions.	Have you eaten **yet**?
	I haven't eaten **yet**.
Already comes before the past participle or at the end of the sentence. *Yet* usually comes at the end of the sentence.	

B. *Ever* and *Never*

Ever means "at any time before now." Use it in questions and negative statements.	Have you **ever** traveled?
	I haven't **ever** traveled.
Never means "at no time before now."	I have **never** traveled.
Ever and *never* come before the past participle.	
(See Chapter 1, Grammar Briefing 3, for more information about *ever* and *never*.)	

C. *Recently* and *Just*

Recently and *just* both mean "a short time ago." *Just* means "a very short time ago."	He has **recently/just** traveled to Asia.
Recently can come at the beginning of a sentence, just before the participle, or at the end of a sentence. *Just* comes before the participle.	He has traveled to Asia **recently**.
	Recently, he has traveled to Asia.
	He has **just** eaten.

D. Time Expressions for Exact/Indefinite Number of Times

1. *Once, twice, three times,* etc., count the number of times in the indefinite past.	I have seen that movie **four times**.
2. *A few/many/several times* (*days, years,* etc.) are used for an indefinite number of times.	I have eaten in that restaurant **many times**. (I'm not sure how many times, but I've eaten there a lot.)

Remember! *Ever* and *yet* are used with the present perfect in questions and **negative** statements about indefinite time. They are not used in affirmative statements.

Have you eaten **yet**? I haven't eaten **yet**.
  NOT: I have eaten ~~yet~~.

Have you **ever** traveled? I haven't **ever** traveled.
  NOT: I have ~~ever~~ traveled.

GRAMMAR PRACTICE 4

Time Expressions with the Present Perfect

10 Position of Time Expressions: Bigfoot or Big Fake?

A. Draw arrows (↓) to mark all the correct positions for the time expressions in parentheses.

1. ↓Jack Jones has↓seen Bigfoot in the forest near Portland, Oregon.↓(recently)

2. Jack has seen this monster. (several times)

3. Jack has taken photos of Bigfoot. (already)

4. But he hasn't had his photos developed. (yet)

5. Jack has told the police about the monster. (just)

6. The police have heard many similar stories. (recently)

7. But they have seen Bigfoot. (never)

8. No one has proved the existence of Bigfoot. (ever)

 B. Discuss as a class: Is there really a Bigfoot? What do you think?

11 Time Expressions: Monsters of the Deep

Complete the paragraphs with the time expressions in the box. Use each time expression only once.

many times	never	✓ since

Have dinosaurs really disappeared from the earth? ___Since___ 1933, many people have talked
                                                         1

about a monster in Loch Ness, a lake in Scotland. They have named this monster Nessie, and they have

tried to photograph her _____. But the photos have _____
                                   2   3

been very good.

already	recently	yet

_____ , people have reported a Nessie look-alike in Lake Champlain, a lake in the
　　4

United States. They have named this monster Champ. More than 250 people have

_____ seen this monster, but nobody has proved his existence _____ .
　　5　　　　　　　　　　　　　　　　　　　　　　　　　　　　　　　　　　　6

ever	for	just

An international group of researchers has _____ begun looking for more evidence of
　　　　　　　　　　　　　　　　　　　　　　7

Nessie and Champ. _____ several months, they have searched for these creatures in
　　　　　　　　　　　　8

Loch Ness and Lake Champlain. They haven't found them, but they haven't _____
　　　　　　　　　　　　　　　　　　　　　　　　　　　　　　　　　　　　　　9

doubted that they are real.

Do you believe in sea monsters? See the *Grammar Links* Website for some interesting
theories about sea monsters like Champ and Nessie.

12 Questions and Answers with Time Expressions: Talking to a Believer

Use the words to write questions to ask someone who has seen Champ. Then use the
words in parentheses to write the person's answers. Write complete sentences. Use the
present perfect tense.

1. How long/Champ/live in Lake Champlain? (for several centuries)

   Q: *How long has Champ lived in Lake Champlain?*

   A: *He's lived in Lake Champlain for several centuries.*

2. How many times/you/see Champ? (10 times)

   Q: _____

   A: _____

3. He/ever/see you? (several times)

   Q: _____

   A: _____

   We're friends.

4. How long/Champ/be your friend? (for several years)

   Q: _____

   A: _____

5. You/see Champ/recently? (twice this week)

   Q: _____

   A: _____

6. You/take a good picture of Champ/yet? (not yet)

   Q: _____

   A: _____

7. How many times/you/try? (several times)

   Q: _____

   A: _____

   But Champ doesn't like photos. He's a very shy guy.

13 Questions and Answers with the Present Perfect: More About You

Work with a partner. Take turns asking and answering questions. Use the words given with the present perfect and *ever* in your questions. Respond with a short answer and a sentence in the present perfect. Use *ever* or *yet* in negative answers.

1. buy a car

   Question: Have you ever bought a car?
   Answer: Yes, I have. OR No, I haven't. I haven't bought one yet, but I will someday.

2. read a science-fiction story

3. travel to Mars

4. see a bionic woman or man

5. use electronic banking

6. watch a science-fiction movie

7. see a monster like Bigfoot

8. (Add three questions of your own.)

Present Perfect Versus Simple Past

FUNCTION

A. Connection to the Present

The present perfect expresses a **connection to the present**. The simple past does not.

PAST	NOW	FUTURE
has lived		

Georgina **has lived** in Texas for three years. (She still lives there now and may continue to live there in the future.)

PAST	NOW	FUTURE
lived		

Georgina **lived** in Texas for three years. (She doesn't live there now.)

B. Indefinite and Definite Past

1. For the **indefinite past**, use the present perfect or the simple past.

   She**'s lived** in France.

   She **lived** in France. (We don't know when she lived in France.)

2. For the **definite past**, use the simple past.

   I **went** to France in 1999.
   NOT: I~~'ve gone~~ to France in 1999.

TALKING THE TALK

We usually use the present perfect with *just* and *recently* to describe the recent indefinite past. Sometimes, in less formal English, we use the simple past instead. The meaning is the same.

MORE FORMAL	LESS FORMAL
I**'ve just bought** a new house.	I **just bought** a new house.
John **has recently found** a new job.	John **recently found** a new job.

Present Perfect Versus Simple Past

14 **Writing Sentences with the Simple Past and the Present Perfect:**
Angela Then and Now

A. Angela Santiago is a scientist. Read the information about her in the chart.
Complete the sentences about her past and her present. Use the simple past and
the present perfect.

In the 1970s	Since then
1. be a student	1. become a scientist
2. work in a cafe	2. work at a college and in a lab
3. believe many myths and legends	3. change her mind
4. believe in unicorns	4. learn more about them
5. believe in mermaids	5. decide they aren't real
6. see Bigfoot	6. not see him again

1. In the 1970s, _she was a student_____. Since then, _she has become a scientist_____.

2. In the summer of 1978, _____.

    Since that summer, _____.

3. During college, _____.

    Since that time, _____.

4. For several years, _____.

    _____ recently.

5. At one time, _____.

    Recently, _____.

6. In 1979, _____.

    Since then, _____.

B. Now write about your own past and present. Describe your life in the 1990s and
your life now. Use the simple past and the present perfect.

See the *Grammar Links* Website for a complete model paragraph for this assignment.

15 Simple Past Versus Present Perfect: Mermaids Then and Now

Complete the article with the words in parentheses. Use the correct form—simple past or present perfect—of the verb.

Since ancient times, people __have told__ stories about

1 (tell)

mermaids. Hollywood movie producers _____ many

2 (make)

movies about mermaids as well. Each year they make more of these movies

because mermaids fascinate both children and adults.

Until the 1800s, most people _____ mermaid stories. At that time, sailors

3 (believe)

_____ sure they saw these magical creatures on rocks. One sailor even

4 (be)

_____ into the sea to follow the mermaid of his dreams! Now, however, most

5 (jump)

people do not really believe in mermaids. Scientists at the Pacific Oceanic Institute

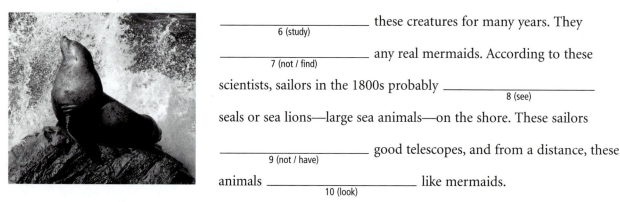

_____ these creatures for many years. They

6 (study)

_____ any real mermaids. According to these

7 (not / find)

scientists, sailors in the 1800s probably _____

8 (see)

seals or sea lions—large sea animals—on the shore. These sailors

_____ good telescopes, and from a distance, these

9 (not / have)

animals _____ like mermaids.

10 (look)

16 Simple Past Versus Present Perfect: Dragons Then and Now

A. Audrey Light, a TV reporter, is interviewing Mister Merlin, a dragon expert. Complete their conversation with the words in parentheses. Use the simple past or the present perfect of the verbs. Remember: With *just* or *recently*, the simple past and the present perfect are both possible.

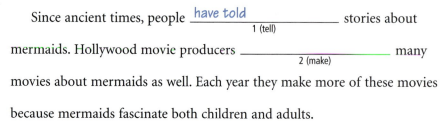

Audrey: Dragons _____ us for

1 (fascinate)

centuries. They _____ the

2 (be)

subjects of many folktales and legends. We still enjoy

stories about dragons today. Mister Merlin, you study

modern-day dragons. Is that right?

Komodo Dragon

Mister Merlin: Yes, I do. I _____ from a trip to Komodo Island

3 (just return)

in Indonesia. I lived with Komodo dragons while I _____ there.

4 (be)

Audrey: What _____ these "dragons" _____ like?
          5   (look)

Mister Merlin: Well, they _____ about nine feet long. They _____
                          6 (be)   7 (have)

          long tails and forked tongues. They _____ like . . . dragons, of course!
                                              8 (look)

Audrey: Of course! Well, how long _____ "dragons" _____ on
                                    9   (live)

          Komodo Island?

Mister Merlin: Dragons _____ on Komodo Island since prehistoric
                       10 (live)

          times. And each Komodo dragon lives a very long life.

Audrey: Really? How old _____ the lizards . . . uh . . . the dragons you saw?
                        11 (be)

Mister Merlin: They _____ at least a hundred years old. But I _____
                    12 (be)   13 (recently see)

          a two-hundred-year-old Komodo dragon.

Audrey: Think of it! That animal _____ for two centuries!
                                 14 (already live)

          How long _____ you _____ about this,
                   15   (know)

          Mister Merlin?

Mister Merlin: I _____ about that fellow. But I
                16 (just learn)

          _____ another dragon for about two hundred
          17 (know)

          and fifty years. He died last spring.

Audrey: What's that? Two hundred and fifty years? You must be very old then!

Mister Merlin: That's right. I'm a wizard. I'm three hundred and fifty years old.

          _____ you ever _____ a wizard before?
          18   (meet)

> *folktale* = a traditional story. *legend* = a very old story, often believed to be
> historically true. *prehistoric* = belonging to the time before written history.

B. Discuss as a class: What stories have you heard about dragons
or wizards? Are any of the stories similar? If so, why?

Wizard

17 Simple Past and Present Perfect: Searching for the Truth

 Work with a partner. Read the information in the chart from the record book. Use the simple past and the present perfect. Take turns asking and answering the questions about the four researchers and the creatures they've seen.

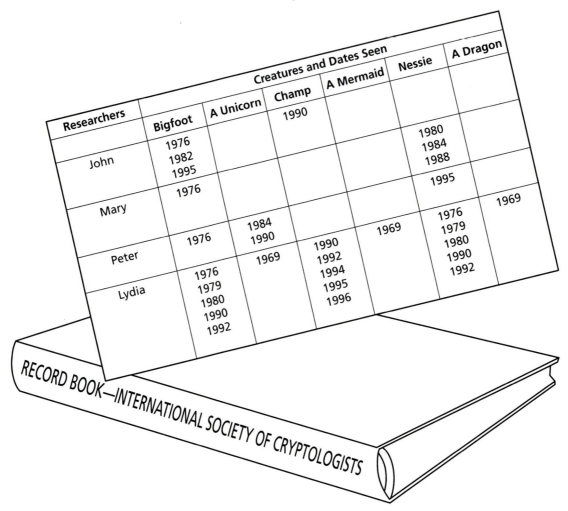

Researchers	Bigfoot	A Unicorn	Champ	A Mermaid	Nessie	A Dragon
John	1976 1982 1995		1990		1980 1984 1988	
Mary	1976				1995	1969
Peter	1976	1984 1990		1969	1976 1979 1980 1990 1992	
Lydia	1976 1979 1980 1990 1992	1969	1990 1992 1994 1995 1996			

RECORD BOOK—INTERNATIONAL SOCIETY OF CRYPTOLOGISTS

Examples: Has Mary ever seen Champ? No, she hasn't.
When did Peter see Nessie? Peter saw Nessie in 1995.
How many times has Lydia seen a unicorn? She's seen a unicorn once.
Has everyone seen a unicorn? No. Lydia and Peter have seen a unicorn, but the other researchers have never seen one.

Check your progress! Go to the Self-Test for Chapter 15 on the *Grammar Links* Website.

Present Perfect Progressive Tense; Present Perfect Versus Present Perfect Progressive

Introductory Task: News About the Universe

A. Read the news flashes.

News Flash 400 BC: Greek philosophers **have given** a name to the space around us. They **have named** it the universe. Some Greek philosophers **have begun** to study the universe. They call themselves astronomers. Astronomers study everything in the universe.

News Flash AD 200: Greek astronomer Ptolemy **has been studying** the universe. He **has found** the center. It is the earth.

News Flash AD 1890: Once again, the facts about the universe **have changed**. Astronomers **have** now **proved** this: The sun is not the center of the universe. The universe contains many galaxies. Each galaxy is a collection of stars and planets. Our sun is a star in a galaxy called the Milky Way. All galaxies together make up the universe.

News Flash AD 1543: Ptolemy was wrong. Polish astronomer Nicholas Copernicus **has been looking** at the stars and the planets. He **has discovered** the true center of the universe. It is the sun!

The Daily News

News Flash AD 1940: Astronomers **have been discovering** new things about the universe. And their old "facts" **have been changing** to "fiction" with each new discovery. Recently, astronomers **have been asking** themselves some new questions: "Did the universe have a beginning? Will it have an end? They **have been finding** answers to these questions. . . .

Milky Way Galaxy

B. Look at the **boldfaced** verbs in Part A.

1. Some of these verbs are in the present perfect tense. Write them here.

   have given
   _____

2. Write the other **boldfaced** verbs in the chart below. Write each verb part in the correct column.

have/has	been	main verb + -ing
has	been	studying

C. Discuss as a class: The verbs in the chart are in the present perfect progressive tense. How is the form of this tense similar to the form of the present perfect tense? How is it different?

D. Discuss as a class: These passages give examples of science "facts" that have become science "fiction." People used to believe them, but they don't believe them anymore. Can you think of any other examples of science facts becoming science fiction?

GRAMMAR BRIEFING 1

Present Perfect Progressive Tense I

FORM

A. Affirmative Statements

SUBJECT	HAVE/HAS	BEEN	MAIN VERB + -ING
I			
You	have		
We	've		
They		been	traveling.
He	has		
She	's		
It			

(continued on next page)

B. Negative Statements

SUBJECT	HAVE NOT/HAS NOT	BEEN	MAIN VERB + -ING
I			
She	have not		
We	haven't		
They		been	traveling.
He	has not		
She	hasn't		
It			

(See Appendix 3 for the spelling rules for *-ing* verbs.)

FUNCTION

A. Past Continuing to Present

The present perfect progressive (sometimes called the present perfect continuous) describes actions that were in progress in the past and are still in progress now. The present perfect progressive focuses on the **ongoing** action itself, not on its completion.

I have been working in Texas for a very long time. I'm still working there. (emphasis on duration of working)

PAST   NOW   FUTURE

have been working

B. Actions That Have Just Ended

The present perfect progressive also describes actions that have **just ended in the recent past**. We can see or feel the results of these actions now.

Her eyes are red. She **has been crying**. (Action = crying; result = red eyes now.)

PAST   NOW   FUTURE

has been crying   eyes are red

C. Time Expressions with the Present Perfect Progressive

Time expressions used with the present perfect progressive include *for, since,* and the other time expressions used with the present perfect.
(See Chapter 15 for more information about these time expressions.)

For several days, Angela has been trying to call her brother.

Exams don't start for two weeks, but Peter has **already** been studying.

Present Perfect Progressive Tense I

1 **Affirmative and Negative Statements; Past Continuing to Present: Our Place Among the Stars**

A. Complete the sentences with the present perfect progressive tense of the verbs in parentheses. Use contractions in negative statements and with pronouns.

Throughout time, humans __have been asking__ themselves:
1 (ask)

"What is our place among the stars? How did the universe begin?" For some time now, scientists

_____ about a theory called the "big bang
2 (talk)

theory." They _____ the universe with their
3 (explore)

telescopes. They _____ on mathematics and
4 (rely)

physics to help them, too. These astronomers believe the universe began with a big explosion— "a big

bang." Since then, they say, the universe _____
5 (get)

bigger. Galaxies _____ in one place.
6 (not / stay)

They _____ away from one another.
7 (move)

Recently, other astronomers _____
8 (think)

about a different theory. They _____
9 (not / work)

with telescopes. They _____ with some
10 (work)

new mathematical theories. They_____
11 (develop)

a new idea. Stephen Hawking, a British physicist, introduced this idea.

Astronomers _____ Hawking's theory.
12 (use)

It is the theory of "quantum gravity." According to this theory, the universe did not begin

with a big bang. It _____ larger because
13 (not / grow)

of a big explosion. In fact, it _____
14 (grow)

larger forever.

> *theory* = strong belief. *explosion* = large blow-up.

B. Discuss as a class: What do you think? Is one of the theories in Part A a fact? Is the other theory fiction? Or are both theories incorrect?

2 Actions That Have Just Ended: What Have They Been Doing?

A. Work with a partner. Imagine that you and your partner are riding the bus. There are several other people on the bus. You are watching them. Make guesses. What have they just been doing? Discuss, and write sentences with the present perfect progressive.

You see:

1. a man with very red eyes.

   He's been crying. OR *He's been reading without his glasses.* OR

   He's been rubbing his eyes.

2. a couple. They seem tired.

   _____

   _____

3. a woman with grease and oil all over her hands.

   _____

   _____

4. a student carrying five astronomy books. One is open. She's sleeping.

   _____

   _____

5. a very thin man. His clothes are all too large.

   _____

   _____

6. a teenage boy with a towel around his neck. He looks hot and sweaty.

   _____

   _____

7. two women with wet hair.

   _____

   _____

B. Share your explanations with the rest of the class. Discuss: Which ones are similar? Which are different? Which are the most original? Why do you think so?

Present Perfect Progressive Tense II

FORM

A. *Yes/No* Questions and Short Answers

QUESTIONS

HAVE/ HAS	SUBJECT	BEEN	MAIN VERB + -ING
Have	I		
	you		**traveling?**
	we		
	they	**been**	
Has	he		
	she		**working?**
	it		

SHORT ANSWERS

YES			NO		
	I			I	
	you	**have.**		you	**have not.**
	we			we	**haven't.**
Yes,	they		No,	they	
	he			he	
	she	**has.**		she	**has not.**
	it			it	**hasn't.**

B. *Wh-* Questions and Answers

Wh- Questions About the Subject

QUESTIONS

WH- WORD	HAS	BEEN	MAIN VERB + -ING
Who	has		**traveling?**
What	's	**been**	**happening?**

ANSWERS

Frank and Ellen.
Something wonderful!

Other *Wh-* Questions

QUESTIONS

WH- WORD	HAVE/HAS	SUBJECT	BEEN	MAIN VERB + -ING
What	have	you		**studying?**
Why	has	he		**traveling?**
How long	has	she	**been**	**working?**
How often	have	they		**calling?**
Who(m)	have	you		**visiting?**

ANSWERS

We've been studying art.
He enjoys it very much!
For several years.
Three times a day.
My parents.

Present Perfect Progressive Tense II

3 *Yes/No* **Questions and Short Answers:** Interview with Two Astronomers

You are interviewing two astronomers, Dr. Graves and Dr. Jones. Dr. Graves believes in quantum gravity. Dr. Jones believes the "big bang" theory. Write *yes/no* questions and short answers with the present perfect progressive tense. Use contractions in negative short answers.

1. Q: you / study the universe for a long time?

   Have you been studying the universe for a long time?

   A: Dr. Graves: Yes, I have.

   Dr. Jones: Yes, I have.

2. Q: you/learn many new facts?

   _____

   A: Dr. Graves: Yes, _____

   Dr. Jones: Yes, _____

3. Q: you and your colleagues/use quantum gravity?

   _____

   A: Dr. Graves: Yes, _____

   Dr. Jones: No, _____

4. Q: universe/expand since the big bang?

   _____

   A: Dr. Graves: No, _____

   Dr. Jones: Yes, _____

5. Q: other scientists/use your ideas?

   _____

   A: Dr. Graves: Yes, _____

   Dr. Jones: Yes, _____

4 *Wh-* Questions and Answers: Full-Moon Madness

A. Doctor Thompson studies the moon, but he's not an astronomer. He's a psychologist. Complete this interview with Doctor Thompson. Write *wh-* questions in the present perfect progressive.

1. Q: How long / you / study the moon?

   <u>How long have you been studying the moon?</u>

   A: For about three years.

2. Q: Why / you / study the moon?

   _____

   A: It changes my patients' personalities, and I want to know why.

3. Q: How has the moon changed your patients' personalities? What / they / do?

   _____

   A: Crazy things. They've been taking unplanned vacations, quitting their jobs,

   howling at the moon, dancing and singing with no music . . . things like that.

   We call this illness "full-moon madness."

4. Q: How many of your patients / act this way?

   _____

   _____

   A: Almost all of them.

5. Q: How long / this "full-moon madness" / bother people?

   _____

   _____

   A: For thousands of years!

   | *howl* = make a loud, long, sad sound. |

B. Discuss as a class: Have you ever heard of "full-moon madness"? Do you think it is fact or fiction?

See the *Grammar Links* Website for more information about the moon and our personalities.

5 Present Perfect Progressive: Full-Moon Madness and You

 Imagine that you have been suffering from full-moon madness; you have been doing crazy but fun things. Write about these things. Use the present perfect progressive tense.

Example: *I've been standing on my head at work. I've been howling at the moon. . . .*

See the *Grammar Links* Website for a complete model paragraph for this assignment.

GRAMMAR BRIEFING 3

Present Perfect Versus Present Perfect Progressive

FUNCTION

A. Completed Versus Continuing Actions

Use the present perfect to describe actions or states **completed** in the indefinite past.	I **have read** that book. (I finished the book.)

PAST — NOW ▼ — FUTURE
▲
have read

Use the present perfect progressive to describe actions that began in the past and are still **in progress now**.	I **have been reading** that book. (I am still reading it now.)

PAST — NOW ▼ — FUTURE
have been reading

B. Actions Completed in the Recent Past

Use the present perfect progressive to describe actions **completed in the very recent past** when you can still feel or see their results now. Do not use the present perfect.	Her eyes are red. She **has been crying**. NOT: She ~~has cried~~.

C. Repeated Actions

Use the present perfect to describe **repeated actions.** Do not use the present perfect progressive.	I **have read** that book five times. NOT: I ~~have been reading~~ that book five times.

(continued on next page)

D. The Present Perfect and the Present Perfect Progressive with *For* and *Since*

With *for* and *since*, the present perfect and the present perfect progressive have very similar meanings. They both describe actions that began in the past, continue to the present, and might continue to the future. The present perfect progressive emphasizes the ongoingness of the action or its duration.

I **have walked** to work for 20 years. (and I continue to walk to work now)

I **have been walking** to work for 20 years. (and this action is ongoing)

GRAMMAR HOTSPOT!

Be careful! Verbs with stative meaning are not usually used in the present perfect progressive.

(See Chapter 3, Grammar Briefing 2, for a review of verbs with stative meaning.)

I **have known** him for a long time.
NOT: I ~~have been knowing~~ him for a long time.

GRAMMAR PRACTICE 3

Present Perfect Versus Present Perfect Progressive

6 **Present Perfect Versus Present Perfect Progressive:** Star Gazing

Read the first sentence in each pair. Then decide if the second sentence is true or false. Circle **T** or **F**.

1. Cornelius Clark has been watching the stars for hours.
   He's still watching the stars.   (T)   F

2. He's been studying astronomy for several months.
   He's not studying astronomy this month.   T   F

3. Cornelius has read several books about the stars.
   Cornelius finished these books.   T   F

4. Cornelius' professor has written a book about the zodiac.
   The professor is still writing the book.   T   F

5. Cornelius has been reading this book.
   He is still reading this book.   T   F

6. He has been learning a lot about the zodiac.
   He finished learning about the zodiac.   T   F

7. Cornelius learned this: The sun has been passing through
   12 groups of stars for millions of years.
   The sun doesn't pass through these groups of stars anymore.   T   F

8. People have named these stars the *zodiac*.
   People are still naming these stars.   T   F

7 Present Perfect Versus Present Perfect Progressive: More About the Zodiac

Read this passage from a book about the zodiac. Circle the correct verb.

All through history, humans (**have had**/ have been having) the zodiac as
1
a guide. For example, sailors of the past (have used / have been using) the
2
zodiac as a guide on the sea. The zodiac (has also been / has also been being)
3
important to astronomers for centuries. They (have relied / have been relying)
4
heavily on the zodiac; it (has helped / has been helping) them discover the
5
secrets of the universe.

For the past two years, computer scientists (have been designing / have designed)
6
a new computer program to guide sailboats. When they complete this program,
sailors will not need the stars anymore. Throughout the centuries, sailors
(have liked / have been liking) to use the stars of the zodiac as a guide. Up to now,
7
most sailors (have not seemed / have not been seeming) very excited about this
8
new technology.

> *computer scientist* = a person who studies computers. *computer program* = software;
> instructions that control the operation of a computer.

8 Present Perfect Versus Present Perfect Progressive: Astrology and Astrologers

A. Complete the article. Use the present perfect or the present perfect progressive of
the verbs in parentheses.

Astrology is the study of the stars and their influence on people. People _____
1 (know)

about the zodiac for centuries. They _____ the zodiac to design
2 (use)

astrology. The zodiac has 12 parts or "signs," one for each month. Your birthday tells you your sign.

People with different signs have different personalities and different futures. One famous

astrologer, Jay Swoboda, _____ several popular books about
                                    3 (write)

astrology. For the past three years, he _____ a new book
                                                    4 (write)

about astrology for the twenty-first century. Many people _____
                                                                      5 (read)

Mr. Swoboda's other books. They liked them very much. Now they are waiting for his new book.

They _____ to use it as their guide to the future.
            6 (decide)

B. Discuss as a class: Have you ever read your horoscope? Do you know your sign?
Is astrology fact, or is it fiction? What do you think?

What's your sign? See the *Grammar Links* Website for information about your horoscope.

9 **The Present Perfect and the Present Perfect Progressive: Test Yourself**

Complete the sentences. Use the present perfect or the present perfect progressive of
the verbs in parentheses. When both are possible, write them both in the blank. Add
time expressions where indicated.

1. Reza _has lived/has been living_____ in Washington since he was five years years old.
              (live)

2. John is just opening his eyes. He _____.
                                              (sleep)

3. Leonard _____ a new computer.
                (recently / buy)

4. Paul _____ a job since January.
              (look for)

5. Paul _____ a job.
              (still / not find)

6. Arthur's hands are covered with flour. He _____.
                                                      (bake)

7. Angela _____ a scientist for several years.
                  (be)

8. Dasha _____ to work for several weeks.
                  (walk)

**Check your progress! Go to the Self-Test for
Chapter 16 on the *Grammar Links* Website.**

Wrap-up Activities

1 **The Beast of Exmoor:** EDITING

Read the letter. Correct the 12 errors. There are present perfect, present perfect progressive, and simple past errors. There are also errors with time expressions. The first one is corrected for you. (Sometimes there is more than one possible correction.)

Exeter, June 18

Dear Mom and Dad,

    Well, here I am in England, looking for the Beast of Exmoor. I ~~have~~ **haven't** seen it yet, but I've only been here since a couple of weeks. I've heard a lot of stories about this "monster" yet. Many people have seen recently it. It has frightening them. People have been chasing this beast for a long time, but they yet haven't caught it. Have you ever heard of the Beast of Exmoor? Well, it's a giant catlike animal. It has being lived in this area for many years now.

    Last week I met another cryptozoologist. He is looking for the Beast of Exmoor, too. His name is Clyde Cray. He's famous; he's been writing several articles about this beast, and I've read all of them. Clyde has came here several weeks ago. He recently saw the monster; he has been taking several pictures of it, but they weren't good ones.

    Clyde and I have been working together for yesterday. This morning, just after we finished our breakfast, we heard a loud noise and saw a giant cat shadow. We think it has been the Beast of Exmoor, but it escaped again! I hope I see it soon!

                    Wish me luck!

                    Love,

                    Flora

Looking into the Future: SPEAKING

Step 1 Below are some predictions about the future. What is true about the predictions? Write the correct letter next to each prediction.

    a. This has already happened.

    b. This hasn't happened yet.

    c. This has started to happen but hasn't finished happening.

    d. This will never happen!

Predictions:

1. People will live underground. _____

2. Books will disappear. Computers will give us all our information. _____

3. By cloning, we will save animals and plants in danger of dying and becoming extinct. _____

4. More and more people over the age of 30 will go to college. _____

5. Everyone will stop eating meat. People will eat only fruits and vegetables. _____

6. A very dangerous new illness will threaten the population of the earth. _____

7. We will find a cure for all pain. _____

8. Computers will become intelligent. They will have their own thoughts. _____

9. People will communicate only with their minds (telepathically). They will not need language anymore. _____

10. People will not work in office buildings anymore. Their homes will become their offices. _____

11. Each student will have his or her own teaching machine. Colleges and universities will disappear. Teaching machines will do the teacher's work. _____

Step 2 Compare your answers. Discuss as a class. Explain your answers. Use the present perfect or the present perfect progressive tense.

3 **Create a Beast:** SPEAKING/WRITING

Step 1 Have you ever seen a monster or creature like those discussed in this unit? If so, draw a picture of it. If not, create your own.

Step 2 Work with a partner. Show your partner your picture. Ask and answer some of the questions. Write your partner's answers on a piece of paper.

How long has this beast been alive?

How many times have you seen it?

Has anyone else seen it? If so, who?

Have you talked to it? Has it talked to you?

Where has it been living recently?

What has it been doing recently?

What interesting things have happened to your beast during its life?

What was your life like before you met/saw this beast?

What has your life been like since you met or saw it?

Add any other interesting information you want to share. Use the present perfect, present perfect progressive, and simple past tenses.

Step 3 Show the class your partner's picture. Tell the class about your partner's creature. Are any of your descriptions the same or similar? If so, what does that mean? Are these beasts fact or are they fiction? Discuss.

4 Carnac: SPEAKING/WRITING

Carnac is a village in France. In the village and all around it are thousands of giant megaliths, or tall stones. They have been in Carnac for over 7,000 years. Someone put them there. No one knows why. There are three groups of stones. One group has over 1,000 stones in it. The other two groups are smaller. They are connected to the large group.

Step 1 Look at this picture of the stones of Carnac. Write a short story about Carnac. Who put the stones there? Why? What happened in Carnac? What has been happening or has happened there since then? Tell a story about the people and the stones of Carnac. Use the present perfect, the present perfect progressive, and the simple past.

Examples:

Seven thousand years ago, the leader of Carnac became very worried. He had a bad dream. . . .

Since ancient people put the stones in Carnac, many wonderful things have happened there. . . .

See the *Grammar Links* Website for a complete model paragraph for this activity.

Step 2 Read your story to the rest of the class. Discuss your stories.

Unit Eight

Modals, Related Expressions, and Imperatives

TOPIC FOCUS
Language

UNIT OBJECTIVES

- **modal auxiliary verbs**
  (*I **can't** speak Chinese. You **should** say "please."*)

- **phrasal modals and modal-like expressions**
  (*I **am not able to** speak Chinese. You **ought to** say "please."*)

- **imperative sentences**
  (***Say** "please." **Don't worry** about your grammar.*)

Grammar in Action

 Reading and Listening: The Mysteries of Language

Read and listen.

---

174 Language

The Mysteries of Language

1   When did language begin? Humans **could** probably speak about 30,000 years ago. However, they **could** not write until five or six thousand years ago, so there is no real evidence of language until then. But they **were able to** paint pictures a long time before that.

2   There **could** be as many as 4,000 languages in the world today. How do we learn them? The answer is a mystery in some ways, but some things are certain. Children **ought to** learn their first language before they are three or four years old, or they **may** never learn to speak. Children **can** learn perfect pronunciation in a few years, but adults who learn a second language **are** often not **able to** do this.

3   Another thing is certain: Language is very powerful in society. Language **can** make us laugh and cry. It **may** win political elections or start wars; we **must** use it carefully. Different cultures **may** use language differently to show friendship and politeness. When we don't know the culture, we **could** make serious mistakes.

4   With more research, we **should** know much more about language in the future. Some languages **could** die or combine with other languages. New artificial languages **may** appear. With research, perhaps we **will be able to** solve more of the mysteries of language.

---

evidence = a way of knowing about something. *artificial* = not natural; made by humans.

Think About Grammar

Look at the **boldfaced** words and phrases in the passage. What are these words and phrases used to talk about? Write them in the correct columns.

The past (paragraph 1)	The present (paragraphs 2 and 3)	The future (paragraph 4)
	could	

Modals and Related Expressions; Ability; Possibility

Introductory Task: Language—Gift or Headache?

A. Read the conversation.

Son: Daddy, what's that?

Dad: Hmm . . . I think it's a stegosaur, son.

Son: St-steg-

Dad: Or no, wait. It **could** be a *Tyrannosaurus rex*. Or it **might** be a brontosaur.

Son: Brunt-bront-

Dad: No, it **couldn't** be a brontosaur. They don't fly! I know. Yes, that's right. It **must** be a pterodactyl.

Son: Pter- Oh, Daddy, I **can't** learn language! It's too hard.

B. Match the **boldfaced** words in Part A with the explanations.

Explanations:

1. This word shows that the speaker is sure about the idea. _must_

2. These two words show that the speaker is not sure about the idea. _____ and _____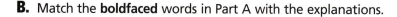

3. This word shows that the speaker does not have enough knowledge or ability.

   _____

4. This word shows that the idea is impossible. _____

Overview of Modals and Related Expressions
One-Word Modals

FORM

A. Overview

1. One-word modals are auxiliary verbs; they come before the main verb in a sentence.

   Modals include *can, could, may, might, must, should, will,* and *would.*

   > modal verb (main)
   > We **might see** you at the concert.

2. Modals don't change form.

   > This **could** be a difficult test.
   > **NOT:** This ~~coulds~~ be a difficult test.

3. Modals are followed by the base form of the main verb.

   > modal verb (main)
   > She **should say** no sometimes.

B. Affirmative Statements

SUBJECT	MODAL	BASE VERB	
You	**may**		
He	**can**	**go**	now.
We	**should**		

C. Negative Statements

SUBJECT	MODAL + *NOT*	BASE VERB	
You	**may not**		
He	**cannot** **can't**	**park**	here.
We	**should not** **shouldn't**		

D. *Yes/No* Questions and Short Answers

QUESTIONS			
MODAL	SUBJECT	BASE VERB	
Should	she	**stay**	here?

SHORT ANSWERS	
YES	*NO*
Yes, she **should**.	No, she **shouldn't**.

(continued on next page)

E. *Wh-* Questions and Answers

Wh- Questions About the Subject

QUESTIONS				ANSWERS
WH- WORD	MODAL	BASE VERB		
Who	can	swim?		They can.
What	could	go	wrong?	Everything.

Other *Wh-* Questions

QUESTIONS				ANSWERS
WH- WORD	MODAL	SUBJECT	BASE VERB	
Who(m)	should	I	ask?	The director.
What	can	they	do?	Take the test again.

GRAMMAR **HOT**SPOT!

1. Remember! *May + not* is usually not contracted in American English.

   > You **may not** park here.
   > **NOT:** You ~~mayn't~~ park here.

2. Be careful! *Can + not* is spelled as one word: *cannot*. The contraction of *can + not* has only one *n*: *can't*.

   > I **cannot** speak Chinese.
   > I **can't** speak Chinese.

■ Modal-Like Expressions

FORM and FUNCTION

Overview

1. Modal-like expressions include *ought to, had better (not),* and *let's (not).* Like one-word modals, these expressions do not change form.

   Modal-like expressions are followed by the base verb.

   > base verb
   > We **ought to** leave now.
   >
   > base verb
   > We **had better** go soon.
   >
   > base verb
   > **Let's** go.

(continued on next page)

Overview (continued)

2. The contracted form of *had better* is *'d better*.	We**'d better** go soon.

3. *Ought to* and *had better* are not normally used in questions. *Ought to* is not normally used in negatives.	**Should** we go?
	   NOT: ~~Ought~~ we ~~to~~ go?
	
	We'd **better not** stay.
	   NOT: We ~~ought not to~~ stay.

■ Phrasal Modals

FORM

A. Overview

1. Phrasal modals begin with *be* or *have* and end with *to*. The *be* and *have* change form. Phrasal modals include *be going to*, *be able to*, and *have to*.	We **are going to** leave now. You **don't have to** stay.
2. Like modals, phrasal modals are followed by the base verb.	base verb He **was able to finish** the job.

B. Affirmative Statements

SUBJECT	PHRASAL MODAL	BASE VERB	
I	**was able to**	**finish**	the job.
He	**has to**	**leave**	now.

C. Negative Statements

SUBJECT	PHRASAL MODAL + *NOT*	BASE VERB
You	**don't have to**	**pay**.
They	**'re not going to**	**arrive**.

D. *Yes/No* Questions and Short Answers

QUESTIONS	SHORT ANSWERS
Have you ever **had to pay**?	No, I **haven't**.
Were you **able to finish**?	Yes, I **was**.
Did she **have to get up** early?	Yes, she **did**.

E. *Wh-* Questions

Wh- *Questions About the Subject*	Other Wh- *Questions*
Who **will have to pay**?	When **are** they **going to arrive**?

(For more on tense formation and for question formation in all tenses, see Units 1, 2, 3, and 7.)

Overview of Modals and Related Expressions

1 **Identifying Modals and Related Expressions:** Language Planning

Underline the 14 modals and related expressions in the passage. The first modal is underlined for you.

Can governments control language? Many governments have tried. For example, in the sixteenth century, the English government told Irish people: "You must not speak Irish. You had better learn English." In Spain in the 1930s, everybody had to speak Spanish.

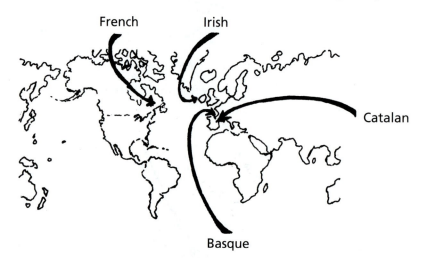

French   Irish

Catalan

Basque

Sometimes, governments have not been able to succeed with their language plans. Now, for example, all Irish school children learn Irish, and in the north of Spain, students can learn Basque and Catalan in the schools. In fact, anyone who wants a job in these places ought to learn these languages.

However, sometimes language planning can be successful. In Quebec, Canada, the French-speaking government started a bilingual education plan in the 1960s. Now most English-speaking children in Quebec can also speak French. Some people think the United States should try this plan. They say that bilingual education could help children who don't speak English and could also help English speakers who want to learn other languages. Do you think this is ever going to happen in the United States? Let's wait and see!

2 Statements with Modals and Related Expressions:
Which Language, and Why?

Complete the sentences with the words in parentheses. Use correct tenses where appropriate.

1. Why is language planning important to governments? First, language means power. Governments

    cannot govern countries or make laws if people _are not able to_____
                                                   (not / be able to)

    understand those laws.

2. Second, many governments believe language brings people together. If people speak different

    languages, they _____ live or work together easily.
                           (not / might)

3. When countries form governments, they often look for a "lingua franca"—a language that

    everybody _____ speak.
                      (be able to)

4. This _____ be easy.
              (not / may)

5. One country _____ have many small groups, or minorities,
                        (could)

    who speak different languages.

6. This was true, for example, in the former Soviet Union and in India. When the groups

    came together under one government, they _____ speak
                                                    (not / be able to)

    one another's languages.

7. Some say the government _____ choose the language of the
                                   (ought to)

    majority (the largest group), for example, Russian or Hindi.

8. Another idea is to choose a new language. The government _____
                                                                    (may)

    choose one language that has international power.

9. Perhaps one day the world will have one lingua franca. What do you think?

    _____ we _____ all speak
                                    (be going to)

    the same language someday?

3 Contractions and Full Forms: English in North America

A. People have very different opinions about English. Read the opinions. Write contractions above the **boldfaced** words where possible.

OPINION: The United States is one country. We **should not** [*shouldn't*] have more than one

language.

DISAGREEMENT: Many Americans speak different languages. Some of them **may not** want

to speak English. They should choose for themselves.

OPINION: English is very important for all American children. They **will have to**

speak it when they look for jobs. They **had better** learn English as fast as

possible. We **must not** waste school time on other languages.

DISAGREEMENT: American children need English, but they **do not have to** give up other

languages. Teach them in two languages! Then they **will be able to** get

better jobs.

OPINION: English is the most important language in the world. You **cannot** travel or

do business without English. Ask people in young countries like Ghana or

India or Belize. Many of them **could not** speak English before, but they

have had to choose English as a lingua franca.

DISAGREEMENT: English **may not** always be the most important language. There are

more Chinese speakers than English speakers in the world today. We

should not forget that.

B. Work in small groups. Discuss: What do you think about the statements in Part A? Do you agree more with the "opinion" side or with the "disagreement" side? Give examples to support your opinions.

4 *Yes/No* **Questions and Short Answers:** Ideas About Language Learning

A. People have different ideas about language learning. Read the statements. Change the statements into *yes/no* questions.

1. You can learn any language in the world.

   Can you learn any language in the world?

2. People should learn one language at a time.

   _____

3. Every language learner has to study grammar.

   _____

4. You could forget your first language one day.

   _____

5. We have to speak a language before we can read it.

   _____

B. Work with a partner. What do you think about the statements in Part A? Take turns asking and answering the questions. Share your answers with the class.

5 *Wh-* **Questions:** Children and Language

Read the statements. Write *wh-* questions about the **boldfaced** words. (You will find the answers later in Exercise 6.)

1. You could do **something** before you could speak.

   What could you do before you could speak?

2. People have **sometimes** been unable to learn language.

   _____

3. **Some people** can help children.

   _____

4. They should do **one important thing**.

   _____

5. **This** could be the most important secret of language.

   _____

6 Editing: Language Learning

Correct the errors in the passage. There are ten errors with modals and related expressions. The first error is corrected for you.

All humans can ~~to~~ learn languages. Any human may learns any language, and we don't have learn them separately; people sometimes learn two, three, or four languages at the same time. Young children don't have to study grammar. However, they have to speak the language they are learning, or they mayn't remember it. Adults are different. Sometimes an adult might learning a language from a book and read it very well but never speak it.

Children can communicate before they can speak. They use their voices and faces. Soon, they are going learn language too—but only after they hear it from other people. When people have never heard language, they have be unable to learn it.

So, parents, let's to help our children. We have better do one important thing: we ought talk to our babies. This could be the most important secret of language learning. ◆

See the *Grammar Links* Website for more information about language learning.

GRAMMAR BRIEFING 2

Ability

FORM and FUNCTION

A. *Can*

Use *can* to express ability (power, knowledge, or skill) in the present.	**Can** you swim? (Do you have the skill?)
	I **can't** answer the question. (I don't have the knowledge.)

B. *Could*

Use *could* to express general ability in the past (but see **C2**).	I **could** run much faster when I was younger.

(continued on next page)

C. Be Able To

1. Because *be* changes form, you can use *be able to* to express ability in all tenses.

Are you **able to** answer the question?

I **wasn't able to** read.

Will I **be able to** swim after one class?

What **has** she **been able to** tell you so far?

2. To talk about **single events in the past**, use *be able to* (not *could*) for affirmative statements. (Use either *be able to* or *could* for negative statements.)

Last week, I had two exams. I **was able to** finish the first exam early.

    NOT: I ~~could~~ finish the first exam early.

I **couldn't** finish the second one at all.

Ability

7 **Ability with *Can*: Children, Adults, and Language**

Replace *be able to* with *can/can't* or *could/couldn't*. Write the words above the sentences.

1. When you were a baby, you were a super language student. You <u>were able to</u> *could* make

   all the language sounds in the world!

2. It's true that you <u>were not able to</u> speak or write.

3. But when you wanted something, you cried, and everybody <u>was able to</u> understand you.

4. You <u>were able to</u> ask questions with intonation (the music of your voice).

5. And when your family <u>wasn't able to</u> answer, you repeated the question more loudly!

6. By the time you were four months old, you <u>were able to</u> hear important sound

   differences in your language.

7. Now, you're learning a second language—English. Perhaps you <u>are not able to</u>

   communicate as easily in this language.

8. Maybe people <u>are not able to</u> understand you all the time.

9. <u>Are</u> you <u>able to</u> hear all the differences between sounds in English—like *l* and *r*, or *p*

   and *b*, or *b* and *v*? Probably not.

10. But you make sounds in your language that an English speaker <u>is not able to</u> make.

8 | **Ability with *Can* and *Be Able To*:** Adults and Language—The Good News

Replace *be able to* with *can/can't* or *could/couldn't* where possible. Write the words above the sentences.

    Can
1. <u>Are</u> adults <u>able to</u> learn language as quickly as children? Here's some good news.

2. In some ways, adults <u>are not able to</u> learn new languages as easily as children.

    But in other ways, it's easier for adults.

3. Since we were babies, we <u>have been able to</u> learn many useful skills. These skills help

    us now when we learn new languages.

4. For example, you <u>are able to</u> study the grammar rules in this book. Since you started

    Chapter 1, you have probably learned hundreds of new rules!

5. You <u>were not able to</u> learn so quickly when you were a baby.

6. The last time you learned a new song, I'm sure you <u>were able to</u> learn all those new

    words at once.

7. But most babies <u>are able to</u> learn only about 20 words in their first year.

8. You <u>have</u> probably <u>been able to</u> learn more than that in the last three days!

9 | **Future Ability with *Be Able To*:** Teach Your Baby to Read!

Sometimes advertisements promise crazy and impossible things. Complete this advertisement with *will be able to.* Use affirmative or negative forms as appropriate.

Is Your Baby Six Months Old?

    Then he or she can start reading today!

Just leave your baby with us at the Baby Wonder Institute. You'll be amazed! After just

two weeks at the Baby Wonder Institute, your baby <u>will be able to</u> _____
                                                         1

read simple stories. After a month or two, your baby _____ choose all the right books
                                                        2

for a nine-month-old child. He or she will <u>love</u> books—your baby _____ stay away
                                                        3

from the library! By the time your baby is a year old, you _____ invite your friends
                                                        4

to poetry readings by your baby! And after 18 months, you _____ read your
                                                        5

newspaper in peace; your baby will want to read it first!

---

10 Past Ability: Then and Now

A. Write a paragraph about things you could do and couldn't do when you were a young child—things that are different now. Write five or six sentences with *could* and *couldn't*.

Examples:
I could wear baby clothes, but I couldn't dress myself....

See the *Grammar Links* Website for a complete model paragraph for this assignment.

B. Share your paragraph with the class. Did your classmates think of the same things?

TALKING THE TALK

It is often difficult to hear the difference between *can* and *can't*. In conversation, *can* sounds shorter (more like *cn*). *Can't* sounds slightly longer (you can hear the *a* sound).

⏑ (= short)
I **can** come tomorrow.

— (= longer)
I **can't** come tomorrow.

---

11 Listening: *Can* or *Can't?*

A. Listen to the sentences. Do you hear *can* or *can't*? Circle the word you hear.

1. I can / can't go with you tomorrow.

2. You can / can't leave your bags here.

3. I can / can't tell you how much I enjoyed the party!

4. You can / can't take your bags into the library.

5. I can / can't choose which class to take.

6. You can / can't try too hard.

B. Work with a partner. Take turns reading and listening to the sentences in Part A. The reader uses *can* for some sentences and *can't* for other sentences. If the listener hears *can*, he or she raises one finger. If the listener hears *can't*, he or she raises two fingers.

Present Possibility and Belief

FORM and FUNCTION

Expressing Certainty in the Present

1. Modals of possibility and related expressions (*ought to* and *have to*) are used for guesses and conclusions about present situations. Different expressions express different strengths of belief: how certain the speaker feels.

> That **could** be Fred at the door. Or it **could** be Colin. (A guess; the speaker is not sure.)
>
> You **couldn't** have a son. You're too young! (A strong conclusion; the speaker is very certain.)

2. Adverbs of possibility express similar degrees of certainty.

> You **should** know a lot of English by now.
>
> adverb of possibility
> OR You **probably** know a lot of English by now.

CERTAINTY	MODAL	RELATED EXPRESSION	ADVERB
Strong	**must**	**have to**	**almost certainly**
	should	**ought to**	**probably**
	may		**perhaps/maybe**
Weak	**might, could**		**possibly**
	might not		**possibly not**
	may not		**perhaps/maybe not**
	should not		**probably not**
	must not		**almost certainly not**
No possibility	**cannot, could not**		**certainly not**

(For more on adverbs of possibility, see Chapter 11, Grammar Briefing 2.)

3. Use *could* to ask questions about possibility or certainty in the present.

> **Could** this really be true?

1. Be careful! *May + be* is a modal + verb (two words). *Maybe* is an adverb (one word).

She **may be** a teacher.

Maybe she is a teacher.
  NOT: She ~~maybe~~ a teacher.

2. Be careful! *Could* and *might/may* express a similar degree of certainty in affirmative statements. But in negative statements, *could not* has a much stronger meaning than *might not* or *may not*. *Could not* expresses impossibility, strong disbelief, or strong disagreement.

She's definitely a teacher, but she **might not** be Kim's teacher. (possibly not)

She **couldn't** be a teacher. She told me she was a student! (certainly not)

Present Possibility and Belief

12 **Present Possibility:** Biological Grammar?

Here are some theories about language learning. Complete the sentences with modals of possibility or related expressions. Use each of the modals and related expressions in Grammar Briefing 3 at least once. Use the adverbs in parentheses to help you.

1. Most children _____should_____ speak quite
   (probably)

   well before they are five years old.

2. And most children _____ have a high level of grammar by
   (probably)

   the time they are five or six!

3. Young children _____ not use grammar perfectly.
   (perhaps)

4. But in most cases, they _____ not make the same mistakes
   (probably)

   that foreign language learners make.

5. When these children speak, they _____ produce sentences
   (possibly)

   that they have never heard before.

6. For these reasons, many linguists have a "biological" theory of grammar. According to this

   theory, grammar _____ come from our biological nature—
   (almost certainly)

   just like eating or standing on two legs.

7. Humans _____ come into the world with grammar.
(almost certainly)

8. Other linguists think this _____ be true.
(certainly not)

9. These linguists have a "social" theory of grammar. According to this theory, children

_____ have a natural ability for grammar.
(perhaps)

10. But this ability _____ be automatic, like eating or standing up.
(certainly not)

11. Language and grammar _____ be social, not biological;
(almost certainly)

we need to learn them from other people.

12. Both theories _____ be partly true.
(possibly)

> *linguists* = people who study language scientifically.

13 Questions About Present Possibility: What Could It Be?

This is a word that many native English speakers have heard before:
supercalifragilisticexpialidocious.

A. Work in small groups. Try to guess where this word comes from and what it means. Write questions with *could*. Use the ideas below, and add two questions of your own.

supercalifragilisticexpialidocius	
1. Could it mean "painful"?	("painful")
2.	(another language)
3.	(nothing at all)
4.	(a scientific word)
5.	
6.	

B. Work as a class. Share your group's questions. Does anyone know the answer? If not, look at the bottom of this page.

This word comes from the movie *Mary Poppins.* Although no one really explains the word, it seems to suggest a very good feeling!

14 *May Be* Versus *Maybe*; Negative Forms with Modals of Possibility:
What's Going On?

A. Masa is not doing well in his English grammar class this semester.
He doesn't speak in class and doesn't finish his work. What's the
problem? Make guesses. Add *maybe* or *may be* to the words in
parentheses to make your sentences. Do not add any other words.

1. (he/feels shy in class)

   <u>Maybe he feels shy in class.</u>

2. (the homework/too difficult)

   <u>The homework may be too difficult.</u>

3. (he/doesn't like grammar)

   _____

4. (the questions in class/unclear)

   _____

5. (he/lonely)

   _____

6. (the class/boring)

   _____

7. (he/has a problem with his teacher)

   _____

B. It's the next semester. Masa is very different now. Complete the conclusions
and guesses about Masa. Use *must not* if you feel certain about your
conclusion and *may not/might not* if you are only guessing.

Now Masa asks and answers questions in class. He completes all
his homework successfully. He is always smiling, and he talks to all
his classmates. He also has an English-speaking girlfriend.

1. He <u>must not</u> feel shy now.

2. The homework <u>may not/might not</u> be difficult.

3. The teacher's questions _____ be unclear.

4. He _____ have a problem with his teacher.

5. Masa _____ be so lonely now.

6. He _____ be speaking Japanese all weekend.

7. He _____ be doing all his homework by himself.

C. Work as a class. Share your sentences from Part B. Discuss: Did you have the same
guesses and conclusions? If not, how were they different? Why did you choose
must or *may/might* for these sentences?

15 Possibility, Impossibility, and Surprise: Sign Language

Sign languages are languages that use hand movements instead of spoken words.
Read the conversation and circle the correct words in parentheses.

Casey: See you later, Anne.

Anne: Are you going out in this weather? You ((can't) / might not) be serious! There's a
                                                    1
hurricane out there!

Casey: It's not too bad. I have to go to my American Sign Language class.

Anne : Are you really taking a sign language class? That's great!

Casey: Yeah. I met a terrific deaf woman named Sarah. I want to be able to communicate

better with her. And anyway, a lot of people learn sign language these days. In fact,

ASL (could / might not) be one of the most popular foreign languages in America.
           2

Anne: But it (couldn't / might not) be a foreign language! It's not even a real language!
                    3

Casey: Well, you (couldn't / might not) know this, but linguists say it *is* a real language.
                        4
It (might / might not) be exactly the same as spoken languages, but it has words
        5
and grammar. Some signs (might / could not) look like pictures, but others have
                                6
grammatical meaning.

Anne: Well, do all sign language users understand each other?

Casey: No. For example, a British Sign Language user (might / might not) understand
                                                            7
everything an American Sign Language user says.

Anne: Are there a lot of signs?

Casey: Oh, yes. There (couldn't / might) be as many as 4,000 signs in ASL.
                            8

Anne: Four thousand signs? That (couldn't / could) be an easy language! Oh, and I'd like to
                                      9
meet your friend Sarah. She must be very special if you're going to all this trouble.

Casey: She is.

---

deaf = not able to hear.

See the *Grammar Links* Website for more information about American Sign Language.

16 **Present Possibility:** Can You Translate?

Look at these signs from American Sign Language. They mean "separate," "yellow," "push," and "secret." But which means which? Write five or six sentences about your guesses and conclusions. Use modals of possibility. Give reasons for your guesses. The correct answers are at the bottom of this page.

1.   2.   3.   4.

Example:

Number 3 can't mean "yellow." The signer is not pointing at anything that's yellow.
Number 1 could mean "push." The signer is pushing his face with his hand.

| *signer* = a person who communicates through sign language. |

Future Possibility

FORM and FUNCTION

Expressing Certainty About the Future

1. Modals of possibility and related expressions (*will, be going to, should, ought to, may, might,* and *could*) express belief and certainty about the future.

> It **ought to** be sunny tomorrow.
> We **may** (**not**) be here next year.
> It **shouldn't** take long to finish.

CERTAINTY	MODAL	RELATED EXPRESSION	ADVERB
Strong	will	be going to	definitely, certainly
	should	ought to	probably
	may		perhaps/maybe
Weak	might, could		possibly
	might not		possibly not
	may not		perhaps/maybe not
	should not		probably not
No possibility			

2. Use *will* or *could* to ask questions about possibility in the future.

> **Will** we see each other again?
> **Could** it really happen one day?

The signs have the following meaning: 1. secret; 2. yellow; 3. push; 4. separate.

Future Possibility

17 **Future Possibility:** A Global Language?

Sociolinguists study language and the ways that humans use it. Read this interview with a sociolinguist. Circle the correct words.

Interviewer: Dr. Brown, (**will**/ must) we ever have a global language?
                           1

Dr. Brown: Probably. The world (ought to / couldn't) have a lingua franca one day.
                                    2

             After all, we are a global society now. The question is: Which language?

             There are several possibilities. It (might / must) be an artificial language
                                                        3

             like Esperanto, or it (could / has to) be English.
                                    4

Interviewer: Yes. English is the biggest international language, right?

Dr. Brown: Right. And I'm certain it (will / might) continue to be—at least for business
                                          5

             and technology. But actually, more people in the world speak Chinese than

             English. You can be very sure that Chinese (is going to / might not) become
                                                            6

             more important.

Interviewer: Well, (could / may) Chinese become the worldwide language?
                      7

Dr. Brown: Not yet. It (shouldn't / might) happen in the near future because Chinese
                          8

             has many different spoken dialects and the Chinese don't all understand

             each other. Also, Chinese (might not / could) be a lingua franca for the
                                          9

             Internet anytime soon because Chinese characters are very difficult to type

             on a computer. But the Chinese are trying to make their spoken and

             written language simpler. It (shouldn't / mustn't) take too long. Who
                                            10

             knows? We (may / ought to) all be Chinese speakers in the future!
                          11

---

global = worldwide; connecting people all over the world. *characters* = letters or
other signs in a writing system.

**Check your progress! Go to the Self-Test for
Chapter 17 on the *Grammar Links* Website.**

Chapter

18

Social Modals and Imperatives

Introductory Task: Politeness

A. Frank Suave is the author of a famous book, *How to Manage People with Language.* He is giving a lecture about politeness. Read the lecture.

Politeness is very important. When you work with other people, **you must use the**
a
right words. You want to live happily with your family, right? Then **you must think**
about politeness with your family, too.

Adult politeness means questions, not statements. **You should *ask* people things**;
don't *tell* them. Also, politeness is indirect. **You should let people know things**, but
don't be too direct. Finally, politeness is friendly. **You should be friendly**, but don't
act too friendly, or people may think you don't respect them.

But most of all, when you're dealing with difficult people, **you mustn't lose**
control—that's the worst possible thing. When you feel angry, there are several things
you could do. **You could smile** and say, "I see." Or **you might say nothing**. Or **you**
might just walk away. But **you mustn't say unkind things** to hurt the person. **You**
mustn't destroy your relationship with the person, or you will be sorry later.

---

indirect = not completely straight and clear.

B. Look at the **boldfaced** words and ideas in the lecture. Which of the descriptions below matches these ideas best? Write *a*, *b*, *c*, or *d* above the **boldfaced** words. The first one is done for you.

Descriptions:

Frank thinks that this idea is:

a. very important	**b.** a good idea	**c.** one idea (but there are others)	**d.** a bad idea

C. Circle the correct modals below.

This modal shows that an idea is:

a. very important	must	should	could	might	mustn't
b. a good idea	must	should	could	might	mustn't
c. one idea (but there are others)	must	should	could	might	mustn't
d. a bad idea	must	should	could	might	mustn't

Permission and Offers

FORM and FUNCTION

A. Asking, Giving, and Refusing Permission

More formal

may

could

can

Less formal

1. Use *may*, *could*, or *can* to ask for permission.

   Can we eat here?

   May I have a cookie?

2. Use *can* or *may* to give or refuse permission. Do not use *could*.

   A: Could I have a cookie?

   B: Yes, you **can**. OR No, you **may not**.
   NOT: No, you ~~could~~ not.

   You **cannot** eat here.
   NOT: You ~~could not~~ eat in here.

   May is very formal. It is often used for impersonal public messages.

   Visitors **may not** park outside the building.

3. Phrases like *Sorry, but . . .* , *I'm afraid you can't . . .* , and *I'm afraid not* make refusals of permission more polite and friendly.

   A: Could I borrow your car?

   B: **Sorry, but** my brother is using it. OR **I'm afraid not**.

4. Phrases like *Of course (you may)*, *Sure (you can)*, *Okay*, and *Go ahead* make affirmative answers (giving permission) friendlier.

   A: Could I borrow your car?

   B: **Of course you can**. OR **Go ahead**.

(continued on next page)

B. Making Offers

More formal ▼ Less formal	may
	could
	can/will

1. Use *may*, *could*, or *can* to make polite offers in questions.

OFFER	RESPONSE
May I help you?	Yes, please
Could I do that for you?	No, thanks.
Can I get you a drink?	Thank you.

2. Use *can* or *will* to make offers in statements.

OFFER	RESPONSE
I **can** do that for you.	Thanks.
I'll help you.	

Permission and Offers

1 Giving and Refusing Permission: Library Talk

A. Dave works in a library. He sometimes has to deal with difficult people! Listen to Dave's conversation with a visitor to the library and write the words you hear.

Visitor: Hey, I want to check out these books.

Dave: Yes, sir. May I see your library card?

Visitor: What card? I don't have a card. I just want these books.

Dave: __I'm sorry, sir, but_____ you can't take out books without a card.
　　　　　　　　　　　　　　1

Visitor: This is a public library. I'm a member of the public, so I can use the library. Right?

Dave: _____. But all library members need a card.
　　　　　　　　　　　2

　　　And another thing: _____ eat that hot dog in here.
　　　　　　　　　　　　　　　　　　3

Visitor: What do you mean? I can't eat this little snack?

Dave: _____. Do you see that sign? It says, "Visitors
　　　　　　　　　　　4

may not eat in the library."

Visitor: I can eat when and where I want.

Dave: _____. But not in the library.

5

Visitor: Look, can I get these books or not?

Dave: _____!

6

 B. Discuss as a class: Did Dave become more polite or less polite during the conversation? How do you know? Why do you think this happened?

2 | **Asking Permission and Making Offers:** Practicing Politeness

A. Al is following a rule of politeness: Don't tell people; ask them. What is he going to say in these situations? Write sentences asking permission and making offers. Use *may*, *can*, and *could* at least once.

1. He wants to borrow a book from a good friend.

   Can I borrow your book? _____

2. He is standing in line behind a stranger at the supermarket. He only has a bottle of milk. The stranger has many items. Al wants to go in front of the stranger.

   Excuse me. _____

3. He wants to sit next to someone in a crowded fast-food restaurant. He doesn't know the person, so he asks very politely.

   _____

4. His classmate wrote a very good paper for homework. Al would like to read it.

   _____

5. He visits his friend's parents for dinner. He knows them fairly well. He offers to wash the dishes for them.

   _____

6. He offers to show his vacation photographs to his sister. He is very close to his sister.

   _____

7. He drives past his teacher in the street. The teacher is much older than Al, and Al doesn't know her very well. He offers to give her a ride.

   _____

 B. Discuss your sentences in Part A as a class: Did you use *may*, *can*, and *could* in the same sentences? If not, why did you choose different words?

Requests

FORM and FUNCTION

Making and Responding to Requests

More formal ▼	
	would
	could
Less formal	**can/will**

1. Use *would*, *could*, *can* or *will* to make requests.

   Possibly (with *could*) and *please* add politeness to any request.

   > **Can** you help me?
   >
   > **Could** you **possibly** lend me a dollar?
   >
   > **Would** you **please** pass the salt?

2. Use *can* or *will* to respond to requests. Do not use *could* or *would*.

   > *A:* Would you make me a sandwich?
   >
   > *B:* Yes, I **can**. OR Yes, I **will**.
   > **NOT:** Yes, I ~~could~~. OR Yes, I ~~would~~.

3. Phrases like *I'm sorry, but . . .* , and *I'm afraid I can't . . .* make negative responses to requests more polite and friendly.

   > *A:* Could you help me?
   >
   > *B:* **I'm afraid I can't.** I have to go now.

4. Phrases like *Of course* (*I will*), *Sure*, and *Certainly* make affirmative responses friendlier.

   > *A:* Can you lend me a dollar?
   >
   > *B:* **Sure** (**I can**).

Requests

3 **Making and Responding to Requests:** An Interview

A. Here is an exercise from Frank Suave's book *How to Manage People with Language*. The exercise helps people use the appropriate language during job interviews.

Complete the exercise. Write appropriate requests with *can*, *will*, *could*, and *would*. Use formal modals for conversation between the interviewer and yourself. Use less formal modals for conversation between the interviewer and her colleague. Use *please* to make requests more polite.

---

176   Language

Help Yourself at Interviews!

1. *The interviewer wants to know something about your experience.*

   Interviewer:

   <u>Could you please tell me something about your experience?</u>

   You: Certainly.

2. *The phone rings. The interviewer asks you to excuse her for a moment.*

   Interviewer:

   _____

   You: Of course.

3. *A colleague comes into the office. He and the interviewer are good friends. The interviewer asks him to come back and see her after the interview.*

   Interviewer:

   _____

   Colleague: Sure I will.

4. *The interviewer asks the colleague to close the door when he goes out.*

   Interviewer:

   _____

   Colleague: Okay.

5. *The interviewer didn't hear your question. She asks you to repeat the question.*

   Interviewer:

   _____

   You: Yes, of course.

B. Finish the interview in Part A. Write appropriate responses to requests. Use *I'm afraid / I'm sorry* to soften negative responses. Use the information in parentheses to help you.

Help Yourself at Interviews!

1. Interviewer: Would you please pass the sugar?

   You: _Certainly._ _____ (Yes)

2. Interviewer: Could you please give me the phone number of your last employer? I'll need a reference from him.

   You: _____ (Yes)

3. You: Could you possibly let me know your decision next week?

   Interviewer: _____

   _____

   (No, she won't know until next month.)

4. Interviewer: I'd like my supervisor to meet you too, but he's not here. Could you possibly come back tomorrow?

   You: _____

   _____

   (No, you'll be out of town tomorrow.)

5. You: Well, thank you for your time. It was a pleasure to meet you. Oh, I need to get to the station. Could your secretary possibly call a taxi for me?

   Interviewer: _____ (Yes)

Imperatives for Offers and Requests

FORM and FUNCTION

Making Direct Offers and Requests

1. Use the imperative form of verbs for direct offers and requests:

AFFIRMATIVE OFFERS AND REQUESTS		NEGATIVE REQUESTS		
BASE VERB		DO + NOT	BASE VERB	
Help	me.	**Don't**	**tell**	me.
Have	a cookie.	**Do not**	**walk**	on the grass.

2. Imperative sentences do not usually contain a subject. The understood subject of an imperative verb is *you*.

Help me.
   NOT USUALLY: ~~You,~~ help me.

3. Imperatives are often used for impersonal public requests.

Do not walk on the grass.

4. *Please* adds politeness to any imperative request.

Don't tell me, **please.**

Please do not walk on the grass.

Imperatives are also used to give strong advice and instructions. See Grammar Briefing 5 in this chapter.

TALKING THE TALK

Imperatives are much stronger and more direct than modals. They are not normally used for requests that may be difficult for the listener to agree to. For difficult requests, use (*please*) *could* or *would*.

Pass the sugar. (simple request)

Would you help me with my homework?
   (difficult request)
   NOT: ~~Help~~ me with my homework.

Could you **please** lend me your car?
   (difficult request)
   NOT: ~~Lend~~ me your car.

Imperatives for Offers and Requests

4 **Imperatives:** After a Long Day

Dave has just come home after a hard day of work at the library.

Work in pairs. Complete Dave's conversation with his wife. Write affirmative and negative imperative sentences. Choose appropriate verbs from the box.

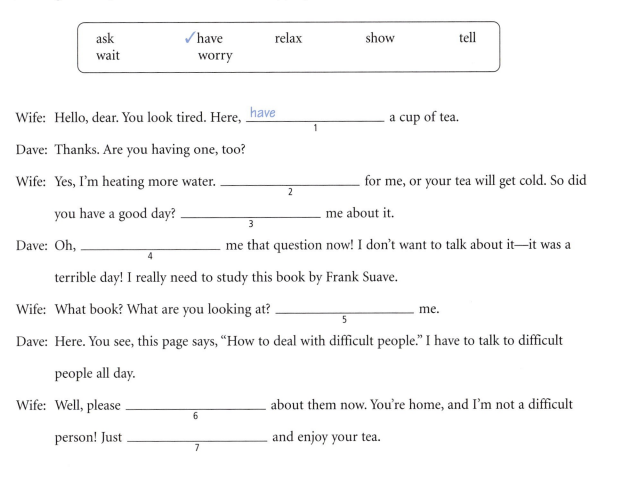

| ask | ✓have | relax | show | tell |
| wait | worry | | | |

Wife: Hello, dear. You look tired. Here, ___*have*___ a cup of tea.
                                                1

Dave: Thanks. Are you having one, too?

Wife: Yes, I'm heating more water. _____ for me, or your tea will get cold. So did
                                                   2

    you have a good day? _____ me about it.
                                     3

Dave: Oh, _____ me that question now! I don't want to talk about it—it was a
                       4

    terrible day! I really need to study this book by Frank Suave.

Wife: What book? What are you looking at? _____ me.
                                                   5

Dave: Here. You see, this page says, "How to deal with difficult people." I have to talk to difficult

    people all day.

Wife: Well, please _____ about them now. You're home, and I'm not a difficult
                                  6

    person! Just _____ and enjoy your tea.
                       7

5 Using Requests, Offers, and Imperatives: Reading Between the Lines

Politeness is sometimes indirect; people don't say exactly what they mean. Read these situations. Speaker A is indirectly asking for something. Speaker B responds incorrectly. Write the question that Speaker A is really asking. Then write a better response for Speaker B. Use polite offers or imperatives for B's response.

1. A is carrying a lot of books. B is walking with A.

   A: These books are so heavy!

   B: Yes, they look heavy.

   Real meaning: A: _Could you help me with these books?_

   Better response: B: _Can I carry some of those books for you?_____ OR

   Here. Give me some of your books.

2. B is eating a big pizza all by herself. A is watching.

   A: That looks delicious!

   B: Yes, it's great.

   Real meaning: A: _____

   Better response: B: _____

3. A needs a pen. He sees an extra pen on B's desk. He wants to take it.

   A: Is that an extra pen?

   B: Yes.

   Real meaning: A: _____

   Better response: B: _____

4. B responds to A's invitation to go to a movie downtown after class.

   B: Okay, but I don't have a car.

   A: Oh.

   Real meaning: A: _____

   Better response: B: _____

5. A visits B's house. She comes in and sits down.

   A: Oh, it's so hot outside! I'm really thirsty.

   B: Really?

   Real meaning: A: _____

   Better response: B: _____

Necessity and Advice
Overview

FORM and FUNCTION

Expressing Necessity and Advice

Some modals and related expressions are often used to tell people what to do. Different modals show the speaker's strength of feeling by expressing necessity or prohibition (strong), advice, or suggestions (weak).

You **must** show your passport at immigration. (Strong advice; the action is necessary.)

You **should** visit Canada while you're in the United States. (General advice; the action is a good idea but not necessary.)

STRENGTH	MODAL	RELATED EXPRESSION	MEANING
Strong	must, must not	have to	necessity/obligation, prohibition
	should (not)	ought to	advice, opinion
	might, could		suggestion
Weak		do not have to	non-necessity

Necessity and Obligation; Non-Necessity; Prohibition

FORM and FUNCTION

A. Expressing Necessity and Obligation

1. Use *must* or *have to* for necessity in the present.

   I **must** go now.

2. Use *have to* in all tenses.

   In conversation, *have to* is more common than *must*.

   I **have to** go now.

   They **had to** leave yesterday.

   I'm sorry; you**'ll have to** leave soon.

   I**'ve had to** work hard all my life.

B. Expressing Non-Necessity

Use *not have to* to say that something is not necessary.

You **don't have to** carry your passport within the United States.

C. Expressing Prohibition

Use *must not* to say that something is prohibited (not allowed) or to give strong negative advice.

You **must not** leave the country without your passport.

(continued on next page)

■ Advice and Opinions; Suggestions

FORM and FUNCTION

A. Giving Advice and Opinions

1. Use *should* and *ought to* for general advice and opinions, when you think something is a good idea.

   You **ought to** read Frank Suave's book. (advice)

   People **should** read more. (opinion)

2. *Should* is normally used (not *ought to*) in negative statements and in questions about advice.

   You **shouldn't** worry so much.

   Should I read that book?

B. Making Suggestions

1. Use *might* and *could* for suggestions when you do not have a strong opinion.

   You **might** try this restaurant when you are in town.

   In conversation, *could* is more common than *might*.

   We **could** go to a movie if you like.

2. Use *should* (not *might* or *could*) for questions about suggestions.

   Which movie **should** I see?

3. *Might* and *could* are often used with *or* to express different choices.

   A: I'm so angry! I don't know what to do.

   B: Well, you **could** take a deep breath. **Or** you **could** just walk away.

Necessity and Advice

6 Necessity and Advice: Learning a Culture

Complete the sentences with *you* + an appropriate modal or related expression.
Use the words in parentheses to help you.

1. When you learn a new language, _you must_____ learn a new

   culture, too. _You don't have to_____ speak with perfect grammar.

(necessary)

(not necessary)

2. But _____ learn the social and cultural

(advice; a good idea)

   rules as soon as possible. Sometimes this is the hardest part of life in a new culture,

   and it can cause problems. We call these problems "culture shock."

3. But _____ worry too much about culture

(not necessary)

   shock. Culture shock usually goes away after a while. Here are some ideas about

   dealing with culture shock.

4. First, _____ try to make some friends in

(advice; a good idea)

   the new culture. Culture shock is easier when you don't feel lonely.

5. Second, _____ try to ask advice from people

(suggestion; one choice)

   who understand the culture. Or _____ laugh

(suggestion; another choice)

   about it sometimes. Laughing will always make you feel better!

See the *Grammar Links* Website for more information about culture shock.

7 Necessity and Obligation: Culture Shock

A. Complete the conversation with *must* or *have to*. Use *must* for sentences about the
present. Use *have to* in other tenses.

Alice: Did you have culture shock when you came to America, Lienh?

Lienh: I didn't at first. I _had to_____ do so many things—like find an apartment

1

   and get a social security number.

Alice: What about later?

Lienh: Well, I was lonely for a while. I had no friends, so I _____ talk to

2

   myself! I used to say, "You _____ try, Lienh. You can't go home now."

3

Alice: Were people friendly?

Lienh: Yes, but I didn't always understand them. For example, they sometimes said, "You

_____ come to my house some time." But then they didn't invite
                4

me. Or sometimes people said, "How are you doing?" But when I started to tell them,

they said, "I _____ go now." I used to think they didn't like me.
                          5

Alice: And what about school?

Lienh: Well, the teacher used to say, "You _____ speak more, Lienh."
                                                          6

But I couldn't speak. I _____ get some confidence first.
                                    7

Lienh: And now?

Alice: I feel much better now. I have learned more about American culture, and I have made some

good friends. It hasn't been easy, but I _____ change since I came
                                                        8

here. I _____ become more outgoing and less shy. But that's okay. It's
                  9

been good for me!

Alice: That's great. Look, Lienh. I'm sorry, but I _____ go now. But you
                                                                  10

_____ come to dinner one evening.
          11

Lienh: Thank you, Alice. Let's do it tomorrow night. Eight o'clock?

B. Discuss as a class: What do you think—did Alice really invite Lienh to dinner?
What do you think Alice's answer was to Lienh's suggestion? Have you ever
experienced culture shock? Describe what happened to you.

GRAMMAR HOTSPOT!

Remember! *Must not* and *don't have to* have very different meanings.

You **must not** leave the country. (You must stay.)

You **don't have to** leave the country. (You can stay or leave.)

8 Non-Necessity and Prohibition: Body Language

A. Complete the article with *mustn't* or *don't have to*.

More Mysteries of Language

Language is communication, and words are part of language. However, we <u>don't have to</u> speak every time we
         1

communicate. Often, we communicate silently—with body language.

With people from our own culture, we _____
         2

think about this too much. But with people from different cultures, we

_____ forget one very important thing:
     3

The same body language communicates different ideas to different people.

For example, eyebrows say a lot in most cultures!

When you pull your eyebrows together toward your nose,

you _____ say,
     4

"I'm angry." Everybody knows. When you move your eyebrows up

and smile, people know you're friendly. But in some cultures, you

_____ do this to strangers—
     5

especially to strangers of the opposite sex—or they may get upset.

B. Work in small groups. Discuss body language in different cultures you know. Talk about things you mustn't do in your culture and things you don't have to worry about.

See the *Grammar Links* Website for more information about body language.

9 **Giving Advice:** Interview Skills

College admissions officers interview people who want to go to their colleges. They often give advice about interview skills. Read the information and write sentences with *should*, *shouldn't*, or *ought to*. Use each form at least once.

Central College Student Services

How to Have a Good Interview

1. Sometimes our candidates don't answer our questions directly. Then we don't get the information we want.

   You ought to answer questions directly.

2. Good candidates are not too shy.

   You shouldn't be too shy.

3. Our best candidates always ask questions after the interview.

   _____

4. Good candidates speak confidently.

   _____

5. They talk about their future plans after college.

   _____

6. But sometimes candidates talk too much or try too hard. This isn't good.

   _____

7. We like it when candidates look straight into our eyes when they speak. Eye contact is good.

   _____

8. They don't look at the floor while they are talking.

   _____

---

candidates = people who are applying for something, for example, a job or a place at a college. *eye contact* = looking directly into another person's eyes.

See the *Grammar Links* Website for more information about interview skills.

10 **Expressing Opinions:** What's Important?

A. Different cultures have different opinions about language. What do you think about these opinions? Write sentences with *shouldn't* or *ought to* and the words given. Then decide how important these opinions are for you. Number the opinions from 1 (the most important) to 6 (the least important).

1. *People shouldn't talk too much.* _____
   (not talk too much)

2. *People ought to tell the truth all the time.* _____
   (tell the truth all the time)

3. _____ _____
   (not say "I'm sorry" when they don't mean it)

   _____

4. _____ _____
   (think before they speak)

   _____

5. _____ _____
   (not interrupt each other)

   _____

6. _____ _____
   (agree with each other)

   _____

B. Work with a partner. Compare your answers in Part A. Did you have the same opinions about language? Discuss any differences.

11 Advice and Suggestions: Making a Good Impression

A. An American friend has invited you to dinner at his or her parents' house for the first time. You want to make a good impression. Complete this letter to Frank Suave, the politeness expert. Ask for advice about spoken language and body language. Think of five questions. Use the ideas in the box or your own ideas.

> ask a lot of questions?
>
> how/say goodbye?
>
> what/talk about?
>
> kiss my friend's mother?
>
> how often/make eye contact?
>
> how much/talk about myself?
>
> tell jokes?

Dear Mr. Suave:

An American family has invited me to dinner at their home. Please give me some information about American culture. For example, some Americans hug each other when they meet and say goodbye. Others shake hands.

1. _Should I hug my hosts? Or should I shake hands with everybody?_

I have several other questions. For example,

2. _____

3. _____

4. _____

5. _____

6. _____

Thank you very much for your help.

Sincerely,

_____

B. Now imagine you are Mr. Suave. Write his reply to the letter in Part A. Write at least six suggestions. Use *could* and *might*. Use *should* for negative suggestions. You don't have to be too serious!

Examples:
> You could bring flowers for your friend's mother. She'll probably like that.
> Or you might bring chocolates. . . .

 See the *Grammar Links* Website for a complete model paragraph for this assignment.

C. Work in small groups. Share your letters from Parts A and B. Choose the best letter and share it with the whole class.

Imperatives for Orders; *Had Better* (*Not*) for Warnings

FORM and FUNCTION

A. Giving Orders

Imperatives are sometimes used to give orders. Orders are a very direct form of advice.

> **Go** home now. **Don't stay.**

For more information on imperatives, see Grammar Briefing 3 in this chapter.

B. Give Warnings with *Had Better* (*Not*)

You	HAD BETTER	(NOT)	BASE VERB	
	had better	**not**	**go**	outside.
	'd better		**stay**	inside.

Had better (*not*) is a modal-like expression that is often used to give warnings. A warning is a kind of strong advice. It implies something bad will happen if the advice is not followed.

> You**'d better** stay inside (or you'll catch a cold).
>
> You **had better not** drive so fast (or you'll get a ticket).

Imperatives for Orders; *Had Better* (*Not*) for Warnings

12 **Giving Orders and Warnings:** Be Careful!

A. Imagine you are going to live in a new country. Your friends and family are worried about you. They give you lots of warnings—many of them about language. What are the warnings? Change the imperative orders into warnings with *You'd better* (*not*).

1. Don't talk to strangers. _You'd better not talk to strangers._

2. Say "please" when you ask for something.

   _____

3. Don't make friends too quickly.

   _____

4. Don't tell people too much about yourself at first.

   _____

5. Learn the language quickly.

   _____

6. Don't stay with people from your country.

   _____

7. Stay with people from your country.

   _____

B. Work as a class. Discuss the warnings in Part A: Why do people give them? What may happen to people who do not listen to the warnings?

Example: *You'd better not talk to strangers. You may get into trouble.*

C. Write a paragraph of advice for someone who is coming to live in this culture. What warnings would you give? Would you agree or disagree with the warnings in Part A? What other warnings have people given you? Write at least five warnings.

Example: *If you want to feel comfortable in this country, you'd better not be too shy. . . .*

See the *Grammar Links* Website for a complete model paragraph for this assignment.

Let's (*Not*) for Suggestions

FORM and FUNCTION

Making Suggestions with *Let's* (*Not*)

LET'S	NOT	BASE VERB	
Let's		**try**	that restaurant.
Let's	**not**	**do**	it now.

1. In conversation, *let's* (*not*) is often used for suggestions that include the speaker.

   Let's go. We'll be late.

2. The understood subject of *let's* (*not*) is *you and I*.

   Let's not do it now. You and I are both tired.

Let's (*Not*) for Suggestions

13 **Suggestions with *Let's* (*Not*): Doing Things Together**

A. One good way to make friends is to suggest doing activities together. Write suggestions with *let's* (*not*) for the ideas given. Then write two suggestions of your own.

1. It's a beautiful day. _Let's take a walk._

2. There's a good movie at the theater, but it's very long.

   _____

3. You can get coffee in the cafeteria downstairs.

   _____

4. You love camping.

   _____

5. You both need to go to the supermarket.

   _____

6. _____

7. _____

 B. Discuss as a class: Could you make all these suggestions to everybody? Which suggestions would you make, or not make, to different people: for example, your teacher, a member of the opposite sex, someone older than you?

Check your progress! Go to the Self-Test for Chapter 18 on the *Grammar Links* Website.

Wrap-up Activities

1 Tricky Language: EDITING

Correct the errors in this student composition. There are 11 errors with modals, related expressions, and imperatives. The first error is corrected for you.

The Language of Advertising

Advertising is everywhere: on street signs, on TV, in newspapers, in the supermarket, and in your mailbox. You ~~mustn't~~ _don't have to_ look for it—it will find you! You can't to get away from advertising.

When we hear or read advertisements, we mayn't think too much about the language in them. But advertisers must thinking about it very carefully. They has to find the words and phrases that sell their products. These words maybe very ordinary, but advertisers know how to use them well. Let's will look at some of these words. For example, the most common word in advertisements is <u>new</u>. That seems like a very ordinary word. But advertisers are able give that word many meanings. In a clever advertisement, <u>new</u> could be mean "exciting," "special," or "better."

Advertisements often use words like <u>may</u> and <u>can</u>—for example, <u>Our toothpaste may make your teeth whiter than any other toothpaste.</u> You have better be careful with these words. Don't to take them too seriously. <u>May</u> means "perhaps," not "definitely," so this advertisement isn't really promising you anything!

2 Yes/No Game: SPEAKING

Can you talk for one minute without saying *yes* or *no*? Find out!

Step 1 One student volunteers to answer questions.

Step 2 The teacher (or another student) quickly asks the volunteer lots of easy questions with modals (for example, "Can you swim?" "Could you swim when you were a child?" "Will you help me with my homework?")

Step 3 The volunteer must answer all the questions quickly (for example, *I can swim. I couldn't swim then. Certainly.*). But the volunteer **must not** say "yes," or "no," or make any sign that means the same, for example, moving your head or saying "Uh-huh"!

Step 4 Classmates watch the clock. If the volunteer stops to think or says *yes* or *no*, the teacher wins. If the volunteer answers successfully for one minute, he or she wins.

3 Language Planning: WRITING

What do you think about language planning in the United States? Should English be the official language, or should the government also use other languages that many Americans speak, like Chinese or Vietnamese? Should we teach non-English-speaking children in English only or also in their first language? Do you think Spanish might become the official language in the United States one day?

Write a paragraph about your opinion. Write at least six sentences with modals and related expressions. Use the opinions in Chapter 17, Exercise 3, to help you.

> *official* = used for all public and government communication.

Example:
   I think English is important, but it shouldn't be the only language in the United States. We ought to have several public languages. . . .

See the *Grammar Links* Website for a complete model paragraph for this activity.

4 Language Learning: SPEAKING

Step 1 Prepare a two-minute speech for the class: *My Language*.

Explain what your first language is like. What should we know when we try to learn your language? Talk about these topics:

The grammar: Can we learn it easily?

How long should it take to learn simple conversation?

Which sounds could be difficult for English speakers?

Body language: We may make mistakes. What may happen then?

Cultural values: Which questions could we ask freely? Which questions shouldn't we ask?

Step 2 Present your speech to the class. Record your speech on audiotape or videotape.

Step 3 Work with a partner. Listen together to each other's recordings. How many modals did each of you use? Did you use them all correctly?

Gerunds and Infinitives

TOPIC FOCUS
Making It

UNIT OBJECTIVES

- **gerunds**
  (*Working* is necessary.)

- **infinitives**
  (It is difficult *to work* for a big company.)

- **choosing between gerunds and infinitives**
  (I *enjoy working* alone. Fred *needs to work* with other people.)

Grammar in Action

🎧 Reading and Listening: Making It

Read and listen.

1   What does *making it* mean? In general, it means "**succeeding**" or "**doing** well." But *making it* and *succeeding* can mean different things to different people. For some people, *making* it means **making** money. For others, it means **doing** something they enjoy, sometimes without **earning** much money. One person might be interested in **having** a business that makes money and also helps solve the problems of the world. Another person might enjoy **working** at home for himself or herself. For yet another person, *making* it means **having** a job that allows free time for family and friends.

2   Whatever your ideas about making it, one thing is for sure: It isn't always easy **to find** a job you like in today's world. People must sometimes struggle **to succeed**. Career counselors have advice for people choosing jobs. It is important **to think** about two questions: What do you really want **to do** with the rest of your life? And what skills do you like **to use**? You need **to find** a job that matches your answers to these two questions. When people do this, they usually succeed in making it.

Think About Grammar

A. Look at the **boldfaced** words in paragraph 1. These words are gerunds. Circle **T** if the statement is true and **F** if the statement is false.

1. A gerund is the *-ing* form of a verb.   T   F

2. A gerund never comes after a preposition.   T   F

3. A gerund never comes right after a verb.   T   F

4. A gerund is sometimes the subject of a sentence.   T   F

B. Look at the **boldfaced** words in paragraph 2. These words are infinitives. Circle **T** if the statement is true and **F** if the statement is false.

1. An infinitive contains the base form of a verb.   T   F

2. An infinitive is sometimes used in a sentence   T   F
   beginning with *It*.

3. An infinitive sometimes comes right after a verb.   T   F

4. An infinitive sometimes comes after a preposition.   T   F

Gerunds and Infinitives

Introductory Task: Friendly Advice

A. Dolores is worried about making it. For her, *making it* means finding her first job. Read this letter from one of her friends who has just found a job.

Dear Dolores,

I know you are worried about finding a job, but you shouldn't worry. It's easy to find a job. It might seem important to look hard for a job. But it is really more important to have good luck. I found a great job yesterday by bumping into an old friend. He was just leaving his job, and I took it. So you see, finding a job is easy. Looking hard for a job might seem important. But having good luck is really more important. Relax. Take it easy. Go out for a walk and see who you bump into!

Good luck,

Charlene

---

bump into = meet unexpectedly.

B. There are three pairs of sentences in the letter that have the same meaning. Write them here:

It's easy to find a job. _____ and Finding a job is easy. _____

_____ and

_____

_____ and

_____

C. Discuss as a class: What is more important, looking hard for a job or having good luck? Do you think it is easy to "make it" in today's world? Why or why not?

GRAMMAR BRIEFING 1

Gerunds I

FORM and FUNCTION

A. Gerunds and Negative Gerunds

1. A gerund (base verb + -*ing*) is a verb form that functions like a noun.

   gerund object
   I enjoy **working**.

   gerund subject
   Reading is fun.

2. The form for a negative gerund is *not* + gerund.

   Not relaxing is bad for your health.

   I suggest **not working** on weekends.

   (See Appendix 3 for the spelling rules for -*ing* verb forms. See Appendix 12 for more about noun functions.)

B. Gerunds as Subjects and After *Be*

1. Like a noun, a gerund or a gerund phrase can be the subject of a sentence.

   Reading is fun.

   A gerund can also come after the verb *be*.

   My favorite sport is **swimming**.

2. When they are subjects, gerunds and gerund phrases take singular verbs.

   Swimming in lakes **is** fun.
     NOT: Swimming in lakes ~~are~~ fun.

(continued on next page)

Gerunds and gerund phrases can be the objects of certain verbs. These include *avoid, keep, consider, practice, dislike, risk, enjoy,* and *suggest*.

verb   object
I **dislike buying** expensive clothes.

verb   object
Joyce **enjoys walking** to work.

verb   object
Frank **considered looking** for a new job.

(See Appendix 20 for more verbs that can be followed by gerunds.)

Note: Are any of the verbs above new to you? Find them in your dictionary.

GRAMMAR PRACTICE 1

Gerunds I

1 **Identifying Gerunds and Negative Gerunds:** Bill Gates—Doing What He Likes

Read the article. Underline the gerunds and negative gerunds. There are 11 of them. The first two are underlined for you.

The Story of Bill Gates

by Edith Parker

When he was a child, Bill Gates' favorite pastime was <u>using</u> computers. In his opinion, <u>not having</u> a computer was worse than not having a library or a school. For Bill, making it in life meant doing what he liked best: working with computers. In 1975, when he was only 19 years old, Bill quit college. With his high school friend, Paul Allen, he started writing computer software. Bill and Paul enjoyed working together. They started their own small software company, Microsoft Corporation. When they first began, they knew a lot about computers but not much about business. They risked losing everything. However, they kept trying. Not giving up their dream was very important to them, and, finally, they "made it." Now Microsoft Corporation is one of the most profitable computer software companies in the world.

pastime = an activity done for fun. *profitable* = money-making.

See the *Grammar Links* Website for more information about Bill Gates.

2 Understanding Gerunds and Negative Gerunds: Advice for Making It

A. Mr. Mack, a successful businessperson, is giving advice for making it. Does he give the following advice? Listen and check *yes* or *no.*

Mr. Mack advises:

		Yes	No
1.	taking business classes at a college or university.	☑	☐
2.	not working alone.	☐	☐
3.	starting with big goals.	☐	☐
4.	not getting a loan.	☐	☐
5.	growing as fast as possible.	☐	☐
6.	doing something you enjoy.	☐	☐

> *goal* = purpose you are working for; objective. *loan* = money you borrow and must repay.

B. Discuss as a class: Do you agree with Mr. Mack's advice? Why or why not?

3 Gerunds as Subjects and After *Be*: Ice Cream for the People

Read the article. Fill in the blanks with the gerund form of the verbs in parentheses. Circle the correct form of the **boldfaced** verbs.

The Story of Ben and Jerry
by Sheela Bavikatty

When Ben Cohen and Jerry Greenfield started their ice cream business in 1978, they had three goals. __Earning__ a living **was** / **were**
1 (Earn)

one of these goals. Another was _____ fun. And a
2 (have)

third goal was _____ something to the people in their community.
3 (give)

_____ their third goal **was** / **were** very important to Ben and Jerry.
4 (Reach)

In the beginning, ice cream was the only thing they had. _____ free
5 (Offer)

ice cream to people **was** / **were** the only way Ben and Jerry could give to the community. Now Ben and

Jerry's is a very successful ice cream business. _____ the community
6 (Help)

is / **are** still important to Ben and Jerry. In their opinion, _____ back
7 (not / give)

to the community **mean** / **means** _____ a responsible business.
8 (not√be)

4   Gerunds as Objects of Verbs: Why Ice Cream?

Complete the story with the gerund form of the verbs in the box. Use each verb only once. Underline the verbs that take gerunds as objects.

> ✓ apply   make   practice
> eat   open   work

Why did Ben and Jerry start an ice cream business? They were looking for work.

They <u>considered</u> <u>applying</u> _____ for jobs in big companies, but they both
                              1

disliked _____ for other people. Ben and Jerry loved food.
                    2

They especially enjoyed _____ ice cream. So their friends
                                        3

suggested _____ an ice cream shop. Ben and Jerry liked this idea.
                        4

They practiced _____ ice cream for a long time. At first it didn't
                          5

taste very good. But they kept _____ until their ice cream was
                                            6

delicious. Then they opened their business. It was a success. Making ice cream helped Ben and

Jerry reach two of their goals: earning a living and having fun.

See the *Grammar Links* Website for more interesting facts about Ben and Jerry's
ice cream.

Gerunds II

FORM and FUNCTION

A. Gerunds After Prepositions

1. Gerunds can be the objects of prepositions.
   (See Chapter 11 for more about prepositions.)

   prep   object
   My ideas **about working** are different from yours.

2. Many verb + preposition combinations can be followed by gerunds—for example, *believe in, concentrate on, count on, dream of, learn about, profit from, succeed in, talk about,* and *work on.*

   She believes in **exercising**.

   Jack talked about **leaving**.

   We dreamed of **winning**.

3. Many adjective + preposition combinations can be followed by gerunds—for example, *afraid of, famous for, fond of, good at, interested in, known for, proud of, sorry about/for,* and *worried about.*

   They were afraid of **failing**.

   Sheila is fond of **swimming**.

   Alex is sorry for **being** late.

4. We use *by* + gerund to talk about how something is done.

   We relax **by reading**. (How do we relax? We read.)

B. *Go* + Gerund

1. *Go* + gerund describes activities—for example, *go bowling, go fishing, go jogging, go shopping, go skiing,* and *go swimming.*

   They **go bowling** every weekend.

   Fred **went swimming** last Saturday.

2. In *go* + gerund sentences, *go* can be in any tense.

   We **go fishing** every summer.

   We **have always gone skiing** in Vermont.

GRAMMAR HOTSPOT!

Don't confuse gerunds with progressive verbs.

Gerund: **Reading** is my favorite hobby.

Progressive verb: I'm **reading** a good book right now.

Gerunds II

5 Gerunds After Prepositions: More Reasons for Ice Cream

Complete the story. Use the prepositions in the box and the gerund forms of the verbs in parentheses. You may use each preposition more than once.

about	by	from	of
at	for	in	on

By making _____ ice cream, Ben and Jerry were reaching two of their goals:
       1 (make)

earning a living and having fun. They were proud _____ in the ice
               2 (succeed)

cream business. But Ben and Jerry were still worried _____ their
               3 (reach)

third goal. They talked a lot _____ something to the people in
         4 (give)

their community. They really believed _____ this. How could they
           5 (do)

use the ice cream business for this purpose? One way was _____
               6 (give)

away free ice cream. Almost everyone is fond _____ ice cream.
            7 (eat)

So Ben and Jerry became famous _____ free ice cream to people
           8 (provide)

in their community. But they dreamed _____ more. They were
           9 (do)

sorry _____ more people. Ben and Jerry were not afraid
     10 (not / help)

_____ hard. So they worked _____
    11 (work)   12 (become)

a "values-led" company, a company that does things that help many people around the world.

> *values* = beliefs or principles.

6 *Go* + Gerund: Making It?

A. Kate and Pete are opening a new business. Kate is talking to her mother on the phone. Complete their conversation with the correct tense of *go* + gerund.

Mother: Congratulations, Kate! When can I _go shopping_____ at your
                                                                     1 (shop)

new store?

Kate: Well, let's see. On Monday morning, Pete _goes swimming_____ and
                                                                     2 (swim)

I always _____ in the park. So that's not a good time.
                        3 (jog)

Mother: Hmm. And Monday afternoons? You _____ every
                                                                     4 (bowl)

Monday afternoon, don't you?

Kate: That's right. And on Tuesdays, we go to the lake. Our friends Angela and Jaime meet

us there. They _____ in the morning, and we
                                5 (fish)

_____. Then, in the afternoon, we all
                6 (sail)

_____ together. So Tuesday isn't a good day either.
                7 (water ski)

Mother: Well, what about Wednesday, then?

Kate: We'll usually be in the store on Wednesday. But next Wednesday we're going to

go to the mountains. Pete _____, and I
                                                8 (ski)

_____.
                9 (ice skate)

Mother: Okay. So you'll be in the store on Thursday?

Kate: Well, you know, Pete and I _____ together since
                                                10 (not / hiking)

last August. So we're going to go to the state park on Thursday. We'll stay until Sunday,

so we can _____, too.
                        11 (sightsee)

Mother: Listen Kate. Maybe you should think a little more about opening your store. I'm not

sure you're going to make it.

Kate: What makes you think that, Mom?

B. Discuss as a class: Why does Kate's mother say Kate won't make it? How can
Kate and Pete succeed in making it in their new business? Use *by* + gerund in
your answers.

Example: *Kate and Pete can succeed by working more.*

C. Write three sentences about your favorite activities. Tell when you usually enjoy them. Use *go* + gerund.

Example: In the winter, I go skiing on weekends.

7 Gerunds Versus Progressive Verbs: Jeff's Problem

A. Read the story. Circle the six *-ing* forms that are gerunds. Underline the eight *-ing* forms that are progressive verbs.

Jeff Jones has been <u>working</u> at the same job for twenty years. He has been getting up every morning at seven o'clock and going to work at eight. He has been working all day and coming home at five o'clock. Jeff is tired of (doing) the same thing and seeing the same people all the time. He is thinking about changing jobs. But when Jeff complains to his wife about not being happy, she says, "Jeff, you are making it in your job. Earning money is important. Paying the bills is important. You have been working at the same job for 20 years. You can't change jobs now. It's too late!"

B. Discuss as a class: Do you agree with Jeff or with Jeff's wife? Is changing jobs after 20 years easy or difficult? What should Jeff and his wife talk about doing next?

8 Writing with Gerunds: About You

Write a paragraph of at least five sentences about yourself. Use the words in the box or choose other verbs, verb + preposition combinations, or adjective + preposition combinations. Use a progressive verb in at least two sentences.

verbs	verbs + prepositions	adjectives + prepositions
dislike	believe in	afraid of
enjoy	dream of	good at
practice	talk about	interested in
risk	work on	proud of

Example: I never risk falling asleep in class. I'm working on learning English, so I'm very interested in studying.

See the *Grammar Links* Website for a complete model paragraph for this assignment.

Infinitives I

FORM and FUNCTION

A. Infinitives and Negative Infinitives

1. An infinitive (*to* + base verb) is a verb form that can function like a noun.

   (See Appendix 12 for more about noun functions.)

   > infinitive subject
   > **To work** in a college is her dream.
   >
   > infinitive object
   > Pedro loves **to work**.

2. The form for a negative infinitive is *not* + *to* + base verb.

   > Kathy tries **not to work**.

B. Infinitives as Subjects and After *Be*

1. Infinitives can be the subjects of sentences. However, sentences with *it* + infinitive are more common.

   > infinitive subject
   > *Less common*: **To work** in a college is her dream.
   >
   > *It* + infinitive
   > *More common*: **It** is her dream **to work** in a college.

2. Sentences with *it* + infinitive often have the same meaning as sentences with gerund subjects.

   > **Driving** home takes about an hour. = **It** takes about an hour **to drive** home.

3. Infinitives can come after the verb *be*.

   > *be* infinitive
   > Her dream **is to work** in a college.

C. Infinitives After Verbs

Verb + Infinitive

Some verbs follow the pattern **verb** + **infinitive**—for example, *agree, claim, decide, fail, hope, learn, manage, offer, plan, pretend, refuse, seem,* and *struggle.*

> I **hope to buy** a new car.
>
> John **agreed to pay** for my new car.
>
> Maya **struggled to pay** for her new stereo.

Verb + Noun/Pronoun + Infinitive

Some verbs must have a noun or pronoun before the infinitive. These verbs follow the pattern **verb + noun/pronoun + infinitive**—for example, *advise, cause, convince, encourage, force, hire, invite, persuade, remind, require, teach, tell, urge,* and *warn.*

> They **hired John to solve** the problem.
>
> Her brother **convinced her not to buy** a new car.
>
> Their friend **told them to write** a letter.

(continued on next page)

Verb + Infinitive or Verb + Noun/Pronoun + Infinitive

Some verbs follow both patterns: **verb + infinitive** or **verb + noun/pronoun + infinitive**—for example, *ask, beg, choose, expect, need, pay, promise,* and *want.*

VERB + INFINITIVE	VERB + NOUN/PRONOUN + INFINITIVE
I **want to see** the new car.	I **want him to see** the new car.
We **asked to talk** to the doctor.	We **asked Greg to talk** to the doctor.

GRAMMAR **HOT**SPOT!

Remember! Form infinitives and negative infinitives correctly.

INFINITIVES	NEGATIVE INFINITIVES
She wants to go. **NOT:** She wants ~~go.~~ **NOT:** She wants to ~~goes.~~ **NOT:** She wants ~~going.~~	She prefers not to eat. **NOT:** She prefers ~~not eat.~~ **NOT:** She prefers not to ~~eats.~~

GRAMMAR PRACTICE 3

Infinitives I

9 **Infinitives and Negative Infinitives:** Tim's Dream

A. Read the first part of the story. Underline the infinitives and negative infinitives. There are 14 of them. The first two are underlined for you.

On Friday, February 13, Tim Cullins decides <u>to go</u> to work early. It is important <u>not to hurry</u> this morning. He wants to have some time alone. He needs to prepare for a meeting with his boss. Tim works for the giant company, ADX, and he is very loyal. Once, the company failed to give him a raise because they didn't have enough extra money. Another company offered to give Tim a job, but Tim decided not to leave ADX. He has always struggled not to hurt the company.

Tim's dream is to become a vice president at ADX. And he knows that his boss wants to promote him. Tim's boss wants to see him today. Tim expects to talk to his boss about his promotion to senior vice president. It is important not to be nervous, but it is hard not to be excited.

---

loyal = faithful. *raise* = pay increase.

B. Continue reading the story. Circle the verb + infinitive combinations. There are six of them. The first one is circled for you. Draw a box around the verb + object + infinitive combinations. There are seven of them. The first box is done for you.

On Friday morning, Mitsu Tanaka forces himself to get out of bed. He doesn't want to think about this day. Mitsu's boss, the owner of ADX, is requiring him to offer a senior vice president position to a new employee. Mitsu has begged his boss not to do this. He has reminded his boss to look at Tim Cullins' good record. He has encouraged his boss to offer the position to Tim instead. But Mitsu's boss wants to make some changes. The company needs to think about the future. He asks Mitsu not to wait. He wants him to tell Tim the news this morning. Mitsu agrees to do it. He has no choice.

When he arrives at the office, Mitsu calls Tim. He asks to see him right away. Tim arrives quickly. He pretends not to be nervous. But Mitsu knows him. Tim is very excited. Mitsu looks at Tim. It is difficult to speak.

C. Discuss as a class: Have you ever heard a true story like this one? Does this ever happen in the real business world? Is it right, is it wrong, or is it "just business"? What do you think?

10 *It* **+ Infinitive:** Tim's New Dream

Tim Cullins wants a new job. He and his wife, Maria, are talking. Complete their conversation. Change the underlined sentences to *it* + infinitive sentences.

1. Tim: I'm leaving ADX. Staying there now is uncomfortable.

     It is uncomfortable to stay there now.

2. Maria: I understand. But leaving ADX is a big decision.

     But it's a big decision to leave ADX.

3. Tim: Yes, it is. But now I will never be happy there again. Becoming a vice president was very important.

     _____

     _____

4. Maria: You're right. But staying at ADX for a while is important.

     _____

5. Tim: Don't worry. I won't leave until I find another job. Leaving right away isn't necessary.

     _____

6. Maria: Right. <u>Finding a new job might take a long time.</u>

   _____

7. Tim: I know. <u>And paying the bills is still important.</u>

   _____

8. Maria: Right. I just thought of something wonderful about this. <u>Now working on weekends</u>
   <u>won't be necessary</u>!

   _____

   Tim: That's right!

9. Maria: <u>Spending more time together might be possible!</u>

   _____

10. Tim: That's true, Maria. I can slow down and enjoy my life a little more.
    <u>Maybe not getting promoted wasn't a bad thing.</u>

    _____

11 Verb + Infinitive and Verb + Object + Infinitive: Making It on Stage

A. Ginger Carrera is an actress. Complete the passage from Ginger's journal.
Use the correct forms of the words in parentheses.

I love acting in front of a live audience. That kind of acting <u>teaches me to be</u>
1 (teach / me / be)

a better actress. Each audience _____ something a
2 (seem / want)

little different. That's exciting. My agent often _____ other
3 (encourage / me / try)

kinds of acting. He _____
4 (warn / all of his actors / not / stay)

with one thing. Once, in the past, he _____ in a movie.
5 (convince / me / act)

But I didn't enjoy it. Now my agent _____ working in
6 (tell / me / keep)

the movies. He _____ me "strike it rich" someday.
7 (hope / see)

But I _____ about other things besides money!
8 (remind / him / think)

I _____ about money for a while. I just
9 (decide / not / worry)

_____ something new every day and become a better actress.
10 (plan / learn)

> *live audience* = people attending and watching a performance. *agent* = a person
> who helps others get jobs.

B. Discuss as a class: What does *making it* mean for Ginger Carrera? What do you
think of her ideas?

12 **Verb + Infinitive or Verb + Object + Infinitive:** The Wrong Agent or the Wrong Actress?

Read the short conversations. Then complete the sentences. Use a verb + infinitive or a verb + object + infinitive combination.

1. Agent: Welcome to my office. Please come in and sit down.

    Actress: Thank you very much.

    The agent invites _the actress to sit down._

2. Agent: Please try to act in more movies.

    Actress: Sorry. I'm not interested.

    The actress refuses _____

3. Agent: Please don't stop acting in movies! You are making a lot of money!

    Actress: I don't care about money.

    The agent warns _____

4. Agent: Okay. So you don't want to act in movies. Will you meet with the new producer for

              CBN television?

    Actress: I'll think about it.

    The agent encourages _____

    _____

5. Agent: Have you thought about the offer to act in the new mystery movie?

    Actress: I'm not going to accept the offer.

    The actress has decided _____

    _____

6. Agent: I think maybe you need to find a new agent.

    Actress: I agree.

    The actress has agreed _____

Infinitives II

FORM and FUNCTION

A. Infinitives of Purpose

1. *In order* + infinitive is the infinitive of purpose. It is an adverb telling **why**.	*in order* infinitive	He studied medicine **in order to become** a doctor. (Why did he study medicine? Because he wanted to become a doctor.)
2. We often omit *in order* with infinitives of purpose. The meaning stays the same.		He studied medicine **in order to become** a doctor. = He studied medicine **to become** a doctor.
3. Don't use *for* before infinitives of purpose.		I went to the store to buy some milk. **NOT:** I went to the store ~~for~~ to buy some milk.

TALKING THE TALK

	WRITING	SPEAKING
1. Infinitive *to* is often pronounced "*tuh*."	Pete needs to find a new job.	Pete needs **tuh** find a new job.
2. *Want to* is often pronounced "*wanna*."	I want to go home.	I **wanna** go home.

Infinitives II

13 Listening to Infinitives; Infinitives of Purpose: Helping Companies Make It

A. A business consultant is talking about the problems that some companies are having today. Listen and write the full forms of the words you hear.

It's a real struggle for some big companies _to survive_ (1) these days.

Things are different now in the business world than they were ten years ago. Big companies are not doing as well. So big companies are hiring me _____ (2) them.

These big companies _____ (3) survive. But _____ (4) that, they need to make very hard decisions. They _____ (5) force themselves to do things that sometimes seem unkind in the short term. Usually, for example, I advise them to downsize. _____ (6) companies usually need _____ (7) some people go, that is, _____ (8) them.

It's tough. They don't like _____ (9) that, and I don't either. But I _____ (10) help these big companies. I _____ (11) see them succeed. When they succeed, there are more jobs for everybody. _____ (12) well in the long term, and _____ (13) the most people over time, companies need _____ (14) tough in the short term.

> *in the short term* = at the moment. *downsize* = get smaller.

B. Look again at the infinitives you wrote in Part A. Write *in order* above all the infinitives of purpose.

C. Discuss with a partner: Do you agree with the consultant's ideas? Why or why not?

14 Infinitives of Purpose: In Order to Make It...

A. What should people do in order to make it in different jobs? Write sentences using the words given. Use an infinitive of purpose with *to* or *in order to* in the **boldfaced** part of each sentence. Use *you need to* for the other part of each sentence.

1. work night and day/**have your own successful business.**

   You need to work night and day in order to have your own successful business ___ OR

   You need to work night and day to have your own successful business. ___

2. **be a college professor**/earn a Ph.D. in a specialized field of study

   To be a college professor, you need to earn a Ph.D. in a specialized field of study. ___ OR

   In order to be a college professor, you need to earn a Ph.D. in a specialized field of study. ___

3. **be a clerk in a store**/enjoy working with people ___

   ___

   ___

4. enjoy acting/**have a career as a film star** ___

   ___

   ___

5. **be an elementary school teacher**/enjoy children ___

   ___

   ___

6. understand numbers/**work in a bank** ___

   ___

   ___

7. **manage a large company**/make difficult decisions ___

   ___

   ___

8. work hard/**succeed in any job** ___

   ___

   ___

B. Discuss as a class: Do you agree with the sentences in Part A? Why or why not?

15 Infinitives of Purpose: About You

 Work with a partner. Ask and answer the questions below. Use an infinitive of purpose with *to* or with *in order to* in your answer. Then ask two questions of your own.

Example: Question: You went to the library. Why?
Answer: I went to the library to borrow a book. OR I went to the library in order to borrow a book.

1. You went to the cafeteria. Why?

_____

2. You bought a new suit. Why?

_____

3. You applied for a new job. Why?

_____

4. You are studying English. Why?

_____

5. You wrote a letter to your friend. Why?

_____

6. You bought an airplane ticket. Why?

_____

7. You came to this school. Why?

_____

8. You went to the gym. Why?

_____

Check your progress! Go to the Self-Test for Chapter 19 on the *Grammar Links* Website.

Chapter 20

Gerunds Versus Infinitives

Introductory Task: People and Their Jobs

A. Read this poster hanging in a career counselor's office.

FINDING THE RIGHT JOB

What job interests you the most? Take a minute. **Stop** to think about your career interests. You should never **stop** thinking about your career goals and interests. When you stop thinking about these things, you sometimes find yourself in a job that you do not enjoy at all. Here are some good jobs for different types of people.

Type of Person	Good Job Choice	
Enjoys helping others	teacher, social worker, counselor, nurse	Nurse
Likes working with mechanical things	airplane or car mechanic, electrician, plumber, appliance repairperson	Mechanic
Wants to earn a lot of money	banker, lawyer, businessperson, airline pilot	Lawyer
Likes to create things	artist, advertiser, cook, architect	Artist

Talk to your career counselor NOW about the best job for you!

social worker = person who works for an organization to help others.
appliance = a machine, such as a toaster or dishwasher.

B. Look at the **boldfaced** verbs in the poster. Answer these questions.

1. Which verb is followed only by a gerund? _____

2. Which verb is followed only by an infinitive? _____

3. Which verbs are followed by both gerunds and infinitives? _____

C. Read these two sentences from the poster.

Stop to think about your career interests. You should never **stop** thinking about your career goals and interests.

Discuss as a class: In these sentences, *stop to think* and *stop thinking* do not have the same meaning. What is the difference?

GRAMMAR BRIEFING 1

Gerunds Versus Infinitives

FORM

A. Verb + Gerund

Some verbs can be followed by gerunds, but not by infinitives—for example, *appreciate, avoid, dislike, enjoy, finish, miss, practice, quit, recommend,* and *suggest.*
(See Appendix 20 for a more complete list of these verbs.)

I enjoy **reading**.
  NOT: I enjoy ~~to read~~.

He recommended **calling** her.
  NOT: He recommended ~~to call~~ her.

I miss **talking** to you.
  NOT: I miss ~~to talk~~ to you.

B. Verb + Infinitive

Some verbs can be followed by infinitives, but not by gerunds—for example, *advise, arrange, decide, expect, fail, manage, need, offer, struggle, wait,* and *want.*
(See Appendix 21 for a more complete list of these verbs.)

I want **to go**.
  NOT: I want ~~going~~.

She managed **to find** her watch.
  NOT: She managed ~~finding~~ her watch.

They decided **to move** to Chicago.
  NOT: They decided ~~moving~~ to Chicago.

GRAMMAR HOTSPOT!

Remember! Gerunds can come after prepositions. Infinitives cannot.

I am happy **about going** to Chicago.
  NOT: I am happy about ~~to go~~ to Chicago.

Gerunds Versus Infinitives I

1 **Gerund or Infinitive: Paula's Job Search**

A. Complete the story with the gerund or the infinitive form of the verbs in parentheses.

Paula was a lawyer, but she was unhappy. She was very shy, so she didn't enjoy

<u>talking</u> to people very much. Lawyers need _____
1 (talk)   2 (talk)

to people every day.

Last year, Paula arranged _____ computer programming at the
3 (study)

university in her town. She managed _____ very well, so she decided
4 (do)

_____ a computer programmer. As a computer programmer, she could
5 (become)

avoid _____ to people too much. She could talk to computers instead.
6 (talk)

Paula wanted _____ her new career right away. She was excited
7 (begin)

about _____ her job search. She expected _____
8 (start)   9 (find)

a job quickly. In one day, she finished _____ her résumé to over
10 (send)

100 companies! Then she waited _____ back from all of them.
11 (hear)

Paula was discouraged. She was failing _____ a job. Paula visited
12 (find)

a career counselor. The counselor suggested _____ a different job-
13 (try)

hunting strategy. He recommended _____ to employers directly.
14 (talk)

Then Paula was even more unhappy! She was not good at _____ to
15 (talk)

strangers. The career counselor offered _____ Paula. With him, she
16 (help)

practiced _____ employers and _____
17 (call)   18 (ask)

for job interviews. At first she disliked _____ this. She struggled
19 (do)

_____ more confidence. Soon, however, Paula managed
20 (have)

_____ her shyness. She appreciated _____
21 (overcome)   22 (learn)

this new job-hunting strategy. And it worked! Paula now has a job as a computer programmer.

She talks to computers all day. But Paula is still unhappy. Thanks to her career counselor, Paula

isn't shy anymore. She misses _____ to people!
23 (talk)

B. Discuss in small groups: Have you ever felt like Paula? Have you ever been tired of
one job and ready to try another? What did you do?

Be used to + gerund means "be accustomed to." | I walk to school every day now. **I'm used to walking** to school.
NOT: I'm used to ~~walk~~ to school.

Used to + base verb talks about actions in the past that are not happening anymore.
(See Unit Two for a more about *used to*.) | In the past, I walked to school every day. I **used to walk** to school.
NOT: I used to ~~walking~~ to school.

2 **Be Used To and Used To:** A Personal Career Choice

A. Complete the story with *used to* + the base form or *be used to* + the gerund of the verbs in parentheses.

I ___used to work___ as an editor for a large publishing company, but I
          _{1 (work)}

don't anymore. Now I work at home as a professional writer. My job at the publishing company

was great in many ways, but it was also very difficult. I _____
              _{2 (commute)}

to work every day in heavy rush-hour traffic. Now I _____ at
              _{3 (relax)}

home and _____ a cup of coffee during rush hour. What a difference
      _{4 (enjoy)}

that makes! I _____ to get home before my kids arrived from school,
      _{5 (rush)}

and I often didn't make it. Now my daughter _____ me home every
           _{6 (find)}

afternoon when she gets off the school bus. And my son _____ me
            _{7 (have)}

there to help him with his homework.

I _____ a lot about pleasing my boss and following
      _{8 (worry)}

his work schedule. Now I _____ my own boss and
        _{9 (be)}

I _____ my own work schedule. My life is much less
      _{10 (set)}

stressful than it _____.
      _{11 (be)}

We're a much happier family these days. In the past, we _____
           _{12 (spend)}

only a few hours together each week. Now we _____ together
        _{13 (be)}

several hours a day. My career change was an important personal choice.

> *editor* = a person who helps writers prepare material for publication. *publishing company* = a company that prints books. *commute* = travel between home and work. *rush-hour traffic* = heavy traffic during commuting.

 See the *Grammar Links* Website for more information about jobs you can do at home.

B. Write a paragraph of at least five sentences about things you **used to do** in the past but don't do now and about the things you **are used to doing** now instead. Use *used to* + base form and *be used to* + gerund.

Example:

I used to eat five candy bars every day. Now I'm used to eating five servings of vegetables instead.

See the *Grammar Links* Website for a complete model paragraph for this assignment.

GRAMMAR BRIEFING 2

Gerunds Versus Infinitives II

FORM and FUNCTION

A. Verb + Gerund or Infinitive—Same Meaning

Some verbs can be followed by either a gerund or an infinitive, with little or no difference in meaning. These verbs include *begin, continue, hate, like, love, prefer,* and *start*.	The snow began **falling** late last night. = The snow began **to fall** late last night.

B. Verb + Gerund or Infinitive—Different Meaning

Some verbs can be followed by either a gerund or an infinitive, but there is a difference in meaning. These verbs include *forget, remember,* and *stop*:

• *Forget, remember,* or *stop* + gerund: The gerund describes what happens first. *Forget, remember,* or *stop* describes what happens second.	I'll never **forget going** to the opera. (First I went to the opera; now I'll never forget it.) I **remember mailing** the letters. (First I mailed the letters; now I remember.) I **stopped eating** desserts. (First I ate desserts; then I stopped.)
• *Forget, remember,* or *stop* + infinitive: The infinitive describes what happens second. *Forget, remember,* or *stop* describes what happens first.	I **forgot to go** to the opera. (First I forgot about the opera; so I didnt go.) I **remembered to mail** the letters. (First I remembered; then I mailed the letters.) I **stopped to eat** dessert. (First I stopped what I was doing; then I ate dessert.)

Gerunds Versus Infinitives II

3 **Gerunds and Infinitives:** A Crazy Career

Complete the article with the gerund or the infinitive of the verbs in parentheses. In some blanks, either form might be possible.

A CRAZY CAREER

by James Conley

Gabriel Wasserman, garbologist

Gabriel Wasserman lives in New York City. He is a "garbologist." He collects and sells the valuable garbage of famous people. Most people want ___to get rid of___ their
1 (get rid of)

garbage. Gabriel Wasserman prefers _____
2 (collect)

it. He has succeeded in _____ many priceless treasures in the
3 (find)

garbage cans of famous people. For example, he has found letters written by movie stars.

He has also found old clothing that once belonged to U.S. presidents and their wives.

Gabriel sells this "garbage" to people who enjoy _____ things
4 (collect)

used by famous people.

Some famous people don't like _____ Gabriel looking in
5 (have)

their garbage cans. They hate _____ him in their yards.
6 (see)

The police have even arrested Gabriel for _____ garbage.
7 (take)

But Gabriel Wasserman continues _____ his job. He keeps
8 (do)

_____ to the homes of famous people. He always hopes
9 (go)

_____ good things for his garbage collection. Gabriel Wasserman
10 (find)

has a tough job, but he loves it. He just loves _____ garbage!
11 (pick up)

🌐 Check out the *Grammar Links* Website for more interesting facts about crazy careers!

4 Gerunds and Infinitives: Making It Your Way

A. Complete the sentences below with things that are important to you in a good job.
Use a verb + gerund or a verb + infinitive in each sentence. Write about the ideas
in the box or use your own ideas.

coworkers	a lot of work on weekends	problems
salary	a computer	a lot of meetings
free time for friends	privacy	a long vacation
boss	coffee breaks	
commute	help from other people	

When I am working:

1. I expect _to have friendly coworkers._____

2. I like _having a lot of responsibility._____

3. I hate _____

4. I refuse _____

5. I always want _____

6. I enjoy _____

7. I need _____

8. I prefer _____

9. I don't need _____

10. I hope _____

> *coworker* = person you work with. *privacy* = freedom to keep your own
> affairs secret.

B. Choose the three things in Part A that are the most important to you in a
good job. Write them on the lines in order of importance (1 = most important,
3 = least important).

1. _____

2. _____

3. _____

C. Compare your list with a partner's list. Did you have any of the same ideas?
Now survey the class. Write each person's sentence 1 from Part B on the board.
Discuss: What do most people think is the most important thing in a good job?
Suggest possible jobs for your classmates, based on what they think is important.

5 ***Forget, Remember,*** **and** ***Stop*****:** **The Unlucky Interview I**

Joyce had an interview with the DataWow Company. Write *1* next to what happened first. Write *2* next to what happened second.

1. The night before the interview, Joyce remembered to set her alarm clock for 7:30 a.m.

   ___2___ Joyce set her alarm clock.   ___1___ Joyce remembered.

2. However, she forgot getting a call from the DataWow secretary. DataWow wanted to see her at 8:00 instead of 9:00.

   _____ Joyce got a call.   _____ Joyce forgot.

3. Joyce thought she had plenty of time before the interview, so she stopped to eat breakfast.

   _____ Joyce ate breakfast.   _____ Joyce stopped.

4. Suddenly, Joyce stopped eating her breakfast.

   _____ Joyce was eating breakfast.   _____ Joyce stopped.

5. She remembered receiving the phone call from DataWow to change the interview time.

   _____ She received a call.   _____ She remembered.

6. Joyce was already one hour late for her job interview! She hurried out of the restaurant. But on her way out the door, she remembered to leave a tip for the waitress.

   _____ She left a tip for the waitress.   _____ She remembered.

6 *Forget, Remember,* and *Stop*: The Unlucky Interview II

Joyce's job interview went from bad to worse. Complete the sentences with the correct form—gerund or infinitive—of the verbs in parentheses.

1. Joyce rushed into the DataWow office. She didn't tell the secretary who she was.

    Joyce forgot _____ the secretary who she was.
    (tell)

2. The secretary met Joyce three days ago. She didn't remember this.

    The secretary didn't remember _____ Joyce three days ago.
    (meet)

3. The secretary stopped what she was doing. She asked Joyce to leave.

    The secretary stopped _____ Joyce to leave.
    (ask)

4. Joyce started to explain why she was late. The secretary was busy.

    She looked angry. Joyce stopped.

    Joyce stopped _____ why she was late.
    (explain)

5. Joyce was embarrassed. She thanked the secretary for her time. She rushed out.

    Joyce remembered _____ the secretary for her time.
    (thank)

6. Joyce went home. There was a message on her answering machine. It was from the

    DataWow secretary. She was asking Joyce to come back and try again tomorrow.

    Joyce will never forget _____ to that message. It made her
    (listen)

    the happiest job hunter in the world.

7. Joyce was too excited to think clearly. She forgot an important thing. She didn't write

    down the interview time.

    Joyce forgot _____ the interview time.
    (write down)

7 Gerunds and Infinitives: Group Game

 Divide into three groups. Group 1 has Box 1. Group 2 has Box 2. Group 3 has Box 3. Some of the sentences in each box are correct. Others are incorrect. Mark the correct sentences with a check (✓). Correct the incorrect sentences. The first group to finish everything correctly is the winner.

Box 1

1. We were tired of working, so we stopped to drink a cup of coffee.
2. Raquel and Clara go to hiking together every Saturday.
3. My cousins are afraid of not to have enough money when they retire.
4. It takes patience to find the career you want.
5. They were not ready retire.
6. To find a new career, you need to have more than good luck.
7. By be patient, you will find a good job.

Box 2

1. It takes time to find the right job.
2. Peter is going to skiing tomorrow.
3. We always appreciate to get good business advice.
4. She improved her career chances by working with a career counselor.
5. I used to take work home at night, but I've stopped doing that.
6. My boss asked to me to do some extra work tonight.
7. Sometimes they don't want to eating dinner.

Box 3

1. Hsui and Tsai like to going to the business meeting every Friday.
2. I always remember to lock the car door, but I sometimes forget to remove the keys first.
3. Randy goes shopping on Saturdays.
4. They wanted in order to start a new business in California.
5. Paul is used to have lots of free time.
6. I'll never forget meeting my new boss.
7. They always expect me doing the extra work.

Check your progress! Go to the Self-Test for Chapter 20 on the *Grammar Links* Website.

Wrap-up Activities

1 The Right Job for George: EDITING

Correct the errors in this student essay. There are 12 errors with gerunds and infinitives. The first error is corrected for you.

Essay by: Jahan Bakhtar

English 101

February 12, 2005

The Right Job for George

George Walters is a truck driver. He ~~is~~ used to work in a big factory, but he really disliked working with so many people. He also hated being not his own boss. Working for himself were his dream. Now George's dream has come true, and he has his freedom. George loves to driving his truck. He enjoys to be alone all day, and he loves traveling all over the United States. George never complains about to drive. He is used to be in his truck all day.

George is used to being in his truck all night, too! When he first started drive his truck, George decided to fix it up. He wanted his truck to be his home away from home. By enlarge his cab (where he sits), it was easy for George to making a small bedroom and kitchen in his truck. George now has enough room for live in the back of his cab. When he is too tired to drive anymore, he stops sleeping.

George spends a lot of time alone. But he has a lot of friends, too. George and his truck driver friends stop to visit with one another at rest stops and truck stops all across the United States. The next time you are on the road, look for George. He'll be driving a big black truck with the words "I love my job!" painted on the side.

2 People Like You: WRITING/SPEAKING

Step 1 Complete the descriptions with gerunds or infinitives. Then choose your favorite group of people. Put an X on the line next to that group.

_____ Group A: These people like _____ (work) with machines, tools, plants, or animals, and _____ (be) outdoors.

Mechanic

_____ Group B: These people enjoy _____ (work) with numbers, _____ (carry out) details, and _____ (follow) other people's instructions.

Computer Programmers

_____ Group C: These people prefer _____ (influence) other people. They like _____ (manage), _____ (lead) others in _____ (do) things.

Lawyer

_____ Group D: These people want _____ (work) with other people. They are interested in _____ (inform), _____ (help), _____ (cure), and _____ (teach).

Nurse

_____ Group E: These people love _____ (be) creative. They like _____ (use) their imaginations and _____ (be) artistic. They prefer _____ (work) without too much structure or too many bosses.

Artist

_____ Group F: These people prefer _____ (observe), _____ (learn), and _____ (investigate). They enjoy _____ (solve) problems and _____ (analyze) things.

Scientist

Step 2 Work as a class. Students choosing Group A go to one part of the room. Students choosing Group B go to another part of the room, etc. Talk to the people in your group. Are they interested in having the same kinds of jobs you are? What are those jobs?

Step 3 Write a paragraph of at least five sentences about the jobs that people in your group like doing. Explain why. Use gerunds and infinitives.

Example: Some of the people in my group are interested in teaching. They want to be English teachers.

See the *Grammar Links* Website for a complete model paragraph for this activity.

Step 4 Report to the class. Discuss: Do different groups have different job interests? Or do they all like to do the same things?

3 Selling It!: WRITING/LISTENING/SPEAKING

Imagine that you are a salesperson. You need to sell the objects below.

Step 1 Work in groups. Think of several uses for the objects. Use your imagination! With the other members of your group, write a short paragraph about one of the objects. In your paragraph, give detailed instructions about using your object. Use at least three gerunds and three infinitives.

Example: You can use a paper clip to hold your glasses together. To do this, you need to open the paper clip. Then, . . .

Step 2 Sell your object to the class. Demonstrate all of its uses. If possible, videotape your demonstration.

Step 3 Watch your video. Did you use gerunds? Infinitives?

4 Don't Forget to Remember: WRITING/SPEAKING

Step 1 Use the words given to write interesting sentences about yourself. Then choose one sentence. Add information to write a short story about yourself.

Example: I'll never forget buying my first car. I was 21 years old. It was difficult to choose the right car for me. . . .

1. I'll never forget (+ gerund) _____

_____

2. I once forgot (+ infinitive) _____

_____

3. I'll always remember (+ gerund) _____

_____

4. I always remember (+ infinitive) _____

_____

5. Once I get started, I can never stop (+ gerund) _____

_____

6. I recently stopped on my way to school (+ infinitive) _____

_____

🌐 See the *Grammar Links* Website for a complete model story for this activity.

Step 2 Share your stories as a class.

Appendixes

Simple Present Tense of the Verb *Be*

FORM

A. Affirmative Statements

SUBJECT	BE	
I	**am**	tall.
You		
We	**are**	tall.
They		
He		
She	**is**	tall.
It		

B. Negative Statements

SUBJECT	BE + NOT	
I	**am not** / **'m not**	tall.
You	**are not**	
We	**aren't**	tall.
They	**'re not**	
He	**is not**	
She	**isn't**	tall.
It	**'s not**	

C. *Yes/No* Questions and Short Answers

QUESTIONS

BE	SUBJECT	
Am	I	tall?
	you	
Are	we	tall?
	they	
	he	
Is	she	tall?
	it	

SHORT ANSWERS

YES				NO		
Yes,	I	**am.**		No,	I	**am not.** / **'m not.**
	you				you	**are not.**
Yes,	we	**are.**		No,	we	**aren't.**
	they				they	**'re not.**
	he				he	**is not.**
Yes,	she	**is.**		No,	she	**isn't.**
	it				it	**'s not.**

D. *Wh-* Questions and Answers

QUESTIONS

WH- WORD	BE	SUBJECT
Where	**am**	I?
Who	**are**	you? / we? / they?
Where	**is**	he? / she? / it?

ANSWERS

In the hospital.

Doctors.

In the hospital.

Pronunciation Rules for the Third Person Singular Form of the Simple Present Tense

The -*s* ending is pronounced three different ways:

- /s/ after the voiceless sounds /p/, /t/, /k/, and /f/.

stops	gets	takes	laughs

- /z/ after the voiced sounds /b/, /d/, /g/, /v/, /th/, /m/, /n/, /ng/, /l/, /r/, and all vowel sounds.

robs	gives	remains	hears
adds	bathes	sings	agrees
begs	seems	tells	knows

- /iz/ after the sounds /s/, /z/, /sh/, /zh/, /ch/, /j/, and /ks/.

passes	catches
freezes	judges (ge = /j/)
rushes	relaxes (x = /ks/)
massages (ge = /zh/)	

Spelling Rules for *-ing* Verb Forms

1. Most verbs: Base form of verb + -*ing*

walk → walk**ing**	order → order**ing**

2. Verbs that end in -*e*: Drop -*e*. Add -*ing*.

write → writ**ing**	decide → decid**ing**

3. Verbs that end in -*ie*: Change -*ie* to -*y*. Add -*ing*.

tie → t**ying**	lie → l**ying**

4. Verbs that end in consonant + vowel + consonant: Double the final consonant. Add -*ing*.

run → ru**nning**	permit → permi**tting**

   BUT: Do not double the final consonant when:

   - The last syllable is not stressed.

lísten → listen**ing**

   - The last consonant is *w*, *x*, or *y*.

allow → allow**ing**	box → box**ing**
play → play**ing**	

Spelling Rules for the Simple Past Tense of Regular Verbs

1. Most verbs: Add -ed.	walk → walk**ed** order → order**ed**
2. Verbs that end in -e: Add -d.	live → live**d** decide → decide**d**
3. Verbs that end in a consonant + y: Change -y to -i. Add -ed.	bury → bur**ied**
4. Verbs that end in consonant + vowel + consonant: Double the final consonant. Add -ed.	shop → shop**ped** permit → permit**ted**

BUT: Do not double the final consonant when:

- The last syllable is not stressed.

lísten → listen**ing**

- The last consonant is w, x, or y.

allow → allow**ing**   box → box**ing**

play → play**ing**

Pronunciation Rules for the Simple Past Tense of Regular Verbs

The -d ending is pronounced three different ways:

- /t/ after the voiceless sounds /f/, /k/, /p/, /s/, /sh/, /ch/, and /ks/.

laughed	clapped	wished	waxed
talked	passed	watched	

- /d/ after the voiced sounds /b/, /g/, /j/, /m/, /n/, /ng/, /l/, /r/, /th/, /v/, /z/, /zh/, and all vowel sounds.

robbed	bathed
begged	waved
judged (ge = /j/)	surprised
seemed	massaged (ge = /zh/)
remained	played
banged	enjoyed
called	cried
ordered	

- /ɪd/ after the sounds /t/ and /d/.

started	needed

Irregular Verbs

BASE FORM	PAST	PAST PARTICIPLE	BASE FORM	PAST	PAST PARTICIPLE
be	was, were	been	forget	forgot	forgotten
beat	beat	beaten	forgive	forgave	forgiven
become	became	become	freeze	froze	frozen
begin	began	begun	get	got	gotten
bend	bent	bent	give	gave	given
bite	bit	bitten	go	went	gone
bleed	bled	bled	grow	grew	grown
blow	blew	blown	have	had	had
break	broke	broken	hear	heard	heard
bring	brought	brought	hide	hid	hidden
build	built	built	hit	hit	hit
burn	burned/burnt	burned/burnt	hold	held	held
buy	bought	bought	hurt	hurt	hurt
catch	caught	caught	keep	kept	kept
choose	chose	chosen	know	knew	known
come	came	come	lay	laid	laid
cost	cost	cost	lead	led	led
cut	cut	cut	leap	leaped/leapt	leaped/leapt
dig	dug	dug	leave	left	left
do	did	done	lend	lent	lent
draw	drew	drawn	let	let	let
dream	dreamed/dreamt	dreamed/dreamt	lie	lay	lain
drink	drank	drunk	light	lit/lighted	lit/lighted
drive	drove	driven	lose	lost	lost
eat	ate	eaten	make	made	made
fall	fell	fallen	mean	meant	meant
feed	fed	fed	meet	met	met
feel	felt	felt	mistake	mistook	mistaken
fight	fought	fought	pay	paid	paid
find	found	found	prove	proved	proved/proven
fly	flew	flown	put	put	put
forbid	forbade	forbidden	quit	quit	quit
forecast	forecast	forecast	read	read	read

Irregular Verbs

BASE FORM	PAST	PAST PARTICIPLE	BASE FORM	PAST	PAST PARTICIPLE
rid	rid	rid	spend	spent	spent
ride	rode	ridden	spread	spread	spread
ring	rang	rung	spring	sprang	sprung
rise	rose	risen	stand	stood	stood
run	ran	run	steal	stole	stolen
say	said	said	strike	struck	struck
see	saw	seen	swear	swore	sworn
seek	sought	sought	sweep	swept	swept
sell	sold	sold	swim	swam	swum
send	sent	sent	swing	swung	swung
set	set	set	take	took	taken
shake	shook	shaken	teach	taught	taught
shave	shaved	shaved/shaven	tear	tore	torn
shine	shined/shone	shined/shone	tell	told	told
shoot	shot	shot	think	thought	thought
show	showed	showed/shown	throw	threw	thrown
shut	shut	shut	understand	understood	understood
sing	sang	sung	upset	upset	upset
sink	sank	sunk	wake	woke	woken
sit	sat	sat	wear	wore	worn
sleep	slept	slept	wet	wet	wet
slide	slid	slid	win	won	won
speak	spoke	spoken	wind	wound	wound
speed	sped	sped	write	wrote	written

Simple Past Tense of *Be*

FORM

A. Affirmative Statements

SUBJECT	BE	
I		
He	**was**	tall.
She		
It		
You		
We	**were**	tall.
They		

B. Negative Statements

SUBJECT	BE + NOT	
I		
He	**was not**	tall.
She	**wasn't**	
It		
You		
We	**were not**	tall.
They	**weren't**	

C. *Yes/No* Questions and Short Answers

QUESTIONS

BE	SUBJECT	
Was	I	tall?
	he	
	she	
	it	
Were	you	tall?
	we	
	they	

SHORT ANSWERS

YES		
Yes,	I	**was.**
	he	
	she	
	it	
Yes,	you	**were.**
	we	
	they	

NO		
No,	I	**was not.**
	he	**wasn't.**
	she	
	it	
No,	you	**were not.**
	we	**weren't.**
	they	

D. *Wh-* Questions and Answers

QUESTIONS

WH- WORD	BE	SUBJECT
Where	**was**	I?
		he?
		she?
		it?
Who	**were**	you?
		we?
		they?

ANSWERS

In the hospital.

Doctors.

Spelling Rules for Regular Plural Count Nouns

- Most nouns: Add -*s*.

room → rooms	office → offices
day → days	studio → studios

- Nouns that end in -*ch*, -*sh*, -*ss*, -*x*, or -*z*: Add -*es*.

lunch → lunches	box → boxes
brush → brushes	quiz → quizzes
kiss → kisses	

- Nouns ending in a consonant + -*y*: Drop -*y*. Add -*ies*.

dormitory → dormitories	story → stories

- Nouns ending in -*f* or -*fe*: Drop -*f* or -*fe*. Add -*ves*.

shelf → shelves	knife → knives
Exceptions: belief → beliefs, chief → chiefs, roof → roofs	

- A few nouns ending in a consonant + -*o*: Add -*es*.

hero → heroes	potato → potatoes
mosquito → mosquitoes	tomato → tomatoes

Pronunciation Rules for Regular Plural Count Nouns

The -*s* ending is pronounced as:

- /s/ after the voiceless sounds /p/, /t/, /k/, /f/, and /th/.

cups	hats	books	cuffs	paths

- /z/ after the voiced sounds /b/, /d/, /g/, /v/, /th/, /m/, /n/, /ng/, /l/, /r/, and all vowel sounds.

jobs	knives	bones	bears
kids	lathes	things	days
legs	dreams	bells	potatoes

- /ɪz/ after the sounds /s/, /z/, /sh/, /zh/, /ch/, /j/, and /ks/.

classes	churches
breezes	judges (*ge* = /j/)
dishes	taxes (*x* = /ks/)
massages (*ge* = /zh/)	

Common Irregular Plural Nouns

SINGULAR	PLURAL	SINGULAR	PLURAL	SINGULAR	PLURAL	SINGULAR	PLURAL
child	children	goose	geese	person	people	woman	women
deer	deer	man	men	sheep	sheep		
fish	fish	mouse	mice	species	species		
foot	feet	ox	oxen	tooth	teeth		

Common Noncount Nouns

1. Names of groups of similar items:

baggage	equipment	furniture	jewelry	mail	stuff
cash	food	garbage	luggage	makeup	trash
clothing	fruit	homework	machinery	money	traffic

(**Note:** These groups often have individual parts that can be counted; for example, clothing is made up of different pieces—dresses, shirts, coats, etc.)

2. Liquids:

coffee	gasoline	juice	lotion	oil		sauce	soda	syrup	vinegar	wine
cream	honey	ketchup	milk	rubbing alcohol	shampoo	soup	tea	water		

3. Solids:

aspirin	cabbage	chocolate	garlic	ice cream	meat	seafood	wool
bacon	cake	cotton	glass	jam	paper	soap	yogurt
beef	candy	film	gold	Jell-O	pasta	spaghetti	
bread	cheese	fish	hair	jelly	pie	toothpaste	
butter	chicken (as food)	food	ice	lettuce	pizza	wood	

4. Particles:

cereal	corn	dust	grass	pepper	salt	spice	wheat
chalk	dirt	flour	hair	rice	sand	sugar	

5. Gases:

air	fog	hydrogen	smog	smoke	steam

(continued on next page)

Common Noncount Nouns (continued)

6. Natural phenomena:

cold	electricity	hail	light	mist	rain	snow	temperature	weather
darkness	fire	heat	lightning	space	scenery	sunshine	warmth	wind

7. Abstract ideas:

art	education	happiness	joy	luck	quiet	trouble
beauty	entertainment	health	knowledge	music	space	truth
comfort	freedom	homework	laughter	news*	time	wealth
competition	friendship	honesty	life	noise	traffic	weightlessness
courage	fun	information	love	peace	travel	work

8. Fields of study:

accounting	biology	economics	geometry	literature	physics*	speech
art	business	engineering	journalism	mathematics*	science	writing
astronomy	chemistry	geography	linguistics	music	sociology	

*Some noncount nouns, such as *news*, *mathematics*, and *physics*, end in *-s*. These nouns look plural, but they are not; they always take a singular verb.

APPENDIX 12

Noun Functions

In an English sentence, a noun can be:

- the **subject** of the sentence.

  Henry Ford invented the automobile.

- the **subject complement** (for example, after *be* or *become*), when it renames or identifies the subject.

  Henry Ford was an **inventor**.

- the **direct object**, when it directly receives the action of the verb.

  Henry Ford invented the **automobile**.

- the **indirect object**, when it indirectly receives the action.

  Henry Ford gave his **wife** an automobile. (In this sentence, *automobile* is the direct object. Ford gave an automobile. *Wife* is the indirect object.)

- the **object of a preposition**. Prepositions include words such as *through, in, of, to,* and *on*.

  Henry's wife drove her automobile to the **beach**.

Spelling Rules and Irregular Forms for Adverbs of Manner

- Many adverbs of manner are formed from adjective + -ly.

  | sad → sad**ly** | beautiful → beautiful**ly** |
  | slow → slow**ly** | |

- Adjectives that end in -y: Drop the -y and add -ily.

  | eas~~y~~ → eas**ily** | happ~~y~~ → happ**ily** |

- Adjectives that end in -ic or -ical: Add -ally.

  | tragic → tragic**ally** | physical → physic**ally** |

- Irregular forms (adjective and adverb forms are the same):

  | fast | hard | right | wrong | loud |
  | long | friendly | lively | lonely | lovely |

- The adverbial form of the adjective *good* is *well*.

Common Adjective + Preposition Combinations

| afraid of | crazy about | famous for | full of | jealous of | responsible for | safe from | sorry for |
| bad for | familiar with | fond of | good for | proud of | sad about | similar to | sure about |

Common Phrasal Verbs and Their Meanings

Phrasal Verbs Without Objects

catch up	reach the same place	show up	appear
drop out	leave an activity or group	slow down	become slower
grow up	become adult	take off	start (to fly or move)
run out	come to the end	turn up	come; visit unexpectedly
settle down	become comfortable	work out	exercise

Phrasal Verbs With Objects

bring up	educate (a child)	let down	disappoint; not keep a promise
build up	make stronger	look up	find written facts about
call off	cancel (a plan)	make up	1. invent 2. replace; compensate
check out	find information about		
figure out	discover (an answer)	pick up	get; collect
give up	stop doing (an activity)	point out	tell
keep up	continue		

(continued on next page)

Common Phrasal Verbs and Their Meanings (continued)

Phrasal Verbs With Objects

show off	want people to see	turn down	1. make quieter 2. say no to (an invitation)
sign up	register; add (a name) to a list	turn off	stop from working
take off	make (time) free	turn up	make louder
try out	test	work out	solve (a problem)

APPENDIX 16

Common Verb + Preposition Combinations

believe in	come from	happen to	live on	pay for	think of
belong to	concentrate on	hear about	look after	recover from	wait for
care about	depend on	know about	look at	talk to	worry about
care for	forget about	listen to	look for	think about	

APPENDIX 17

Common Three-Word Verbs and Their Meanings

come up with	discover (an idea)	get down to	begin (work)
cut down on	use or have less	get through with	finish
drop in on	visit unexpectedly	keep up with	go at the same speed as
face up to	confront; meet bravely	meet up with	meet unexpectedly
get along with	enjoy their company	put up with	tolerate

APPENDIX 18

Adjectives ending in *-ing* and *-ed*; *-ed* Adjective + Preposition Combinations

PRESENT PARTICIPLES (*-ING* FORMS)	PAST PARTICIPLES + PREPOSITIONS (*-ED* FORMS)	PRESENT PARTICIPLES (*-ING* FORMS)	PAST PARTICIPLES + PREPOSITIONS (*-ED* FORMS)
amazing	amazed at	depressing	depressed about/by
amusing	amused by	disappointing	disappointed with/in
annoying	annoyed by/with	disgusting	disgusted with
boring	bored with	exciting	excited about
confusing	confused by	exhausting	exhausted from

(continued on next page)

Adjectives ending in -ing and -ed; -ed Adjective + Preposition Combinations (continued)

PRESENT PARTICIPLES (-ING FORMS)	PAST PARTICIPLES + PREPOSITIONS (-ED FORMS)	PRESENT PARTICIPLES (-ING FORMS)	PAST PARTICIPLES + PREPOSITIONS (-ED FORMS)
fascinating	fascinated by	satisfying	satisfied with
frightening	frightened of	shocking	shocked by
inspiring	inspired by	terrifying	terrified of
interesting	interested in	tiring	tired of
pleasing	pleased with	worrying	worried about

APPENDIX 19

Comparative and Superlative Adjectives and Adverbs

ADJECTIVES AND ADVERBS	SIMPLE FORM	COMPARATIVE FORM	SUPERLATIVE FORM	WHAT DO I USE? -ERI-EST OR MORE/MOST?
One-syllable adjectives and adverbs	clean	cleaner	cleanest	Use -er and -est.
	fast	faster	fastest	
	slow	slower*	slowest*	
	big	bigger*	biggest*	
Most two-syllable adjectives and adverbs	active	more active	most active	Use more and most.
	frequent	more frequent	most frequent	
	frequently	more frequently	most frequently	
	quickly	more quickly	most quickly	
Two-syllable adjectives ending in -y, -ow, -er, -some or -ite	lonely	lonelier**	loneliest	Use -er or -est. OR Use more and most.
		more lonely	most lonely	
	narrow	narrower	narrowest	
		more narrow	most narrow	
All adjectives and adverbs of three or more syllables	beautiful	more beautiful	most beautiful	Use more and most.
	spontaneously	more spontaneously	most spontaneously	

*For one-syllable adjectives or adverbs that end with a single vowel + a consonant, double the final consonant before adding -er or -est. Do not double the final consonants x, w, and y.

**For two syllable adjectives ending in a consonant + -y, change the -y to -i and add -er or -est.

Verbs Commonly Followed by Gerunds

admit	consider	endure	finish	involve	miss	recommend	suggest
anticipate	delay	enjoy	forgive	justify	practice	report	support
appreciate	discuss	escape	go	keep (continue)	prevent	resist	tolerate
avoid	dislike	explain	imagine	mention	quit	risk	understand

Verbs Commonly Followed by Infinitives

advise	attempt	demand	hesitate	manage	pretend	struggle
agree	claim	deserve	hope	need	promise	tend
appear	consent	expect	intend	offer	refuse	wait
arrange	decide	fail	learn	plan	seem	want

Grammar Glossary

- **adjective**   A word that modifies a noun. Adjectives often come before the nouns they modify. They also come after linking verbs.

    A **beautiful** cat walked in the door.
    The cows looked **wild**.

- **adverb**   A word that modifies a verb, an adjective, another adverb, or a complete sentence.

    He ran **quickly**.
    Beans are **very** healthy.
    He ran **really** quickly.
    Yesterday, I went fishing.

- **affirmative statement**   A positive sentence. Affirmative statements do not usually include *not*.

    I **like** chocolate.

- **articles**   The words *a/an* and *the*. Articles introduce and identify nouns.

    a dog   **an** apple
    the cat   **the** apples

- **as . . . as**   Used with adjectives, adverbs, nouns, and verbs to talk about two things that are equal or very similar.

    Europe is **as rainy as** North America.
    Boston has **as much snow as** Minneapolis.

- **auxiliary verb** (also called *helping verb*)
  A verb that is used with a main verb to make questions and negative sentences and to help make tenses. *Do, have*, and *be* are often used as auxiliary verbs. The modals (*e.g., can, should, will*) are also auxiliary verbs.

    Rachel **does**n't have time for lunch.
    Peter **has** arrived.
    Is she reading?
    They **can** come with us.

- **base form of a verb**   A verb without *to* in front of it or any endings after it; an infinitive without *to*.

    make   **do**   **eat**   **be**

- **clause**   A group of related words that has a subject and a verb.

    If I call you . . .
    Today is Sunday.
    . . . when he comes.

- **common noun**   A noun that is not the name of a particular person, place, thing, or idea.

    dog   **sugar**   **people**
    houses   **honesty**

- **comparative**   Form of an adjective, adverb, noun, or verb used to describe two things that are different.

    The earth is **bigger than** the moon.
    Jack exercises **more than** Joe does.

- **conditional sentence**   A sentence that contains an *if* clause and a main clause. The *if* clause states the condition. The main clause states the expected or imagined result.

    If you heat water, it boils.
    If you go, I will go, too.

- **contraction**   The combination of two words into one. In contractions, letters are replaced with an apostrophe (').

    They will → **They'll**   We are → **We're**

- **count noun**   A noun that names a person, place, thing, or idea that can be counted. There can be one, two, three, or more.

    a boy   **2 boys**   **3 boys**

- **definite article**   The word *the. The* is used with singular, plural, and noncount nouns when both the speaker and the listener are thinking about the same noun.

    The sun is shining brightly today.

- **direct object**   A noun, pronoun, or noun phrase that directly receives the action of the verb in a sentence.

    Jack ate **the cake**.   Ramon likes **me**.

general quantifier A quantifier that describes a general amount or quantity.

several people **a lot of** sugar
a few days

gerund The *-ing* form of a verb, used as a noun.

I enjoy **working**.
We go **fishing** every summer.

imperative A type of sentence used for making offers and requests and for giving orders. The verb in an imperative sentence is in the base form.

Have a cookie. **Help** me.

indefinite article The word *a* or *an*. *A/An* is used to introduce singular count nouns to a listener and/or a speaker.

a boy **an apple**

indirect object A noun, pronoun, or noun phrase that indirectly receives the action of the verb in a sentence.

Jack gave **Mary** a book.
Mary bought **him** a new ring.

infinitive *To* + the base form of a verb. Infinitives can be used as nouns.

Peter loves **to work**.
To be a ballet dancer is her dream.

information question (See *wh-* question.)

intensifier An adverb that makes the word it modifies stronger or weaker in meaning.

I **really** love chocolate.
He **hardly** thought about his decision.

intransitive verb A verb that does not take an object.

John **runs** every day.

linking verb A verb that takes a subject complement. Linking verbs include *be, appear, feel, seem, smell,* and *become.*

She **is** a teacher. Ralph **feels** ill.

main clause (also called *independent clause*) A clause that is or could be a complete sentence.

Today is Sunday.
When he called, **I wasn't home.**

main verb The verb that can be used alone in a sentence in the simple present and simple past tense and that carries the primary verbal meaning in the sentence. Main verbs often occur with auxiliaries.

Carol **ate** breakfast today.
Carol has already **eaten**.

measure words Quantifiers that express specific or exact amounts.

a cup of sugar **a loaf of** bread
two pounds of apples

modal An auxiliary verb used to express ability or possibility, ask for or give permission or advice, make offers and requests, or express necessity. Modals include *can, could, may, might, should, must, will,* and *would.*

Harriet **can** speak French.
You **should** learn Spanish.

modify To tell more about or change the meaning of a word or phrase. For example, adjectives modify nouns.

the **beautiful** woman

negative statement A sentence that is not positive. Many negative statements contain *not.*

I **do not like** chocolate.

noncount noun A noun that names a person, place, thing, or idea that cannot be counted.

Mrs. Jones **Mel's Diner**
water **honesty**

noun A word that names a person, place, thing, or idea.

king **New York City** **house** **love**

noun phrase A noun and its modifiers.

the beautiful, big, blue ball on the table

object of a preposition A noun, pronoun, or noun phrase that comes after a preposition.

from **Ben** to **them** at **the party**

■ **particle**   The adverb in a phrasal verb.

> Please turn **off** the lights.

■ **past progressive tense** (also called *past continuous tense*)   A verb tense that describes actions in progress in the past.

> At six o'clock last night, the sun **was shining**.

■ **personal pronoun**   A word that replaces a noun or noun phrase and functions as a subject, object, or subject complement in a sentence.

> John is a teacher. **He** is a teacher.
> Tim called Katy. Tim called **her**.
> This is my car. This is **it**.

■ **phrasal verb**   A verb + adverb (particle) combination that has a special meaning. Some phrasal verbs take objects. Others do not take objects.

> John has **made up** the exam.
> I **work out** every day.

■ **phrase**   A group of related words that does not contain both a subject and a verb.

> **on the table**   **the big, black dog**

■ **plural**   More than one. Pronouns and nouns can be plural (e.g., *they, we, two dogs*). Plural verb forms are used with plural subjects.

> · The **books are** on the table.

■ **possessive**   A noun (e.g., *John's*), pronoun (e.g., *mine*), or adjective (e.g., *my*) that shows ownership or possession.

> **John's** car is new.   This book is **mine**.
> This is **my** book.

■ **predicate**   The verb and the words that come after it in a statement.

> I **like movies**.
> Reza **has lived here for several years**.

■ **preposition**   A function word that takes a noun or pronoun as an object. Prepositions often express meanings like time, location, or direction.

> **at** 10 o'clock   **in** the building
> **into** the house

■ **prepositional phrase**   A preposition plus its object.

> **in the building   into the house**

■ **present perfect progressive tense** (also called *present perfect continuous tense*)   A verb tense that describes actions in progress in the past which are continuing now or have just ended.

> They **have been waiting** for over an hour.
> Her eyes are red. She **has been crying**.

■ **present perfect tense**   A verb tense that describes actions and states that began in the past and continue to the present. The present perfect also describes actions and states completed at an indefinite time in the past.

> Susan **has lived** here for 10 years.
> Susan **has read** that book.

■ **present progressive tense** (also called *present continuous tense*)   A verb tense that describes actions happening at the moment of speaking or over a longer period of time in the present.

> I **am writing** postcards right now.
> We **are studying** English this semester.

■ **pronoun**   A word that replaces a noun or noun phrase (See *personal pronoun, possessive, reflexive pronoun*.)

> John is my friend.   **He** is my friend.

■ **proper noun**   A noun that names a particular person, place, thing, or idea. Proper nouns begin with capital letters.

> **Mary Larson   Paris   Christmas**

■ **quantifier**   A word or phrase that comes before a noun and tells *how many* or *how much*.

> **Many** people enjoy walking.
> They don't need **much** equipment to walk.

■ **reflexive pronoun**   A pronoun ending in *-self* or *-selves*. Reflexive pronouns are used when the subject and the object in a sentence are the same.

> I hurt **myself**.
> Angela bought **herself** a new bike.

short answer An answer to a *yes/no* question that includes: *Yes/No*, + subject + auxiliary verb/*be* + (*not*).

> Do you like fish?   **No, I don't.**
> Are you tired?   **Yes, I am.**

simple past tense A verb tense that describes actions and states that began and ended in the past.

> Plato **lived** in ancient Greece.
> John **was** here yesterday.

simple present tense A verb tense that describes habits, routines, and things that are generally or always true.

> We often **meet** for breakfast.
> The earth **is** a planet.

singular One. Pronouns and nouns can be singular (e.g., *I, she, book*). Singular verb forms are used with singular and noncount subjects.

> The **book is** on the table.
> The **sugar is** in the bowl.

stative meaning States, not actions. Verbs with stative meaning do not usually occur in the progressive tenses.

> I **know** the answer.
> NOT: I am knowing the answer.

subject The noun, pronoun, or noun phrase that comes before the verb in a statement. The subject is usually the doer of the action or the experiencer of the state in a sentence.

> **John** is a teacher.   **We** like chocolate.

subject complement A noun, pronoun, noun phrase, or adjective that comes after *be* or another linking verb. A subject complement renames, identifies, or describes the subject of a sentence.

> Lois will become **a doctor** soon.
> John is **handsome**.

superlative Form of an adjective or adverb used to compare three or more things or actions. Form of a noun or verb used to compare three or more quantities.

> The Nile is **the longest** river in the world.
> Jack exercises **the least** of all.

three-word verb The combination of a phrasal verb + a preposition.

> I **met up with** Fred.
> He needs to **get down to** an exercise plan.

time clause A clause that begins with a time expression (e.g., *when, while, before, as soon as, until, after*) and includes a subject and a verb.

> **When I ate**, I felt better.
> John's going to exercise **before he eats**.

transitive verb A verb that can take an object.

> The dog **chased** the cat.

verb + preposition combination A combination formed by certain verbs and certain prepositions. Prepositions in verb + preposition combinations often combine with verbs of thinking, speaking, sensing, or feeling. The preposition always has an object.

> He **thought of** a good idea.
> I was **talking to** my friend this morning.

yes/no question A question that can be answered with *yes* or *no*.

> *Yes/No* Question: **Are you hungry?**
> Answer: Yes.

wh- question (also called *information question*) A question that begins with a *wh-* word (*who, what, where, when, why, how, how much, how many*) and asks for information. *Wh-* questions cannot usually be answered with only *yes* or *no*.

> *Wh-* question: **What do you want to eat?**
> Answer: A hamburger

Index